"A revolutionary new phase of earth history, the *Anthropocene*, has been unleashed by human action, and the prospects for this blue sphere and the mass of humanity are not good. We had best start thinking in revolutionary terms about the forces turning the world upside down if we are to put brakes on the madness. A good place to begin is this book, whose remarkable authors bring together history and theory, politics and ecology, economy and culture, to force a deep look at the origins of global transformation. In short, the enemy to be met is not us, dear Pogo, but capitalism, whose unrelenting exploitation of (wo)man and nature is driving us all to the end(s) of the earth."
—Richard Walker, professor emeritus of geography, University of California, Berkeley, and author of *The Capitalist Imperative*, *The New Social Economy*, *The Conquest of Bread*, and *The Country in the City*

"This volume puts the inadequate term 'Anthropocene' in its place and suggests a much more appropriate alternative. We live in the 'age of capital,' the Capitalocene, the contributors argue, and the urgent, frightening and hopeful consequences of this reality check become apparent in chapters that forces the reader to think. In a time when there is generally no time or space to think (meaning: to go beyond the thoughtlessness that is the hallmark of 'business as usual') we need a book like this more than ever. Confronting and thinking the Capitalocene we must. This book is a great place to start."
—Bram Büscher, professor of sociology, Wageningen University, and author of *Transforming the Frontier: Peace Parks and the Politics of Neoliberal Conservation in Southern Africa.*

"For more than a decade, earth system scientists have espoused the idea of a new geological age, the Anthropocene, as a means of understand the system environmental changes to our planet in recent decades. Yet we cannot tackle the problem of climate change without a full account of its historical roots. In this pioneering volume, leading critics call for a different conceptual framework, which places global change in a new, ecologically oriented history of capitalism—the Capitalocene. No scholar or activist interested in the debate about the Anthropocene will want to miss this volume."
—Fredrik Albritton Jonsson, associate professor of history, University of Chicago, and author of *Enlightenment's Frontier: The Scottish Highlands and the Origins of Environmentalism*

Anthropocene or Capitalocene?

KAIROS

In ancient Greek philosophy, *kairos* signifies the right time or the "moment of transition." We believe that we live in such a transitional period. The most important task of social science in time of transformation is to transform itself into a force of liberation. Kairos, an editorial imprint of the Anthropology and Social Change department housed in the California Institute of Integral Studies, publishes groundbreaking works in critical social sciences, including anthropology, sociology, geography, theory of education, political ecology, political theory, and history.

Series editor: Andrej Grubačić

Kairos books:

In, Against, and Beyond Capitalism: The San Francisco Lectures by John Holloway

Anthropocene or Capitalocene? Nature, History, and the Crisis of Capitalism edited by Jason W. Moore

Birth Work as Care Work: Stories from Activist Birth Communities by Alana Apfel

Wrapped in the Flag of Israel: Mizrahi Single Mothers, Israeli Ultranationalism, and Bureaucratic Torture by Smadar Lavie

We Are the Crisis of Capital: A John Holloway Reader by John Holloway

Anthropocene or Capitalocene?

Nature, History, and the Crisis of Capitalism

Edited by
Jason W. Moore

Anthropocene or Capitalocene? Nature, History, and the Crisis of Capitalism
Edited by Jason W. Moore
© 2016 PM Press.

ISBN: 978-1-62963-148-6
Library of Congress Control Number: 2016930960

Cover by John Yates / www.stealworks.com
Interior design by briandesign

10 9 8 7 6 5 4 3

PM Press
PO Box 23912
Oakland, CA 94623
www.pmpress.org

Printed in the USA

For my father,
Who taught me that it is the conversation that counts

Contents

Acknowledgments

It was a spring day in southern Sweden in 2009. I was talking with Andreas Malm, then a PhD student at Lund University. "Forget the Anthropocene," he said. "We should call it the *Capitalocene!*"

At the time, I didn't pay much attention to it. "Yes, of course," I thought. But I didn't have a sense of what the Capitalocene might mean, beyond a reasonable—but not particularly interesting—claim that capitalism is the pivot of today's biospheric crisis.

This was also a time when I began to rethink much of environmental studies' conventional wisdom. This conventional wisdom had become atmospheric. It said, in effect, that the job of environmental studies scholars is to study "the" environment, and therefore to study the environmental context, conditions, and consequences *of* social relations. The social relations themselves—not least, but not only, those of political economy—were generally outside the field's core concerns. That didn't seem right to me. Weren't all those "social relations" *already* bundled within the web of life? Were not world trade, imperialism, class structure, gender relations, racial orders—and much more—not just producers of environmental changes but also *products* of the web of life? At some high level of abstraction, that argument was widely accepted. But at a practical, analytical level, such ideas were exceedingly marginal.

That has now changed. The idea of the Capitalocene as a multispecies assemblage, a world-ecology of capital, power, and nature, is part of the global conversation—for scholars, but also for a growing layer of activists.

This book is one product of the conversations that germinated in Sweden, beginning that spring of 2009. Those conversations would eventually give rise to the world-ecology perspective, in which the relations of capital, power, and nature form an evolving, uneven, and patterned whole in the modern world. Rather than pursue a "theory of everything," the early world-ecology conversation began with special group of graduate students at Lund University interested in pushing the boundaries of how we think space, geography, and nature in capitalism. These students included: Diana C. Gildea, Erik Jonsson, Cheryl Sjöström, Holly Jean Buck, Bruno Portillo, Geannine Chabaneix, Jenica Frisque, Xiao Yu, and Jessica C. Marx. Holly Buck deserves special credit for insisting that the Anthropocene, for all its many problems, remained a useful way of speaking to a wider audience. *This* is what we call a productive disagreement!

Special thanks go to a number of individuals. First, special thanks to my colleagues at Binghamton University: to Bat-Ami Bar On, the director of the university's Institute for Advanced Studies in the Humanities, and to Donald G. Nieman, provost, for allowing me release time from teaching to complete this book. Thanks also to Denis O'Hearn, my department chair, for providing a congenial atmosphere to complete this project. I would also like to thank the many generous scholars around the world who have invited me for talks, and the audiences who sat patiently through those talks—your responses and conversations have enriched the present dialogue in ways that are often not so obvious, but no less profound for it.

The arguments you find in this book owe everything to a wonderful community of radical intellectuals who encouraged, in large ways and small, the Anthropocene/Capitalocene and world-ecology conversations: Haroon Akram-Lodhi, Elmar Altvater, Gennaro Avallone, Henry Bernstein, Jay Bolthouse, Neil Brenner, Alvin Camba, Christopher Cox, Sharae Deckard, Marion Dixon, Joshua Eichen, Harriet Friedmann, Paul K. Gellert, Aaron Jakes, Fredrik Albritton Jonsson, Ashok Kumbamu, Benjamin Kunkel, Rebecca Lave, Emanuele Leonardi, Kirk Lawrence, Sasha Lilley, Larry Lohmann, Philip McMichael, Michael Niblett, Kerstin Oloff, Andrew Pragacz, Larry Reynolds, Marcus Taylor, Eric Vanhaute, Tony Weis, and Anna Zalik. I am especially grateful for continuing conversations with Diana C. Gildea, Christian Parenti, Raj Patel, and Marge Thomas. Ramsey Kanaan and the team at PM Press were exemplary and encouraging at every step. Naomi Schulz compiled and helped to format the bibliography. And finally, I am inspired by and grateful for Diana's and Malcolm's unflinching joy and love in making life—and in transforming the world as we know it.

INTRODUCTION

Anthropocene or Capitalocene?
Nature, History, and the Crisis of Capitalism

Jason W. Moore

The news is not good on planet Earth. Humanity—and the rest of life with it—is now on the threshold of what earth system scientists call a "state shift." This moment is dramatized in the growing awareness of climate change—among scholars, and also among a wider concerned public. But our moment involves far more than bad climate. We are living through a transition in planetary life with the "potential to transform Earth rapidly and irreversibly into a state unknown in human experience" (Barnosky et al. 2012, 52).

The zeitgeist of the twenty-first century is therefore understandably infused with a sense of urgency, among citizens, activists, and scholars (e.g., Foster et al. 2010; Hansen 2009; Parenti 2011; Klein 2014). The reality is quite real. And, in any reasonable evaluation, the situation is deteriorating. Weekly, even daily, the research mounts. "Human pressures" are pushing the conditions of biospheric stability—climate and biodiversity above all—to the breaking point (Steffen et al. 2015; Mace et al. 2014; Dirzo et al. 2014). Multiple "planetary boundaries" are now being crossed—or soon will be (Rockström et al. 2009). The conditions of life on planet Earth are changing, rapidly and fundamentally.

Awareness of this difficult situation has been building for some time. But the reality of a *crisis*—understood as a fundamental turning point in the life of a system, *any* system—is often difficult to understand, interpret, and act upon. Crises are not easily understood by those who live through them. The philosophies, concepts, and stories we use to make sense of an increasingly explosive and uncertain global present are—nearly always—ideas inherited from a different time and place. The kind of thinking that created today's global turbulence is unlikely to help us solve it.[1]

Modes of thought are tenacious. They are no easier to transcend than the "modes of production" they reflect and help to shape. This collection of essays is one effort to extend and nurture a global conversation over such a new mode of thought. Our point of departure is the Anthropocene concept, the most influential concept in environmental studies over the past decade. The essays in this book offer distinctive critiques of the Anthropocene argument—which is in fact a family of arguments with many variations. But the intention is to move beyond critique. The Anthropocene is a worthy point of departure not only for its popularity but, more importantly, because it poses questions that are fundamental to our times: How do humans fit within the web of life? How have various human organizations and processes—states and empires, world markets, urbanization, and much beyond—reshaped planetary life? The Anthropocene perspective is rightly powerful and influential for bringing these questions into the academic mainstream—and even (but unevenly) into popular awareness.

The work of this book is to encourage a debate—and to nurture a perspective—that moves beyond Green Arithmetic: the idea that our histories may be considered and narrated by adding up Humanity (or Society) and Nature, or even Capitalism plus Nature. For such dualisms are part of the problem—they are fundamental to the thinking that has brought the biosphere to its present transition toward a less habitable world. It is still only dimly realized that the categories of "Society" and "Nature"—Society without nature, Nature without humans—are part of the problem, intellectually and politically. No less than the binaries of Eurocentrism, racism, and sexism, Nature/Society is directly implicated in the modern world's colossal violence, inequality, and oppression. This argument against dualism implicates something abstract—Nature/Society—but nevertheless quite material. For the abstraction Nature/Society historically conforms to a seemingly endless series of *human* exclusions—never mind the rationalizing disciplines and exterminist policies imposed upon extra-human natures. These exclusions correspond to a long history of subordinating women, colonial populations, and peoples of color—humans rarely accorded membership in Adam Smith's "civilized society" ([1776] 1937).

These are certainly questions of oppression. And they are also fundamental to capitalism's political economy, which rests upon an audacious accumulation strategy: Cheap Nature. For capitalism, Nature is "cheap" in a double sense: to make Nature's elements "cheap" in price; and also *to cheapen*, to degrade or to render inferior in an ethico-political sense, the better to make Nature cheap in price. These two moments are entwined at every moment, and in every major capitalist transformation of the past five centuries (Moore 2015a).

This matters for our analytics, and also for our politics. Efforts to transcend capitalism in any egalitarian and broadly sustainable fashion will be stymied so long as the radical political imagination is captive to capitalism's either/or organization of reality: Nature/Society. And relatedly, efforts to discern capitalism's limits today—such discernment is crucial to any antisystemic strategy—cannot advance much further by encasing reality in dualisms that are immanent to capitalist development.

The Anthropocene argument shows Nature/Society dualism at its highest stage of development. And if the Anthropocene—as a historical rather than geological argument—is inadequate, it is nevertheless an argument that merits our appreciation. New thinking emerges in many tentative steps. There are many conceptual halfway houses en route to a new synthesis. The Anthropocene concept is surely the most influential of these halfway houses. No concept grounded in historical change has been so influential across the spectrum of Green Thought; no other socio-ecological concept has so gripped popular attention.

Formulated by Paul Crutzen and Eugene Stoermer in 2000, the Anthropocene concept proceeds from an eminently reasonable position: the biosphere and geological time has been fundamentally transformed by human activity. A new conceptualization of geological time—one that includes "mankind" as a "major geological force"—is necessary. This was a surely a courageous proposal. For to propose humanity as a geological agent is to transgress one of modernity's fundamental intellectual boundaries. Scholars call this the "Two Cultures," of the "natural" and "human" sciences (Snow 1957). At its best, the Anthropocene concept entwines human history and natural history—even if the "why" and the "how" remain unclear, and hotly debated. Such murkiness surely accounts for the concept's popularity. Like globalization in the 1990s, the Anthropocene has become a buzzword that can mean all things to all people. Nevertheless, reinforced by earlier developments in environmental history (e.g., Worster 1988), the Anthropocene as an argument has gradually crystallized: "Human action" plus "Nature" equals "planetary crisis" (Chakrabarty 2009; e.g., Steffen et al. 2007). Green Arithmetic, formulating history as the aggregation of human and natural relations, had triumphed.

Green Arithmetic. It is a curious term, but I can think none better to describe the basic procedure of environmental studies over the past few decades: Society plus Nature = History. Today it is Humanity, or Society, or Capitalism plus Nature = Catastrophe. I do not wish to disparage this model. It has been a powerful one. It has provided the philosophical basis for studies that have delivered a wealth of knowledge about environmental change. These studies, in turn, have allowed a deeper understanding of the *what* of the biosphere's unfolding "state shift." But they have not facilitated—indeed they have stymied—our understanding of *how* the present crisis will unfold in a world-system that is a *world-ecology*, joining power, nature, and accumulation in a dialectical and unstable unity.[2] This book seeks to transcend the limits of Green Arithmetic. This allows us to pursue, in Donna Haraway's words, "wonderful, messy tales" of multispecies history—tales that point to the possibilities "for getting on now, as well as in deep earth history" (see her "Staying with the Trouble" in this volume).

Green Arithmetic works when we assume Society plus Nature add up. But do they? In my view, this "adding up" was necessary—and for a long time very productive. The consolidation of the historical social sciences in the century after 1870s proceeded as if nature did not exist. There were some exceptions (e.g., Mumford 1934), but none that unsettled the status quo until the 1970s. Then, energized by the "new" social movements—not least around race, gender, and environment—we saw an important intellectual revolt. The blank spots in the dominant cognitive mapping of reality were filled in; the old, nature-blind, cognitive map was challenged. In environmental studies, radicals argued for a relational view of humanity-in-nature, and nature-in-humanity (e.g., Harvey 1974; Naess 1973). But that relational critique remained, for the most part, philosophical. Above all, our concepts of "big history"—imperialism, capitalism, industrialization, commercialization, patriarchy, racial formations—remained *social* processes. Environmental consequences were added on, but the conception of history as social history did not fundamentally change.

Today a new conceptual wind blows. It seems we are now ready to ask, and even to begin to answer, a big question about big history: What if these world-historical processes are not only producers, but also products of changes in the web of life? The question turns inside out a whole series of premises that have become staples of Green Thought. Two are especially salient. First, we are led to ask questions not about humanity's *separation* from nature, but about how humans—and human organizations (e.g., empires, world markets)—*fit* within the web of life, and vice versa. This allows us to begin posing situated questions, in Donna Haraway's sense (1988). We start to see human organization as something more-than-human and less-than-social. We begin to see human organization as utterly, completely, and variably porous within the web of life. Second, we can begin asking questions about something possibly more significant than the "degradation" of nature. There is no doubt that capitalism imposes a relentless pattern of violence on nature, humans included. But capitalism works because violence is part of a larger repertoire of strategies that "put nature to work." Thus, our question incorporates but moves beyond the degradation of nature thesis: How does modernity put nature to work? How do specific combinations of human and extra-human activity work—or *limit*—the endless accumulation of capital? Such questions—these are far from the only ones!—point toward a new thinking about humanity in the web of life.

Anthropocene or Capitalocene? An Evolving Conversation

The chapters in this volume defy easy summary. But two common themes emerge. First, the essays all suggest that the Anthropocene argument poses questions that it cannot answer. The Anthropocene sounds the alarm—and what an alarm it is! But it cannot explain how these alarming changes came about. Questions of capitalism, power and class, anthropocentrism, dualist framings of "nature" and "society," and the role of states and empires—all are frequently bracketed by the dominant Anthropocene perspective. Second, the contributors to *Anthropocene or Capitalocene?* all seek to go beyond critique. All argue for reconstructions that point to a new way of thinking humanity-in-nature, and nature-in-humanity.

The first thing I wish to say is that Capitalocene is an ugly word for an ugly system. As Haraway points out, "the Capitalocene" seems to be one of those words floating in the ether, one crystallized by several scholars at once—many of them independently. I first heard the word in 2009 from Andreas Malm. The radical economist David Ruccio seems to have first publicized the concept, on his blog in 2011 (Ruccio 2011). By 2012, Haraway began to use the concept in her public lectures (Haraway 2015). That same year, Tony Weis and I were discussing the concept in relation to what would become *The Ecological Hoofprint*, his groundbreaking work on the meat-industrial complex (2013). My formulation of the Capitalocene took shape in the early months of 2013, as my discontent with the Anthropocene argument began to grow.

The Capitalocene. As I think the contributions to this volume clarify, the Capitalocene does not stand for capitalism as an economic and social system. It is not a radical inflection of Green Arithmetic. Rather, the Capitalocene signifies capitalism as a way of organizing nature—as a multispecies, situated, capitalist world-ecology. I will try to use the word sparingly. There have been many other wordplays—Anthrobscene (Parikka 2014), econocene (Norgaard 2013), technocene (Hornborg 2015), misanthropocene (Patel 2013), and perhaps most delightfully, *manthropocene* (Raworth 2014). All are useful. But none captures the basic historical pattern modern of world history as the "Age of Capital"—and the era of capitalism as a world-ecology of power, capital, and nature.

In Part I, Eileen Crist and Donna J. Haraway take apart the Anthropocene concept and point to the possibilities for an alternative. Crist cautions powerfully against the Anthropocene argument—and other "Promethean self-portrait[s]." These tend to reinvent, and at time subtly recuperate, neo-Malthusian thought. While many defenders of the Anthropocene concept point to the ways it has opened discussion, Crist sees this opening as exceedingly selective. For Crist, the concept "shrinks the discursive space of challenging the [human] domination of the biosphere, offering instead a techno-scientific pitch for its rationalization." Drawing on Thomas Berry, Crist orients us toward a different—and more hopeful—framing of our present and possible futures. This would be not an "age of Man" but an "ecozoic": a vision of humanity-in-nature as a "union-in-diversity," in which humanity may embrace "Earth's integral living community."

Donna J. Haraway elaborates the spirit of Crist's "ecozoic" perspective, taking it—as she so often does—toward a new vision: the *Chthulucene.* Here the autopoietic, closed system mirage of capital (or "society") is revealed as partial and illusory. Such closed system thinking cannot help us to think through the liberatory possibilities of a messy, muddled, interspecies future. This Chthulucene—admittedly a word that does not roll easily off the tongue—is not autopoietic but sympoietic: "always partnered all the way down, with no starting and subsequently interacting 'units.'" For Haraway, the problem of the Anthropocene is fundamentally a problem of thinking humanity's place in the web of life: "*It matters what thoughts think thoughts.*" But, Haraway argues forcefully, even poetically, the issue is not "merely" thinking, it is how thought and messy life-making unfold in ways that are "always partnered." The Anthropocene, then, is not only poor thinking—a narrative of "the self-making Human, the human-making machine of history." It is also poor history: "Coal and the steam engine did not determine the story, and besides the dates are all wrong, not because one has to go back to the last ice age, but because one has to at least include the great market and commodity reworldings of the long sixteenth and seventeenth centuries of the current era, even if we think (wrongly) that we can remain Euro-centered in thinking about 'globalizing' transformations shaping the Capitalocene."

The historical geography of the Capitalocene moves to center stage in Part II. In "The Rise of Cheap Nature," I argue for an interpretive frame for capitalism's history that builds on Haraway's longstanding critique of "human exceptionalism" (2008). Capitalism is a way of organizing *nature as a whole* . . . a nature in which human organizations (classes, empires, markets, etc.) not only make environments, but are simultaneously made by the historical flux and flow of the web of life. In this perspective, capitalism is a world-ecology that joins the accumulation of capital, the pursuit of power, and the co-production of nature in successive historical configurations. I show that the emphasis on the Industrial Revolution as the origin of modernity flows from a historical method that privileges environmental consequences and occludes the geographies of capital and power. Green Thought's love affair with the Industrial Revolution has undermined efforts to locate the origins of today's crises in the epoch-making transformations of capital, power, and nature that began in the "long" sixteenth century (Braudel 1953). The origins of today's inseparable but distinct crises of capital accumulation and biospheric stability are found in a series of landscape, class, territorial, and technical transformations that emerged in the three centuries after 1450.

Justin McBrien agrees that we are living in the Capitalocene, highlighting capitalism's drive toward extinction in a world-ecological sense. Extinction, McBrien argues, is more than a biological process suffered by other species. It signifies also the "extinguishing of cultures and languages," genocide, and spectrum of biospheric changes understood as anthropogenic. McBrien demonstrates that the very conception of these changes as anthropogenic is premised on the systematic conceptual exclusion of capitalism. These conceptions are, in McBrien's narrative, a product of modern science, at once opposing and entwined within webs of imperial power and capital accumulation. Far from merely an output of the system—as in Green Arithmetic—he shows that "accumulation by extinction" has been fundamental to capitalism from the beginning. The Capitalocene, in this view, is also a Necrocene: "The accumulation of capital is the accumulation of potential extinction—a potential increasingly activated in recent decades." Far from embracing planetary catastrophism and the apocalyptic vistas of many environmentalists, McBrien shows how catastrophism itself has been a form of knowledge situated within the successive ecological regimes of postwar and neoliberal capitalism. Catastrophism, in this reading, has rendered both poles of the environmentalist binary—"sustainability or collapse?" (Costanza et al. 2007)—mirror images of each other.

Elmer Altvater moves beyond political economy to include Weber's "European rationality of world domination" and to challenge the core assumptions of modern rationality. On the one hand, Altvater sees the origins of capitalism in the "long" sixteenth century and the invention of Cheap Nature. On the other hand, he sees a decisive shift in the transition from the "formal" to the "real" subsumption of labor by capital in the late eighteenth and early nineteenth centuries. Altvater calls these two periodizations the "Braudel" and the "Polanyi" hypotheses—after Fernand Braudel and Karl Polanyi. Far from competing, these periodizations are best seen in the totality of historical capitalism: *both* positions, Braudel and Polanyi's, are correct. Importantly, for Altvater, the Capitalocene is not only a question of capital accumulation but of rationalization—immanent to the accumulation process. Charting the contradictions between the firm-level calculation of costs—and the microeconomic "rationality" of externalization—he illuminates a broader set of problems within capitalist modernity and its capacity to address climate change. Using geoengineering as an optic, Altvater pinpoints the trap of bourgeois rationality in relation to biospheric change today. The geoengineers'

> task is much greater than building a car or a dam or a hotel; the geoengineers are tasked with controlling whole earth systems in order to combat—or at least to reduce—the negative consequences of capitalist externalization. However, the required internalization of externalized emissions is the internalization of external effects into production costs at the level of the corporation. Then indeed— *in principle*—the prices could "tell the truth," as in the neoclassical

textbooks. But we would not be wiser still. Why? Because many interdependencies in society and nature *cannot be expressed in terms of prices*. Any effective rationalization would have to be holistic; it would have to be qualitative and consider much more than price alone. But that is impossible because it contradicts capitalist rationality, which is committed to fixing the parts and not the whole. In such a scenario, capitalist modernization through externalization would—*inevitably*—come to an end. The Four Cheaps would disappear behind the "event horizon." Would it be possible for geoengineers to bring the necessary moderation of modernization *and* of capitalist dynamics in coincidence? They cannot, for the engineers are not qualified to work holistically.

In Part III, questions of culture and politics in the Capitalocene move to center stage. In Chapter Six, Daniel Hartley asks how culture matters to thinking about the Anthropocene and Capitalocene. Drawing on the world-ecology perspective, he suggests that the concepts "abstract social nature" (Moore 2014b, 2015a) and "cultural fix" (Shapiro 2014) provide rough—yet partial—guides to the history of capitalism in the web of life. Warning of the dangers that might separate "science" and "culture" in capitalist environment-making, Hartley points to the relations between science and culture, capital and nature, as fundamental to the historical geographies of endless accumulation. In this formulation, he argues powerfully for the analytical incorporation of those relations—racism, sexism, and other "cultural" forms—that "appear to have no immediate relation to ecology, but which are in fact" fundamental to humanity's diverse relations within the web of life."

Christian Parenti, in the concluding chapter, takes us from culture to the politics of the Capitalocene. Parenti's innovation is twofold. First, he reconstructs the modern state as fundamentally an environment-making process. The modern state is not only a producer of environmental changes. In equal measure, state power, as Parenti shows in his exploration of early American history, develops *through* environmental transformation. Secondly, the modern state works through a peculiar valuation of nature—what Marx calls value as abstract social labor. Parenti's insight is that power, value, and nature are thinkable only in relation to each other. Thus, the modern state "is at the heart of the value form." Why? "Because "the use values of nonhuman nature are . . . central sources of value, and it is the state that delivers these." Far from operating outside or above "nature," in Parenti's account the state becomes the pivotal organizational nexus of the relation between modern territory, nature as tap and sink, and capital accumulation. The political implications of this analysis are crucial. The state is not only analytically central to the making of the capitalist world-ecology, but is the only institution large enough and powerful enough to allow for a progressive response to the escalating challenges of climate change.

Toward the Chthulucene . . . (and/or) a Socialist World-Ecology?
Reflecting a diversity of perspectives around a common theme—how the modern world has organized human and extra-human natures—the book's essays are joyfully varied. They point toward a new synthesis, even a new paradigm. I have called this paradigm *world-ecology*, although we may yet find a better phrase for it. This new thinking—whatever name we give it— reflects (and shapes?) a certain zeitgeist. The notion that humans are a part of nature, that the whole of nature makes us, is one readily accepted by a growing layer of the world's populations. University students and many activists seem especially receptive; but this zeitgeist reaches well beyond. It is revealed dramatically in many of our era's emergent movements— food sovereignty, climate justice, "right to the city," degrowth, and many others. These movements represent a "new ontological politics" (Moore 2015b). All organize not only for a more equitable distribution of wealth: they call for a *new conception of wealth*, in which equity and sustainability in the reproduction of life (of *all* life) is central to our vision of the future. In these movements, we find hope for the realization of Haraway's sympoietic vision: the *Chthulucene.*

Whatever name we attach to it, the sympoietic vision shares a new ontology that meshes with—and learns from—movements around food sovereignty and climate justice (see e.g., Wittman et al. 2011; McMichael 2013; Bond 2012). The new ontological politics is so hopeful—without waxing romantic—because it offers not merely a distributional, but an ontological, vision. That vision questions the whole model of how capitalism values nature, and humans within it. For food and climate justice movements—of course there are important variations—the questions of equality, sustainable, and democracy are thinkable only through and in relation to each other. They have made, as never before, food, climate, and the web of life fundamental to older radical vistas of equality among humans.

Importantly, these movements' relational vision of humanity-in-nature occurs at a time when the capitalist model is showing signs of exhaustion. If it has been nothing else, capitalism has been a system of getting nature—human nature too!—to work for free or very low-cost. Capitalism's "law" of value—how and what it prioritizes in the web of life—has always been a law of Cheap Nature. (Absurd, yes! For nature is never cheap.) The weird and dynamic process of putting nature to work on the cheap has been the basis for modernity's accomplishments—its hunger for, and it capacity to extract the Four Cheaps: food, energy, raw materials, and human life. These capacities are now wearing thin. Industrial agricultural productivity has stalled since the mid-1980s. So has labor productivity in industry—since the 1970s. The contradictions of capitalism dramatized by biospheric instability reveal modernity's accomplishment as premised on an active and ongoing theft: of our times, of planetary life, of our—and our children's—futures (Moore 2015a).

The breakdown of capitalism today is—and at the same time is not—the old story of crisis and the end of capitalism. As capital progressively internalizes the costs of climate change, massive biodiversity loss, toxification, epidemic disease, and many other biophysical costs, new movements are gaining strength. These are challenging not only capitalism's unequal distribution—pay the "ecological debt"!—but the very way we think about *what* is being distributed. The exhaustion of capitalism's valuation of reality is simultaneously internal to capital and giving rise to the new ontological politics outside that value system—and in direct to response to its breakdown. We see as never before the flowering of an ontological imagination beyond Cartesian dualism, one that carries forth the possibility of alternative valuations of food, climate, nature, and everything else. They are revealing capitalism's law of value as the value of nothing—or at any rate, of nothing particularly valuable (Patel 2009). And they point toward a world-ecology in which power, wealth, and re/production are forged in conversation with needs of the web of life, and humanity's place within it.

Notes
1   A phrase, or some variant, frequently attributed to Albert Einstein.
2   Key texts in world-ecology include Moore 2015a; Bolthouse 2014; Büscher and Fletcher 2015; Camba 2015; Campbell and Niblett 2016; Cox 2015; Deckard 2015; Dixon 2015; El-Khoury 2015; Gill 2015; Jakes forthcoming; Kröger 2015; Lohmann 2016; Marley 2015; Niblett 2013; Oloff 2012; Ortiz 2014; Parenti 2014; Weis 2013.

PART I
The Anthropocene and Its Discontents
Toward Chthulucene?

ONE

On the Poverty of Our Nomenclature

Eileen Crist[1]

"Nature is gone.... You are living on a used planet. If this bothers you, get over it. We now live in the Anthropocene—a geological epoch in which Earth's atmosphere, lithosphere and biosphere are shaped primarily by human forces."

—Erle Ellis (2009)

"When all is said and done, it is with an entire anthropology that we are at war. *With the very idea of man.*"

—The Invisible Committee

The Anthropocene is a discursive development suddenly upon us, a proposed name for our geological epoch introduced at century's turn and now boasting hundreds of titles, a few new journals, and over a quarter million hits on Google. This paper's thesis is an invitation to consider the shadowy repercussions of naming an epoch after ourselves: to consider that this name is neither a useful conceptual move nor an empirical no-brainer, but instead a reflection and reinforcement of the anthropocentric actionable worldview that generated "the Anthropocene"—with all its looming emergencies—in the first place. To make this argument I critically dissect the discourse of the Anthropocene.

In approaching the Anthropocene as a discourse I do not impute a singular, ideological meaning to every scientist, environmental author, or reporter who uses the term. Indeed, this neologism is being widely and often casually deployed, partly because it is catchy and more seriously because it has instant appeal for those aware of the scope of humanity's impact on the biosphere. Simply using the term Anthropocene, however, does not substantively contribute to what I am calling its discourse— though compounding uses of the term are indirectly strengthening that discourse by boosting its legitimacy.

By discourse of the Anthropocene I refer to the advocacy and elaboration of rationales favoring the term in scientific, environmental, popular writings, and other media. The advocacy and rationales communicate a cohesive though not entirely homogeneous set of ideas, which merits the label "discourse." Analogously to a many-stranded rope that is solidly braided but not homogeneous, the Anthropocene discourse is constituted by a blend of interweaving and recurrent themes, variously developed or emphasized by its different exponents. Importantly, the discourse goes well beyond the Anthropocene's (probably uncontroversial) keystone rationale that humanity's stratigraphic imprint would be discernible to future geologists.

The Anthropocene themes braid; the braided "rope" is its discourse. Chief among its themes are the following: human population will continue to grow until it levels off at nine or ten billion; economic growth and consumer culture will remain the leading social models (many Anthropocene promoters see this as desirable, while a few are ambivalent); we now live on a domesticated planet, with wilderness[2] gone for good; we might put ecological doom-and-gloom to rest and embrace a more positive attitude about our prospects on a humanized planet; technology, including risky, centralized, and industrial-scale systems, should be embraced as our destiny and even our salvation; major technological fixes will likely be needed, including engineering climate and life; the human impact is "natural" (and not the expression, as I argue elsewhere, of a human species-supremacist planetary politics [see Crist 2014]); humans are godlike in power or at least a special kind of "intelligent life," as far as we know, "alone in the universe"; and the path forward lies in humanity embracing a managerial mindset and active stewardship of earth's natural systems.

Of equal if not greater significance is what this discourse excludes from our range of vision: the possibility of challenging human rule. History's course has carved an ever-widening swath of domination over nature, with both purposeful and inadvertent effects on the biosphere. For the Anthropocene discourse our purposeful effects must be rationalized and sustainably managed, our inadvertent, negative effects need to be technically mitigated—but the historical legacy of human dominion is not up for scrutiny, let alone abolition (Crutzen and Stoermer 2000, 18).

The commitment to history's colonizing march appears in the guise of deferring to its major trends. The reification of the trends into the independent variables of the situation—into the variables that are pragmatically not open to change or reversal—is conveyed as an acquiescence to their unstoppable momentum. Paul Ehrlich and John Holdren's famous formula (1971) that human Impact ("I") equals Population times Affluence times Technological development ("PAT") encapsulates some of the paramount social trends which appear to have so much momentum as to be virtually impervious to change. The recalcitrant trends are also allowed to slip through the net of critique, accepted as givens, and consequently projected as constitutive of future reality.

In brief, here is what we know: population, affluence, and technology are going to keep expanding—the first until it stabilizes of its own accord, the second until "all ships are raised," and the third forevermore—because history's trajectory is at the helm. And while history might just see the human enterprise prevail after overcoming or containing its self-imperiling effects, the course toward world domination should not (or cannot) be stopped: history will keep moving in that direction, with the human enterprise eventually journeying into outer space, mining other planets and the moon, preempting ice ages and hothouses, deflecting asteroid collisions, and achieving other impossible-to-foresee technological feats:

> Looking deeply into the evolution of the Anthropocene, future generations of H. sapiens will likely do all they can to prevent a new ice age by adding powerful artificial greenhouse gases into the atmosphere. Similarly any drops in CO_2 levels to low concentrations, causing strong reductions in photosynthesis and agricultural productivity, might be combated by artificial releases of CO_2, maybe from earlier CO_2 sequestration. And likewise, far into the future, H. sapiens will deflect meteorites and asteroids before they could hit the Earth. (Steffen et al. 2007a, 620)

The Anthropocene discourse delivers a Promethean self-portrait: an ingenious if unruly species, distinguishing itself from the background of merely-living life, rising so as to earn itself a separate name (anthropos meaning "man," and always implying "not-animal"), and whose unstoppable and in many ways glorious history (created in good measure through PAT) has yielded an "I" on a par with Nature's own tremendous forces. That history—a mere few thousand years—has now streamed itself into geological time, projecting itself (or at least "the golden spike" of its various stratigraphic markers[3]) thousands or even millions of years out. So unprecedented a phenomenon, it is argued, calls for christening a new geological epoch—for which the banality of "the age of Man" is proposed as self-evidently apt.

Descriptions of humanity as "rivaling the great forces of Nature," "elemental," "a geological and morphological force," "a force of nature reshaping the planet on a geological scale," and the like, are standard in the Anthropocene literature and its popular spinoffs. The veracity of this framing of humanity's impact renders it incontestable, thereby *also* enabling its awed subtext regarding human specialness to slip in and, all too predictably, carry the day.

In the Anthropocene discourse, we witness history's projected drive to keep moving forward as history's conquest not only of geographical space but now of geological time as well. This conquest is portrayed in encompassing terms, often failing to mention or nod toward fundamental biological and geological processes that humans have neither domesticated nor control (Kidner 2014, 13).[4] A presentiment of triumph tends to permeate the literature, despite the fact that Anthropocene exponents have understandable misgivings—about too disruptive a climate, too much manmade nitrogen, or too little biodiversity. "We are so adept at using energy and manipulating the environment," according to geologist Jan Zalasiewicz, "that we are now a defining force in the geological process on the surface of the Earth" (quoted in Owen 2010).[5] "The Anthropocene," the same author and colleagues highlight elsewhere, "is a remarkable episode in the history of our planet" (Zalasiewicz et al. 2010). Cold and broken though it be, it's still a Hallelujah. The defining force of this remarkable episode—the human enterprise—must contain certain aspects of its "I," but, in the face of all paradox, PAT will continue to grow, and the momentum of its product will sustain history's forward thrust. Extrapolating from the past, but not without sounding an occasional note of uncertainty, Anthropocene supporters expect (or hope) that this forward movement will keep materializing variants of progress such as green energy, economic development for all, a gardened planet, or the blossoming of a global noosphere.

How true the cliché that history is written by the victors, and how much truer for the history of the planet's conquest against which no nonhuman can direct a flood of grievances that might strike a humbling note into the human soul. Adverse impacts must be contained insofar as they threaten material damage to, or the survival of, the human enterprise, but the "I" is also becoming *linguistically* contained so that its nonstop chiseling and oft-brutal onslaughts on nature become configured in more palatable (or upbeat[6]) representations. The Anthropocene discourse veers away from environmentalism's dark idiom of destruction, depredation, rape, loss, devastation, deterioration, and so forth of the natural world into the tame vocabulary that humans are changing, shaping, transforming, or altering the biosphere, and, in the process, creating novel ecosystems and anthropogenic biomes. Such locutions tend to be the dominant conceptual vehicles for depicting our impact (Kareiva et al. 2011).[7]

This sort of wording presents itself as a more neutral vocabulary than one which speaks forcefully or wrathfully on behalf of the nonhuman realm. We are not destroying the biosphere—we are changing it: the former so emotional and "biased"; the latter so much more dispassionate and *civilized*. Beyond such appearances, however, the vocabulary of neutrality is a surreptitious purveyor (inadvertent or not) of the human supremacy complex,[8] echoing as it does the widespread belief that there exist no perspectives (other than human opinion) from which anthropogenic changes to the biosphere might actually be experienced as devastation. The vocabulary that we are "changing the world"—so matter-of-factly portraying itself as impartial and thereby erasing its own normative tracks even as it speaks—secures its ontological ground by silencing the displaced, killed, and enslaved whose homelands have been assimilated and whose lives have, indeed, been changed forever; erased, even.

And here also lies the Anthropocene's existential and political alliance with history and its will to secure human dominion: history has itself unfolded by silencing nonhuman others, who do not (as has been repeatedly established in the Western canon[9]) speak, possess meanings, experience perspectives, or have a vested interest in their own destinies. These others have been de facto silenced because if they once spoke to us in other registers—primitive, symbolic, sacred, totemic, sensual, or poetic—they have receded so much they no longer convey such numinous turns of speech, and are certainly unable by now to rival the digital sirens of Main Street. The centuries-old global downshifting of the ecological baseline of the historically sponsored, cumulative loss of Life[10] is a graveyard of more than extinct life forms and the effervescence of the wild. But such gossamer intimations lie almost utterly forgotten, with even the memory of their memory swiftly disappearing. So also the Earth's forgetting projects itself into humanity's future, where the forgetting itself will be forgotten for as long as the Earth can be disciplined into remaining a workable and safe human stage. Or so apparently it is hoped, regarding both the forgetting and the disciplining.

Not only is history told from the perspective of the victors, it often also conceals chapters that would mar its narration as a forward march. Similarly, for humanity's future, the Anthropocene's projection of a sustainable human empire steers clear of envisioning the bleak consequences of the further materialization of its present trends. What is offered instead are the technological and managerial tasks ahead, realizable (it is hoped) by virtue of *Homo sapiens*'s distinguished brain-to-body ratio and related prowess. In a 2011 special issue on the Anthropocene, the *Economist* (a magazine sweet on the Anthropocene long before the term was introduced) highlights that what we need in the Age of Man is a "smart planet" (2011a, 2011b). As human numbers and wealth continue to swell, people should create "zero-carbon energy systems," engineer crops, trees, fish, and other life forms, make large-scale desalinization feasible, recycle scrupulously especially metals "vital to industrial life," tweak the Earth's thermostat to safe settings, regionally manipulate microclimates, and so forth, all toward realizing the breathtaking vision of a world of "10 billion reasonably rich people."

When history's imperative to endure speaks, the "imagination atrophies" (Horkheimer and Adorno 1972, 35). There is the small thing of refraining from imagining a world of 10 billion reasonably rich people (assuming for argument's sake that such is possible)—a refraining complied with in the Anthropocene discourse more broadly. How many (more) roads and vehicles, how much electrification, how many chemicals and plastics at large, how much construction and manufacturing, how much garbage dumped, incinerated, or squeezed into how many landfills, how many airplanes and ships, how much global trade[11] and travel, how much mining, logging, damming, fishing, and aquaculture, how much plowing under of the tropics (with the temperate zone already dominated by agriculture), how many Concentrated Animal Feeding Operations (aka factory farms)—in brief, how much of little else but a planet and Earthlings bent into submission to serve the human enterprise?

Ongoing economic development and overproduction, the spread of industrial infrastructures, the contagion of industrial food production and consumption, and the dissemination of consumer material and ideational culture are proliferating "neo-Europes"[12] everywhere (Manning 2005). The existential endpoint of this biological and cultural homogenization is captured by the Invisible Committee's description of the European landscape:

> We've heard enough about the "city" and the "country," and particularly about the supposed ancient opposition between the two. From up close, or from afar, what surrounds us looks nothing like that: it is one single urban cloth, without form or order, a bleak zone, endless and undefined, a global continuum of museum-like hypercenters and natural parks, of enormous suburban housing developments and massive agricultural projects, industrial zones and subdivisions, country inns and trendy bars: the metropolis. . . . All territory is subsumed by the metropolis. Everything occupies the same space, if not geographically then through the intermeshing of its networks. (The Invisible Committee 2009, 52)

This passage describes territory from which wilderness has been thoroughly expunged. The Invisible Committee delivers a snapshot of the domestication awaiting the Earth in the Anthropocene, even as many of the latter's "optimistic" exponents prefer to describe the future's geography as akin to a garden (Kareiva et al. 2011; Shellenberger and Nordhaus 2011; Marris et al. 2011).

The "human enterprise"[13] is what Anthropocene exponents are bent on saving from its self-generated, unwanted side effects:

> One of the key developments in moving from problem definition to solution formulation is the concept of the Anthropocene . . . which cuts through a mass of complexity and detail to place the evolution of the human enterprise in the context of a much longer Earth history. This analysis sharpens the focus on an overarching long term goal for humanity—*keeping the Earth's environment in a state conducive for further human development.* (Steffen et al. 2011b, 741)

Keeping the human enterprise viable is never about rejecting history's trajectory of planetary conquest, but about sustaining that trajectory with the caveat of some urgently needed corrections: most especially, the management of certain biophysical boundaries too risky to breach, so as to stabilize "a safe operating space" where humanity can continue to develop and maneuver (Ellis 2012; Rockström et al. 2009a, 2009b; Steffen 2010; Lynas 2011). The implicit loyalty to history's human-imperialist course is backed by an enthrallment with narratives of human ascent[14] and by the compulsion to perpetuate Earth's reduction into a resource-base (Shepard 2002; Foreman 2007; Crist 2012). "But still," as philosopher Hans Jonas entreated decades ago, "a silent plea for sparing its integrity seems to issue from the threatened plenitude of the living world" (Jonas 1974, 126). The threatened plenitude of Life asks that we view timeworn stories of human ascent with the deep suspicion they deserve, see through the self-serving ontology of the world recoded as "resources," "natural capital," and "ecological services," and question what it is we are salvaging in desiring to sustain the human enterprise. For there is no "human enterprise" worth defending on a planet leveled and revamped to serve the human enterprise.

Mastery and the Forfeiting of Human Freedom

The sixth extinction is a casualty of history, the grand finale of the mowing down of biological diversity over the course of many centuries and accelerated in the last two. As a historical trend with a lot of momentum, the Anthropocene literature emphasizes the facticity of the sixth extinction. It does so in two distinct but connected ways: it sees anthropogenic mass extinction through to its potential completion; and it deploys mass extinction as a keystone stratigraphic marker giving a stamp of approval to its proposed nomenclature. "The current human-driven wave of extinctions," we are informed, "*looks set* to become the Earth's sixth extinction event" (Zalasiewicz et al. 2010, 2229, emphasis added). Will Steffen and his colleagues also note as fact that "the world is likely entering its sixth mass extinction event and the first caused by a biological species" (2011, 850). Mass extinctions qualify as powerful indicators of geological transitions, and thus the sixth is a sound criterion for a new epoch (or even era) demarcation. According to Steffen, the strongest evidence that we have left the Holocene is "the state of biodiversity," since "many periods of Earth history are defined by abrupt changes in the biological past" (Steffen 2010). Indeed, Zalasiewicz and his colleagues maintain that "a combination of extinctions, global migrations . . . and the widespread replacement of natural vegetation with agricultural monocultures is producing a distinctive biostratigraphic signal" (Zalasiewicz et al. 2008, 6). The condition of biodiversity calls for painstaking scientific evaluation: "Care will be needed to say how significant is the current, ongoing extinction event by comparison with those that have refashioned life in the past—and therefore how significant is the Anthropocene, biologically" (Zalasieicz et al. 2010, 2230).

Describing human-driven extinction with detachment (and often in passing), and certainly avoiding by a wide berth a Munchian scream for its prevention, sidesteps a matter of unparalleled, even cosmological significance for a "world of facts,"[15] while also marshaling those facts as favoring the championed geological designator. Detached reporting on the sixth extinction amounts to an absence of clarity about its earth-shattering meaning and avoidance of voicing the imperative of its preemption. This begs some questions. Will the human enterprise's legacy to the planet, and all generations to come, be to obliterate a large fraction of our nonhuman cohort, while at the same time constricting and enslaving another sizable portion of what is left? Might the refusal to flood light on this legacy-in-the-making be judged by future people—as it is judged by a minority today—as a historical bequest of autism[16] to the human collective? And in a world where the idea of freedom enjoys superlative status, why are we not pursuing larger possibilities of freedom for people and nonhumans alike, beyond those of liberal politics, trade agreements, technological innovations, and consumer choices?

What remains unstated in the trend reifications that characterize the Anthropocene discourse (projections of rising human numbers,[17] continued economic development,[18] expanding technological projects and incursions, and a deepening biodiversity crisis) is the abdication of freedom that reifying the trends affirms: the freedom of humanity to choose a different way of inhabiting Earth is tacitly assumed absent. This very assumption, however, does nothing but further reinforce the absence of freedom that it implicitly holds given. The inability to change historical course remains a tacit adhered-to claim within the discourse of the Anthropocene. And not in a way that is altogether innocent of its own framing preferences: were humanity's powerlessness to shift history's direction openly appreciated, it would collide dissonantly with the breathless presentation of the "I" as, on the one hand, "an elemental force" (the human on a par with Nature's colossal powers) and, on the other, the upshot of the uniqueness of *Homo sapiens* (the "God species" with its own distinct powers [Lynas 2011]). Admitting that we are locked into a course beyond humanity's willpower to shift would render the "I" of the human enterprise as something less glamorous than a show of power; as more likely due to blundering into the condition of species arrogance and existential solipsism that holds humanity in its hypnotic sway. Instead of such seemingly uncontroversial empirical assessments as "we are so adept at using energy and manipulating the environment that we are now a defining force in the geological process on the surface of the Earth," factoring in a candid admission of our powerlessness to create (or even imagine) another way of life might yield: "we are so impotent to control our numbers, appetites, and plundering technologies, and so indifferent to our swallowing up the more-than-human world, that we are now a colonizing force in the biosphere stripping it of its biological wealth and potential, as well as of its extraordinary beauty and creative art." "To become ever more masters of the world," wrote Jonas, "to advance from power to power, even if only collectively and perhaps no longer by choice, can now be seen to be the chief vocation of mankind" (Jonas 2010, 17). When he wrote these words, he more than suspected the grave price of mankind's advancing from power to power: the unraveling of the web of Life entailed by the reconstruction of the biosphere to serve one species. But he also did not miss the profound forfeiting of freedom to cultivate another kind of power—the power to let things be, the power of self-limitation, the power to celebrate the Creation—that is the price of mankind's vocation of mastery (Heidegger 1977, 28, 32).[19] "The almighty we, or Man personified is, alas, an abstraction," Jonas insightfully noted. "*Man* may have become more powerful; *men* very probably the opposite" (Jonas 1974, 22). The Anthropocene discourse clings to the almighty power of that jaded abstraction "Man" and to the promised land his God-posturing might yet deliver him, namely, a planet managed for the production of resources and governed for the containment of risks. By the same token, however, the power of Anthropos is herding men willy-nilly into the banished condition of being forced to participate in a master identity where there will be no escaping from the existential and ethical consequences of that identity. That our survival as a species may be in jeopardy is a concern shared by all, but is not *who* we are on Earth also of paramount significance? As Jonas cryptically observed: "The image of man is at stake" (ibid. 24). If in our popular fictions we make archetypal villains those who assimilate others in order to inflate their own enterprise—the Borg—what will men make of themselves when they finally get around to facing Man's assimilating mode of operation?

Deconstructing the Anthropocene

Modes of thinking mesh with how people act and with the ways of life they embrace. Modes of thinking themselves are made possible and structured through *concepts*, among which those Ian Hacking dubbed "elevator concepts" are especially potent (Hacking 2000).[20] Thus ways of life are, to a large extent, manifestations of concepts—of the ideas they foster and the possibilities of action they afford, delimit, and rule out. We need not go too far afield speculating, nor wait to see what the future holds, to ascertain what way of life "the Anthropocene" steers humanity toward: it is exhibited perspicuously in today's literature of the Anthropocene and its popular extensions, which, in alliance, constitute a discourse in the strong sense of organizing the perception of a world picture (past, present, and future) through a set of ideas and prescriptions. The high profile of this discourse is beholden to the authoritative cadre of experts zealously championing the nomenclature, coupled with the infectiousness of the term's narcissistic overtones, reinforced by a fetishizing of factuality that blindsides normative exploration, all bundled together in the familiar feel of history's unstoppable momentum.

What does the discourse of the Anthropocene communicate? Nothing about it—much less the name—offers an alternative to the civilizational revamping of Earth as a base of human operations and functional stage for history's uninterrupted performance. The discourse subjects us to the time-honored narrative of human ascent into a distinguished species; a naturalized, subtly glamorized rendition of the "I" as on a par with stupendous forces of Nature; a homogenized protagonist named "the human enterprise" undefended for either its singularity (are all humans involved in one enterprise?) or its insularity (are nonhumans excluded from the enterprise?); a reification of demographic and economic trends as inescapable, leaving the historically constructed identity of *Homo sapiens* as planetary ruler undisturbed and giving permission to humanity's expansionist proclivities to continue—under the auspices of just-the-facts—as the independent variables of the situation; a sidestepping of confronting Life's unraveling, representing it instead as a worthy criterion for a new name; and a predilection for managerial and technological solutions, including a partiality for geoengineering, which, if worsening

24

climate scenarios continue to materialize, will likely be promoted as necessary to save civilization (e.g., Crutzen 2006).[21] Not to put too fine a point on it, the Anthropocene discourse delivers a familiar anthropocentric credo, with requisite judicious warnings thrown into the mix and meekly activated caveats about needed research to precede megatechnological experimentations.[22]

A cavalcade of facts is provided in order to display how human impact is, beyond dispute, leaving a legible mark on the Earth's biostratigraphy, chemostratigraphy, and lithostratigraphy. Through the facts thus meticulously rendered, the causal agency of human domination is spectacularly exhibited, and, at the same time, cognitively muted by twisting domination—by means of the relentless overlay of data—"into the pure truth" (Horkheimer and Adorno 1972, 9).

The discourse of the Anthropocene is arguably an ideational preview of how this concept will materialize into planetary inhabitation by the collective. As a cohesive discourse, it blocks alternative forms of human life on Earth from vying for attention. By upholding history's forward thrust, it also submits to its totalizing (and, in that sense, spurious) ideology of delivering "continuous improvement" (L. Marx 1996, 210).[23] By affirming the centrality of man—as both causal force and subject of concern—the Anthropocene shrinks the discursive space for challenging the domination of the biosphere, offering instead a techno-scientific pitch for its rationalization and a pragmatic plea for resigning ourselves to its actuality. The very concept of the Anthropocene crystallizes human dominion, corralling the already-pliable-in-that-direction human mind into viewing our master identity as manifestly destined, quasi-natural, and sort of awesome.[24] The Anthropocene accepts the humanization of Earth as reality, even though this is still contestable, partially reversible, and worthy of resistance and of inspiring a different vision. Yet the Anthropocene discourse perpetuates the concealment that the human takeover is (by now) an unexamined *choice*, one which human beings have it within both our power and our nature to rescind if only we focused our creative, critical gaze upon it.

As Ulrich Beck noted two decades ago, humanity has become threatened by the side effects of its technological and expansionist excesses (1992). The Anthropocene discourse is deeply concerned about this "risk civilization." But cloistered as it remains within a humanistic mindset, it appears unwilling to acknowledge (the significance of the fact) that

nonhuman existence and freedom—and Earth's very art of Life-making—
are menaced by the human enterprise itself, whose potential to emerge
relatively unscathed from its civilizational game of Russian roulette will
only leave humanity stranded on a planet once rich in Life turned into
a satellite of resources. As poet and deep ecologist Gary Snyder wrote
many years ago in *Turtle Island*, "if the human race . . . were to survive at
the expense of many plant and animal species, *it would be no victory*" (1974,
103, emphasis added).

Philosopher Edmund Burke observed that the power of words is to
"have an opportunity of making a deep impression and taking root in
the mind" (1958, 173). There are compelling reasons to blockade the word
Anthropocene from such an opportunity. As a Janus-faced referent, it
points to Man, on the one hand, and to the spatiotemporal reality of Earth,
on the other, presenting as a straightforward empirical match what has
been, to a far greater extent, the upshot of a plundering forcing. The occupation of the biosphere is *constitutive* of the conceptual flavor and pre-
scriptive content of the Anthropocene—which, turned into a way of life,
will enact that occupation for as long as it can be made sustainable. Thus
if the "Anthropocene" were seen as our roadmap forward, it would draw
the human collective—docilely or kicking and screaming—to be partici-
pants in a project of rationalized domination perpetuated into, and *as*, the
future. Such a prospect is a call to arms against the still-ruling idea of Man
and his newfound audacity to engrave his name onto a slice of eternity.

What Henry Thoreau might have thought of "the Anthropocene" is
likely consonant with his perspective on the Flint family of Concord naming
the pond by their farm after themselves. "*Flints' Pond!*" he exclaimed:

> Such is the poverty of our nomenclature. What right had the
> unclean and stupid farmer, whose farm abutted on this sky water,
> whose shores he has ruthlessly laid bare, to give his name to it? Some
> skin-flint, who loved better the reflecting surface of a dollar, or a
> bright cent, in which he could see his own brazen face; who regarded
> even the wild ducks which settled in it as trespassers; his fingers
> grown into crooked and horny talons from the long habit of grasping
> harpy-like;—so it [Flints' Pond] is not named for me. I go not there
> to see him nor hear of him; who never *saw* it, who never bathed in
> it, who never protected it, who never spoke a good word for it, who
> never thanked God that he had made it. (Thoreau 1991, 158–59)

The Anthropocene? Such is the poverty of our nomenclature to bow once more before the tedious showcasing of Man. To offer a name which has no added substantive content, no specific empirical or ethical overtones, no higher vision ensconced within it—beyond just Anthropos defining a geological epoch. If a new name were called for, then why not have a conversation or a debate about *what* it should be, instead of being foisted (for a very long time, I might add) with the Age of Man as the "obvious" choice?[25]

Integration or Takeover?

Indeed, why not choose a name whose higher calling we must rise to meet? We might, for example, opt for ecotheologian Thomas Berry's proposed "Ecozoic," which embraces Earth's integral living community, and invites human history in concert with natural history into uncharted realms of beauty, diversity, abundance, and freedom. "Evaluating our present situation," Berry wrote, "I submit that we have terminated the Cenozoic Era of the geo-biological systems of the planet. Sixty-five million years of life development are terminated. Extinction is taking place throughout the life systems on a scale unequaled since the terminal phase of the Mesozoic Era." Why is this extinction event not all over the news, and why does the culture's intelligentsia follow suit by understating what the mainstream passes over in silence? As Berry argued in all his work, this event might shake humanity out of our disconnection, inaugurating "a period when humans would dwell upon the Earth in a mutually enhancing manner. This new mode of being of the planet," he continued, "I describe as the Ecozoic Era.... The Ecozoic can be brought into being only by the integral life community itself" (Berry 2008 359–60). What it would demand of humanity as a member of that integral life Berry called the Great Work (1999).

Integration within an organism, an ecosystem, a bioregion, a family, or a community signals a state of being within which gifts of wellness can flow. Being integral, along with the kin quality of possessing integrity, mean working harmoniously together, enhancing and complementing one another, supporting mutual flourishing, respecting distinct identities and appropriate boundaries, and experiencing union-in-diversity.

Through ecological connection, evolutionary change, and organisms' partial shaping of environmental chemistry and morphology, wild nature generates diversity, abundance, complexity, and *umwelts* (meaning different sensory modalities and thus different forms of awareness). To integrate the human within this original matrix would signal humanity's living in integrity in the biosphere, and reaping such gifts as elude our anthropocentric civilization which appears incapable of conceiving that the wellness of human mind, emotion, body, and surroundings can be built on anything other than "resources."

Living in integration with wild nature is not a veiled invitation for humanity to return to its pre-Neolithic phase;[26] nor does it automatically signal (in my view) an *a priori* ceiling to technological innovation; nor is it intended to conjure a naive view of life as an Edenic kingdom. It is not my aim here to recommend what human integration within the biosphere might specifically look like, but instead to contend about the *prerequisite* for such a way of life to emerge: namely, catching "a sideways glance of a vast nonhuman world that has been denigrated by the concepts, institutions, and practices associated with 'the human'" (Calarco 2012, 56); and also becoming receptive to the view that if the imperative of respecting the natural world's self-integrity and intrinsic value appears unimposing to the human mind, it is because the human mind has been conditioned and enclosed by a species-supremacist civilization. Only from a perspective of profound deference for the living world can an integrated human life be imagined and created. The Anthropocene discourse makes no gesture in the direction of such deference, opting instead to retread the ruts of human self-concern and self-adulation.

The merger between the social and the natural that we are in the midst of completing is not about mutual integration, nor even about a hitherto socially underappreciated human-nonhuman "composition" (Latour 2011). This merger is about *takeover*, which has supervened from an alienated praxis on Earth wherein civilized humans have wiped out and reconstructed the more-than-human world for purposes of assimilation—purposes that have been (quite specifically and frankly) unilaterally defined to aggrandize the human enterprise, and most especially its privileged subgroups. There is a yawning chasm between assimilation of the natural *by* the social, on one hand, and integration of the natural *and* the social, on the other—a chasm that the Anthropocene discourse unfailingly blankets in its nebulous descriptions of our present condition of "social-natural coupling."[27]

Takeover (or assimilation) has proceeded by biotic cleansing and impoverishment: using up and poisoning the soil; making beings killable;[28] putting the fear of God into the animals such that they cower or flee in our presence; renaming fish "fisheries," animals "livestock," trees "timber," rivers "freshwater," mountaintops "overburden," and seacoasts "beachfront," so as to legitimize conversion, extermination, and commodification ventures. The impact of assimilation is relentless—as we can see all around us—and it is grounded in the experience of alienation and the attitude of entitlement. Assimilation does not signal the "coupling" of society and nature; rather, it breeds scarcity for both. Of course scarcity for humans and nonhumans will, now and then, always arise; but its deepening persistence, and the suffering it is auguring for all life, is an artifact of human expansionism at every level. If the Anthropocene's dream to avert scarcity for ten billion humans (on a gardened smart planet) is somehow realized, scarcity will painfully manifest elsewhere— in homogenized landscapes, in emptied seas, in nonhuman starvations, in extinctions.

For human and biosphere to become integral invites sweeping away the paltry view of the planet as an assortment of "resources" (or "natural capital," "ecosystem services," "working landscapes," and the like), for a cosmic and truer vision of Earth as a wild planet overflowing in abundance and creativity.

The Anthropocene discourse touts the unavoidable merger of the human-natural, which, according to its reports, calls us to the high road of becoming good managers of the standing reserve. It thus masks an invitation to opt for the low road of rationalizing (and relatedly "greening") humanity's totalitarian regime on Earth. But lifting the banner of human integrity invites the *priority* of our pulling back and scaling down, of welcoming limitations of our numbers, economies, and habitats for the sake of a higher, more inclusive freedom and quality of life. Integration calls for embracing our planetary membership; deindustrializing our relationship with the land, seas, and domestic animals; granting the biosphere unexploited and contiguous large-scale geographies to express its ecological and evolutionary arts; and ensuring our descendants the privilege of witnessing Earth's grandeur. In making ourselves integral, and opening into our deepest gift of safeguarding the breadth of Life, the divine spirit of the human surfaces into the light.

Notes

1   This chapter originally appeared in *Environmental Humanities*, vol. 3 (2013): 129–47.

2   Anthropocene exponents invoke the straw-man definition of "wilderness" as a completely untouched-by-humans state; this enables them to make an irrefutable claim that it is entirely gone. Defenders of wild nature, however, regard wilderness as large tracts of relatively undisturbed natural areas. (For discussion of remaining wildernesses, see Sanderson et al. 2002; Caro et al. 2011.) In the words of environmental author Paul Kingsnorth (2013), wilderness defense is not about the illusion of guarding pristine states of nature, but about "large-scale, functioning ecosystems ... worth getting out of bed to protect from destruction."

3   Boundaries in the strata marking transitions from one geological period to another are referred to as golden spikes. In the case of transitioning into the Anthropocene, a glut of such markers are offered—from mass extinction and human and livestock biomass, to climate change and the nitrogen cycle, from manmade chemicals and radioactive materials, to roads and certain cities, which according to its supporters warrant the designation of the proposed geological epoch. See Vince 2011; Jones 2011; Zalasiewicz et al. 2010.

4   Ecological psychologist David Kidner argues this point as follows: "Even a rudimentary ecological awareness makes it clear that nature emerges through the interaction between *many* forms of life; and absolute control by any single species does not signal a unique form of construction, but rather the death of the ecosystem. Thus the notion that humans have 'constructed' the wilderness stems from a delusory anthropocentric arrogance that greatly overestimates human contributions while downplaying those of other life forms almost to the point of nonexistence" (2014, 13).

5   But also compare Lenton: "In a feat unprecedented for a single animal species, humanity's total energy use has now exceeded that of the entire ancient biosphere before oxygenic photosynthesis, reaching about a tenth of the energy processed by today's biosphere" (2008, 691); or the *New York Times* (2011): "We are the only species to have defined a geological period by our activity—something usually performed by major glaciations, mass extinction and the colossal impact of objects from outer space."

6   On the Anthropocene and "eco-optimism" see Wente (2013); Marris et al. (2011).

7   For example, according to Peter Kareiva and his colleagues, "all around the world, a mix of climate change and nonnative species has created a *wealth of novel ecosystems* catalyzed by human activities" (2011, 35, emphasis added; also Ellis 2011).

8   I regard this complex as composed of three mutually reinforcing and widely shared beliefs: the Earth is a collection of resources and services; the planet belongs to people; and humans are different from, and superior to, all other life forms.

9   For analyses, see Manes (1992), Steiner (2005), Crist (2013).

10   I use "Life" (capital L) as shorthand for the interdependent arising of biological diversity, ecological complexity, evolutionary potential, and variety of minds that occurs in terrestrial and marine wildernesses. By "wilderness" I do not refer to the spurious sense of untouched, pristine spaces, but to large-scale natural areas off-limits to excessive interference by civilized people, areas in

which diversity, complexity, speciation, and the wild and free lives of nonhumans may not only exist but *flourish*, and where humans—far from being in charge—can still end up being some other being's lunch.

11 The link between trade and biological decline has been documented for many specific cases (such as Brazilian and Indonesian rainforests), but has recently also been globally estimated: "developing countries find themselves degrading habitat and threatening biodiversity for the sake of producing exports. Among the net exporters a total of 35% of domestically recorded species threats are linked to production for export. In Madagascar, Papua New Guinea, Sri Lanka and Honduras, this proportion is approximately 50–60%" (Lenzen et al. 2012, 109). Add to this current assessment of trade's enormous impact on biodiversity that *more* trade routes are rapidly opening around the world and that existing ones are expanding. For example, in the port of Los Angeles/Long Beach alone, container traffic is expected to double by 2030, while in the next few years, Africa could be China's biggest trade partner (*Economist* 2013a). The frenzy of moving more and more stuff around the world—fueled by growing human numbers and increasing affluence within a capitalist profit-driven system—is at the core of civilization's superficial definition of "prosperity," and a death knell for the more-than-human world.

12 The phrase might also be "Neo North Americas," except that the Old World remains the occidental paragon of the erasure of the wild.

13 The term "human enterprise" is used in publications on the Anthropocene to characterize the trajectory of human development from the hunter-gatherer phase through the industrial revolution, to the post–Second World War period of the "Great Acceleration" into the present time. Sometimes "human enterprise" is used multiple times in a single publication (for example, at least fourteen times in Steffen et al. 2011a). To my knowledge "the human enterprise" is never defined, allowing for the cultural meaning (encouraged also by its hint of Star Trek) of history as unfolding progress to be readable in the term. In this paper, I rhetorically tap into the expression "the human enterprise," not to target Anthropocene exponent Will Steffen and his coauthors (who seem especially partial to it), but to flag the anthropocentric, progress-laden preoccupations and narratives of the Anthropocene discourse that the expression captures.

14 For example, after sketching the emergence of hominid tool-making, rudimentary weapons, control of fire, and a subsequent shift to an omnivorous diet, Will Steffen and his colleagues inform us that the human brain size grew three-fold, giving "humans the largest brain-to-body ratio of any animal on the Earth," which in turn enabled the development of language, writing, accumulation of knowledge, and social learning. "This has ultimately led to a massive—and rapidly increasing—store of knowledge upon which humanity has eventually developed complex civilizations and continues to increase its power to manipulate the environment. No other species now on Earth or in Earth history comes anywhere near this capability" (Steffen et al. 2011a, 846; Ellis 2012).

15 This move of layering so many coats of "the factual" as to smother the call of "the normative" was pointed out by critical theorists as a characteristic of the Enlightenment worldview: "The new ideology has as its objects the world as such. It makes use of the worship of facts by no more than elevating a disagreeable existence into the world of facts in representing it meticulously. This transference makes existence itself a substitute for meaning and right" (Horkheimer and Adorno 1972, 148).

16 Writes Thomas Berry: "Our primordial spontaneities, which give us a delight in existence and enable us to interact creatively with natural phenomena, are being stifled. Somehow we have become autistic. We don't hear the voices. We are not entranced with the universe, with the natural world. We are entranced instead with domination over the natural world, with bringing about violent transformation" (quoted in Jensen 2002, 36).

17 Most publications in the Anthropocene genre offer the rote prediction that human population will increase by at least two billion by mid to end century; they report this as though it were a natural event beyond judgment or human ability to control. For arguments to stabilize and reduce the global population, and why it is achievable, see Cafaro and Crist (2012); Foreman (2011).

18 The Anthropocene literature often embraces Western-style economic development as inexorable and desirable. For example, Kareiva et al. write: "Scientists have coined a name for our era—the Anthropocene—to emphasize that we have entered a new geological era in which humans dominate every flux and cycle of the planet's ecology and geochemistry. Most people worldwide (regardless of culture) welcome opportunities that development provides to improve lives of grinding rural poverty" (2011, 35).

19 Nor did Heidegger miss that implication: "The rule of Enframing [the way of life and mindset locked into the framework of ordering the world as standing-reserve] threatens man with the possibility that it could be denied to him to enter into a more original revealing and hence to experience the call of a more primal truth. . . . Enframing . . . threatens to sweep man into ordering as the supposed single way of revealing, and so thrusts man into the danger of the surrender of his free essence" (1977, 28, 32).

20 Elevator words are "used to say something about the world, or about what we say or think about the world . . . [that] are at a higher level" (Hacking 2000, 22–23). The Anthropocene qualifies as an "elevator concept."

21 Discussion of geoengineering is standard fare in the Anthropocene discourse. In my view, this discourse (in its conjoined scientific, environmentalist, and journalistic venues) has become the chief force of normalizing the expectation of such megatechnological experimentation in (and/or with) the biosphere.

22 "The Anthropocene will be a warning to the world," quips Crutzen (quoted in Kolbert 2011). Why (and how) would a term *with no content* other than the brazen face of "anthropos" stamped over the face of the Earth, be a warning to the world?

23 For an implicit and explicit telling of history as a record of continuous improvement, see Ellis (2011, 2012).

24 A related point is made by conservation biologist Tim Caro and his colleagues regarding the consequences for conservation of adopting the term Anthropocene: "We fear that the concept of pervasive human-caused change may cultivate hopelessness in those dedicated to conservation and may even be an impetus for accelerated changes in land use motivated by profit" (2011, 185). In a different and more caustic vein, Jensen writes the following about the proposed name: "Of course members of this culture, who have named themselves with no shred of irony or humility *Homo sapiens*, would, as they murder the planet, declare this the age of man" (2013, 41).

25 The name Anthropocene was debated in the Spring 2013 issue of *Earth Island Journal*, including contributions from Raj Patel, Gus Speth, Kathleen Dean Moore, and Derrick Jensen among others. Moore and Jensen offer insightful critiques of this nomenclature.

26 Though questing in the wilderness is a birthright that some people are called to seek out (see Drengson 2004). This possibility for those who would choose it is, needless to say, being eclipsed for future people by the destruction of wilderness.

27 Reference to the "tight coupling" of the social and the natural systems occurs frequently in the literature. For example, Steffen and his colleagues describe "the human enterprise [as] now a fully coupled, interacting component of the Earth system itself" (2011b, 740; also Kareiva and Marvier 2012; Kotchen and Young 2007.

28 Donna Haraway's expression (2008, 80ff).

TWO

Staying with the Trouble
Anthropocene, Capitalocene, Chthulucene

Donna J. Haraway[1]

"We are all lichens."[2]

"*Think we must.* We must think."[3]

What happens when human exceptionalism and methodological individualism, those old saws of Western philosophy and political economics, become unthinkable in the best sciences, whether natural or social? Seriously unthinkable: not available to think with. Biological sciences have been especially potent in fermenting notions about all the mortal inhabitants of the earth since the imperializing eighteenth century. *Homo sapiens*—the Human as species, the Anthropos as the human species, Modern Man—was a chief product of these knowledge practices. What happens when the best biologies of the twenty-first century cannot do their job with bounded individuals plus contexts, when organisms plus environments, or genes plus whatever they need, no longer sustain the overflowing richness of biological knowledges, if they ever did? What happens when organisms plus environments can hardly be remembered for the same reasons that even Western-indebted people can no longer figure themselves as individuals and societies of individuals in human-only histories? Surely, such a transformative time on Earth must not be named the Anthropocene!

In this essay, with all the unfaithful offspring of the sky gods, with my littermates who find a rich wallow in multispecies muddles, I want to make a critical and joyful fuss about these matters. I want to stay with the trouble, and the only way I know to do that is in generative joy, terror, and collective thinking.[4]

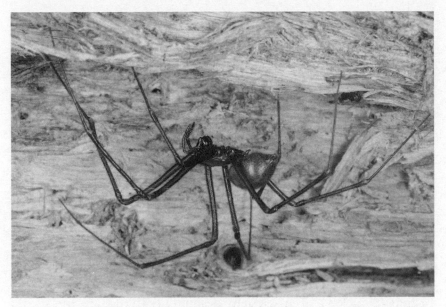

Photo by Gustavo Hormiga, http://araneoidea.lifedesks.org/pages/302

My first demon familiar in this task will be a spider, *Pimoa cthulu*, who lives under stumps in the redwood forests of Sonoma and Mendocino counties, near where I live in North Central California (Hormiga 1994, 549). Nobody lives everywhere; everybody lives somewhere. Nothing is connected to everything; everything is connected to something (van Dooren 2014).[5] This spider is in place, has a place, yet is named for intriguing travels elsewhere. This spider will help me with returns, and with roots and routes.[6] The eight-legged tentacular arachnid that I appeal to gets her generic name from the language of the Goshute people of Utah and her specific name from denizens of the depths, from the abyssal and elemental entities, called chthonic.[7] The chthonic powers of Terra infuse its tissues everywhere, in spite of the civilizing efforts of the agents of sky gods to astralize them and set up chief Singletons and their tame committees of multiples or subgods, the One and the Many. With *Pimoa cthulu*, I propose a name for an elsewhere and elsewhen that was, still is, and might yet be: the Chthulucene. I remember that "tentacle" comes from the Latin "tentaculum," meaning "feeler," and "tentare," meaning "to feel" and "to try"; and I know that my leggy spider has many-armed allies. Myriad tentacles will be needed to tell the story of the Chthulucene.[8]

The tentacular ones tangle me in SF. Their many appendages make string figures; they entwine me in the poiesis—the making—of speculative fabulation, science fiction, science fact, speculative feminism, so far. The tentacular ones make attachments and detachments; they make cuts and knots; they make a difference; they weave paths and consequences but not determinisms; they are both open and knotted in some ways and not others.[9] SF is storytelling and fact telling; it is the patterning of possible worlds and possible times, material-semiotic worlds, gone, here, and yet to come. I work with string figures as a theoretical trope, a way to think-with a host of companions in sym-poietic threading, felting, tangling, tracking, and sorting. I work with and in SF as material-semiotic composting, as theory in the mud, as muddle.[10] The tentacular are not disembodied figures; they are cnidarians, spiders, fingery beings like humans and raccoons, squids, jellyfish, neural extravaganzas, fibrous entities, flagellated beings, myofibril braids, matted and felted microbial and fungal tangles, probing creepers, swelling roots, reaching and climbing tendrilled ones. The tentacular are also nets and networks, IT critters, in and out of clouds. Tentacularity is about life lived along lines—and such a wealth of lines—not at points, not in spheres. "The inhabitants of the world, creatures of all kinds, human and non-human, are wayfarers"; generations are like "a series of interlaced trails" (Ingold 2007, 116–19). String figures all.[11]

All the tentacular stringy ones have made me unhappy with post-humanism, even as I am nourished by much generative work done under that sign. My partner Rusten Hogness suggested compost instead of posthuman(ism), as well as humusities instead of humanities, and I jumped into that wormy pile.[12] Human as humus has potential, if we could chop and shred human as homo, the detumescing project of a self-making and planet-destroying CEO. Imagine a conference not on the Future of the Humanities in the Capitalist Restructuring University, but instead on the Power of the Humusities for a Habitable Multispecies Muddle! Ecosexual artists Beth Stephens and Annie Sprinkle made a bumper sticker for me, for us, for SF: "Composting is so hot!"[13]

The earth of the ongoing Chthulucene is sympoietic, not autopoietic. Mortal Worlds (Terra, Earth, Gaia, Chthulu, the myriad names and powers that are not Greek, Latin, or Indo-European at all)[14] do not make themselves, no matter how complex and multileveled the systems, no matter how much order out of disorder might be produced in generative autopoietic system breakdowns and relaunchings at higher levels of order. Autopoietic systems are hugely interesting—witness the history of cybernetics and information sciences; but they are not good models for living and dying worlds and their critters. Autopoietic systems are not closed, spherical, deterministic, or teleological; but they are not quite good enough models for the mortal SF World. Poiesis is sym-chthonic, sym-poietic, always partnered all the way down, with no starting and subsequently interacting "units."[15] The Chthulucene does not close in on itself; it does not round off; its contact zones are ubiquitous and continuously spin out loopy tendrils. Spider is a much better figure for sympoiesis than any inadequately leggy vertebrate of whatever pantheon. Tentacularity is sym-chthonic, wound with abyssal and dreadful graspings, frayings, and weavings, passing relays again and again, in the generative recursions that make up living and dying.

Imagining that I was somehow original, I first used the term sympoiesis in a grasp for something other than the lures of autopoiesis, only to be digitally handed M. Beth Dempster's Master of Environmental Studies thesis written in 1998 in Canada, in which she suggested the term "sympoiesis" for "collectively-producing systems that do not have self-defined spatial or temporal boundaries. Information and control are distributed among components. The systems are evolutionary and have the potential for surprising change." By contrast, autopoietic systems are "self-producing" autonomous units "with self defined spatial or temporal boundaries that tend to be centrally controlled, homeostatic, and predictable" (Dempster 1998).[16] Dempster argued that many systems are mistaken for autopoietic that are really sympoietic. I think this point is important for thinking about rehabilitation (making livable again) and sustainability amidst the porous tissues and open edges of damaged but still ongoing living worlds, like the planet Earth and its denizens in current times being called the Anthropocene. If it is true that neither biology nor philosophy any longer supports the notion of independent organisms in environments, that is, interacting units plus contexts/rules, then sympoiesis is the name of the game in spades. Methodological individualism amended by autopoiesis is not good enough figurally or scientifically; it misleads us down deadly paths. Barad's agential realism and intra-action become common sense, and perhaps a lifeline for Terran wayfarers.

SF, string figuring, is sympoietic. Thinking-with my work on cat's cradle, as well as with the work of another of her companions in thinking, Félix Guattari, Isabelle Stengers relayed back to me how players pass back and forth to each other the patterns-at-stake, sometimes conserving, sometimes proposing and inventing:

> More precisely, com-menting, if it means thinking-with—that is becoming-with—is in itself a way of relaying. . . . But knowing that what you take has been held out entails a particular thinking 'between.' It does not demand fidelity, still less fealty, rather a particular kind of loyalty, the answer to the trust of the held out hand. Even if this trust is not in 'you' but in 'creative uncertainty,' even if the consequences and meaning of what has been done, thought or written, do not belong to you anymore than they belonged to the one you take the relay from, one way or another the relay is now in your hands, together with the demand that you do not proceed with 'mechanical confidence.' [In cat's cradling, at least] two pairs of hands are needed, and in each successive step, one is 'passive,' offering the result of its previous operation, a string entanglement, for the other to operate, only to become active again at the next step, when the other presents the new entanglement. But it can also be said that each time the 'passive' pair is the one that holds, and is held by the entanglement, only to 'let it go' when the other one takes the relay. (Stengers 2011, 34)

In passion and action, detachment and attachment, this is what I call cultivating response-ability; that is also collective knowing and doing, an ecology of practices. Whether we asked for it or not, the pattern is in our hands. The answer to the trust of the held out hand: think we must.

Marilyn Strathern is an ethnographer of thinking practices. She defines anthropology as "studying relations with relations"—a hugely consequential, mind-and-body altering sort of commitment (1991, 1995, 2005). Nourished by her lifelong work in highland Papua New Guinea (Mt. Hagen), Strathern writes about accepting the risk of relentless contingency, of putting relations at risk with other relations, from unexpected worlds. Embodying the practice of feminist speculative fabulation in the scholarly mode, Strathern taught me—taught us—a game-changing, simple thing: "it matters what ideas we use to think other ideas" (1992, 10; also 1990). I composed a kind of chant from Strathern's SF pattern. I compost my soul in this hot pile. The worms are not human; their undulating bodies ingest and reach, and their feces fertilize worlds.

It matters what thoughts think thoughts.

It matters what knowledges know knowledges.
It matters what relations relate relations.
It matters what worlds world worlds.
It matters what stories tell stories.

It matters what thoughts think thoughts. What is it to surrender the capacity to think? These times called the Anthropocene are times of multispecies, including human, urgency: of great mass death and extinction; of onrushing disasters whose unpredictable specificities are foolishly taken as unknowability itself; of refusing to know and to cultivate the capacity of response-ability; of refusing to be present in and to onrushing catastrophe in time; of unprecedented looking away. Surely, to say "unprecedented" in view of the realities of the last centuries is to say something almost unimaginable. How can we think in times of urgencies *without* the self-indulgent and self-fulfilling myths of apocalypse, when every fiber of our being is interlaced, even complicit, in the webs of processes that must somehow be engaged and repatterned? Recursively, whether we asked for it or not, the pattern is in our hands. The answer to the trust of the held out hand: think we must.

Instructed by Valerie Hartouni, I turn to Hannah Arendt's analysis of the Nazi war criminal Adolf Eichmann's inability to think. In that surrender of thinking lay the "banality of evil" of the particular sort that could make the disaster of the Anthropocene, with its ramped up genocides and speciescides, come true (Arendt 1964; also Hartouni 2012, esp. chapter three).[17] This outcome is still at stake; think we must; we must think! In Hartouni's reading, Arendt insisted that thought was profoundly different from what we might call disciplinary knowledge or science rooted in evidence, or the sorting of truth and belief or fact and opinion or good and bad. Thinking, in Arendt's sense, is not a process for evaluating information and argument, for being right or wrong, for judging oneself or others to be in truth or error. All of that is important, but not what Arendt had to say about the evil of thoughtlessness that I want to bring into the question of the geohistorical conjuncture being called the Anthropocene.

Arendt witnessed in Eichmann not an incomprehensible monster, but something much more terrifying—she saw commonplace thoughtlessness. That is, here was a human being unable to make present to himself what was absent, what was not himself, what the world in its sheer not-oneselfness is and what claims-to-be inhere in not-oneself. Here was someone who could not be a wayfarer, could not entangle, could not track the lines of living and dying, could not cultivate response-ability, could not make present to itself what it is doing, could not live in consequences or with consequence, could not compost. Function mattered, duty mattered, but the world did not matter for Eichmann. The world does not matter in ordinary thoughtlessness. The hollowed out spaces are all filled with assessing information, determining friends and enemies, and doing busy jobs; negativity, the hollowing out of such positivity, is missed, an astonishing abandonment of thinking.[18] This quality was not an emotional lack, a lack of compassion, although surely that was true of Eichmann, but a deeper surrender to what I would call immateriality, inconsequentiality, or, in Arendt's and also my idiom, thoughtlessness. Eichmann was astralized right out of the muddle of thinking into the practice of business as usual no matter what. There was no way the world could become for Eichmann and his heirs—us?—a "matter of care" (Puig de la Bellacasa 2011). The result was active participation in genocide.

The anthropologist, feminist, cultural theorist, storyteller, and connoisseur of the tissues of heterogeneous capitalism, globalism, traveling worlds, and local places, Anna Tsing examines the "arts of living on a damaged planet,"[19] or in the title of her new book, "life in the ruins" (Tsing 2015). She performs thinking of a kind that must be cultivated in the all-too-ordinary urgencies of onrushing multispecies extinctions, genocides, immiserations, and exterminations. I name these things urgencies rather than emergencies because the latter word connotes something approaching apocalypse and its mythologies. Urgencies have other temporalities, and these times are ours. These are the times we must think; these are the times of urgencies that need stories.

Following matsutake mushrooms in their fulminating assemblages of Japanese, Americans, Chinese, Koreans, Hmong, Lao, Mexicans, fungal spores and mats, oak and pine trees, micorrhizial symbioses, pickers, buyers, shippers, restaurateurs, diners, businessmen, scientists, foresters, DNA sequencers and their changing species, and much more, Tsing practices sympoietics in edgy times. Refusing either to look away or to reduce the earth's urgency to an abstract system of causative destruction, such as a Human Species Act or undifferentiated Capitalism, Tsing argues that precarity—failure of the lying promises of Modern Progress—characterizes the lives and deaths of all Terran critters in these times. She looks for the eruptions of unexpected liveliness and the contaminated and nondeterministic, unfinished, ongoing practices of living in the ruins. She performs the force of stories; she shows in the flesh how it matters which stories tell stories as a practice of caring and thinking. "If a rush of troubled stories is the best way to tell contaminated diversity, then it's time to make that rush part of our knowledge practices. . . . Matsutake's willingness to emerge in blasted landscapes allows us to explore the ruins that have become our collective home. To follow matsutake guides us to possibilities of coexistence within environmental disturbance. This is not an excuse for further human damage. Still, matsutake show one kind of collaborative survival" (Tsing 2015, 34, 3–4).

Driven by radical curiosity, Tsing does the ethnography of "salvage accumulation" and "patchy capitalism," the kind that can no longer promise progress but can and does extend devastation and make precarity the name of our systematicity. There is no simple ethical, political, or theoretical point to take from Tsing's work; there is instead the force of engaging the world in the kind of thinking practices impossible for Eichmann's heirs. "Matsutake can catapult us into the curiosity that seems to me the first requirement of collaborative survival in precarious times" (Tsing 2015, 2). This is not a longing for salvation or some other sort of optimistic politics; neither is this a cynical quietism in the face of the depth of the trouble. Rather, Tsing proposes a commitment to living and dying with response-ability in unexpected company. Such living and dying have the best chance of cultivating conditions for ongoingness.

The ecological philosopher and multispecies ethnographer Thom van Dooren also inhabits the layered complexities of living in times of extinction, extermination, and partial recuperation; he deepens our consideration of what thinking means, of what not becoming thoughtless exacts from all of us. In his extraordinary book *Flight Ways*, van Dooren accompanies situated bird species living on the extended edge of extinction, asking what it means to hold open space for another (2014). Such holding open is far from an innocent or obvious material or ethical practice; even when successful, it exacts tolls of suffering as well as surviving as individuals and as kinds. In his examination of the practices of the North American whooping crane species survival plan, for example, van Dooren details multiple kinds of hard multispecies captivities and labors, forced life, surrogate reproductive labor, and substitute dying—none of which should be forgotten, especially in successful projects. Holding open space might—or might not—delay extinction in ways that make possible composing or recomposing flourishing naturalcultural assemblages. *Flight Ways* shows how extinction is not a point, not a single event, but more like an extended edge or a widened ledge. Extinction is a protracted slow death that unravels great tissues of ways of going on in the world for many species, including historically situated people.[20]

Van Dooren proposes that mourning is intrinsic to cultivating response-ability. In his chapter on conservation efforts for Hawaiian crows ('Alalā for Hawaiians, *Corvus hawaiiensis* for Linneans), whose forest homes and foods as well as friends, chicks, and mates have largely disappeared, van Dooren argues that it is not just human people who mourn the loss of loved ones, of place, of lifeways, but also other beings mourn. Corvids grieve loss. The point rests on biobehavioral studies as well as intimate natural history; neither the capacity nor the practice of mourning is a human specialty. Outside the dubious privileges of human exceptionalism, thinking people must learn to grieve-with.

> Mourning is about dwelling with a loss and so coming to appreci-
> ate what it means, how the world has changed, and how we must
> *ourselves* change and renew our relationships if we are to move
> forward from here. In this context, genuine mourning should open
> us into an awareness of our dependence on and relationships with
> those countless others being driven over the edge of extinction. . . .
> The reality, however, is that there *is* no avoiding the necessity of
> the difficult cultural work of reflection and mourning. This work
> is not opposed to practical action, rather it is the foundation of any
> sustainable and informed response. (van Dooren 2013)

Grief is a path to understanding entangled shared living and dying; human beings must grieve *with*, because we are in and of this fabric of undoing. Without sustained remembrance, we cannot learn to live with ghosts and so cannot think. Like the crows and with the crows, living and dead "we are at stake in each other's company" (van Dooren 2014, chapter five).[21]

At least one more SF thread is crucial to the practice of thinking, which must be thinking-with: storytelling. It matters what thoughts think thoughts; it matters what stories tell stories. Van Dooren's chapter on Sydney Harbor's little penguins (*Eudyptula minor*) succeeds in crafting a non-anthropomorphic, non-anthropocentric sense of storied place. In their resolutely "philopatric" (home loving) nesting and other life practices, these urban penguins—real, particular birds—story place, *this* place, not just any place. Establishing the reality and vivid specificity of pen-guin-storied place is a major material-semiotic accomplishment. Storying cannot any longer be put into the box of human exceptionalism. Without deserting the grounding terrain of behavioral ecology and natural history, this writing achieves powerful attunement to storying in penguin multi-modal semiotics. [22]

Ursula Le Guin taught me the carrier bag theory of storytelling and of naturalcultural history. Her theories, her stories, are capacious bags for collecting, carrying, and telling the stuff of living. "A leaf a gourd a shell a net a bag a sling a sack a bottle a pot a box a container. A holder. A recipient" (Le Guin 1989, 166).[23] So much of earth history has been told in the thrall of the fantasy of the first beautiful words and weapons, of the first beautiful weapons *as* words and vice versa. Tool, weapon, word: that is the word made flesh in the image of the sky god; that is the Anthropos. In a tragic story with only one real actor, one real world-maker, the hero, this is the Man-making tale of the hunter on a quest to kill and bring back the terrible bounty. This is the cutting, sharp, combative tale of action that defers the suffering of glutinous, earth-rotted passivity beyond bearing. All others in the prick tale are props, ground, plot space, or prey. They don't matter; their job is to be in the way, to be overcome, to be the road, the conduit, but not the traveler, not the begetter. The last thing the hero wants to know is that his beautiful words and weapons will be worthless without a bag, a container, a net.

Nonetheless, no adventurer should leave home without a sack. How did a sling, a pot, a bottle suddenly get in the story? How do such lowly things keep the story going? Or maybe even worse for the hero, how do those concave, hollowed out things, those holes in Being, from the get-go generate richer, quirkier, fuller, unfitting, ongoing stories, stories with room for the hunter but which weren't and aren't about him, the self-making Human, the human-making machine of history. The slight curve of the shell that holds just a little water, just a few seeds to give away and to receive, suggests stories of becoming-with, of reciprocal induction, of companion species whose job in living and dying is not to end the storying, the worlding. With a shell and a net, becoming human, becoming humus, becoming Terran, has another shape—i.e., the sidewinding, snaky shape of becoming-with.

Le Guin quickly assures all of us who are wary of evasive, senti-mental holisms and organicisms that she is "not, let it be said at once, an unaggressive or uncombative human being. I am an aging, angry woman laying mightily about me with my handbag, fighting hoodlums off. . . . It's just one of those damned things you have to do in order to go on gathering wild oats and telling stories" (1989, 169). There is room for conflict in Le Guin's story, but her carrier bag narratives are full of much else in wonderful, messy tales to use for retelling, or reseeding, possibilities for getting on now, as well as in deep earth history. "It sometimes seems that that [heroic] story is approaching its end. Lest there be no more telling of stories at all, some of us out here in the wild oats, amid the alien corn, think we'd better start telling another one, which maybe people can go on with when the old one's finished. . . . Hence it is with a certain feeling of urgency that I seek the nature, subject, words of the other story, the untold one, the life story" (ibid.).

Le Guin's *The Word for World Is Forest*, published in 1976, is part of her Hainish fabulations for dispersed native and colonial beings locked in struggle over imperialist exploitation and the chances for multispecies flourishing.[24] That story took place on another planet, and is very like the tale of colonial oppression in the name of pacification and resource extraction that takes place on Pandora in the blockbuster 2010 film *Avatar*. Except one particular detail is very different; Le Guin's *Forest* does not feature a repentant and redeemed "white" colonial hero. Her story has the shape of a carrier bag that is disdained by heroes. Also, even as they condemn their chief oppressor to live, rather than killing him after their victory, for Le Guin's "natives" the consequences of the freedom struggle include the lasting knowledge of how to murder *each other*, not just the invader, as well as how to recollect and perhaps relearn to flourish in the tentacular grip of this history. There is no *status quo ante*, no salvation tale, like that on Pandora. Instructed by the struggle on *Forest*'s planet of Athshe, I will stay on Terra, wherewhen the knowledge of how to murder is not scarce, and imagine that Le Guin's Hainish species have not all been of the hominid lineage or web, no matter how dispersed. To think-with is to stay with the naturalcultural multispecies trouble on earth, strengthened by the freedom struggle for a post-colonial world on Le Guin's planet of Athshea. There are no guarantees, no arrow of time, no Law of History or Science or Nature in such struggles. There is only the relentlessly contingent SF worlding of living and dying, of becoming-with and unbecoming-with, of sympoiesis, and so, just possibly, of multispecies flourishing on earth.

Like Le Guin, Bruno Latour passionately understands the need to change the story, to learn somehow to narrate—to think—outside the prick tale of Humans in History, when the knowledge of how to murder each other—and along with each other, uncountable multitudes of the living earth—is not scarce. Think we must; we must think. That means, simply, we *must* change the story; the story *must* change. Le Guin writes, "Hence it is with a certain feeling of urgency that I seek the nature, subject, words of the other story, the untold one, the life story" (1989, 169). In this terrible time called the Anthropocene, Latour argues that the fundamentals of geopolitics have been blasted open. None of the parties in crisis can call on Providence, History, Science, Progress, or any other god trick outside the common fray to resolve the troubles.[25] A common livable world must be composed, bit by bit, or not at all. What used to be called nature has erupted into ordinary human affairs, and vice versa, in such a way and with such permanence as to change fundamentally means and prospects for going on, including going on at all. Searching for compositionist practices capable of building effective new collectives, Latour argues that we must learn to tell "Gaia stories." If that word is too hard, then we can call our narrations "geostories," in which "all the former props and passive agents have become active without, for that, being part of a giant plot written by some overseeing entity" (Latour 2013a, Lecture Three). Those who tell Gaiastories or geostories are the "Earthbound," those who eschew the dubious pleasures of transcendent plots of modernity and the purifying division of society and nature. Latour argues that we face a stark divide: "Some are readying themselves to live as Earthbound in the Anthropocene; others decided to remain as Humans in the Holocene" (Latour 2013b).[26]

In much of his writing, Latour develops the language and imagery of trials of strength; and in thinking about the Anthropocene and the Earthbound, he extends that metaphor to develop the difference between a police action, where peace is restored by an already existing order, and war or politics, where real enemies must be overcome to establish what will be. Latour is determined to avoid the idols of a ready-to-hand fix, such as Laws of History, Modernity, the State, God, Progress, Reason, Decadence, Nature, Technology, or Science, as well as the debilitating disrespect for difference and shared finitude inherent in those who already know the answers toward those who only need to learn them—by force, faith, or self-certain pedagogy. Those who "believe" they have the answers to the present urgencies are terribly dangerous. Those who refuse to be *for* some ways of living and dying and not others are equally dangerous. Matters of fact, matters of concern,[27] and matters of care are knotted in string figures, in SF.

Latour embraces sciences, not Science. In geopolitics, "The important point here is to realize that the facts of the matter cannot be delegated to a higher unified authority that would have done the choice *in our stead.* Controversies—no matter how spurious they might be—are no excuse to delay the *decision* about which side represents our world *better*" (Latour 2013b). Latour *aligns* himself with the reports of the Intergovernmental Panel on Climate Change (IPCC); he does not *believe* its assessments and reports; he *decides* what is strong and trustworthy and what is not. He casts his lot with some worlds and wordings and not others. One need not hear Latour's "decision" discourse with an individualist ear; he is a compositionist intent on understanding how a common world, how collectives, are built-with each other, where all the builders are not human beings. This is neither relativism nor rationalism; it is SF, which Latour would call both sciences and scientifiction and I would call both sciences and speculative fabulation—all of which are political sciences, in our aligned approaches.

"Alignment" is a rich metaphor for wayfarers, for the Earthbound, and does not as easily as "decision" carry the tones of modernist liberal choice discourse, at least in the United States. Further, the refusal of the modernist category of belief is also crucial to my effort to persuade us to take up the Chthulucene and its tentacular tasks.[28] Like Stengers, and like myself, Latour is a thorough-going materialist committed to an ecology of practices, to the mundane articulating of assemblages through situated work and play in the muddle of messy living and dying. Actual players, articulating with varied allies of all ontological sorts (molecules, colleagues, and much more), must compose and sustain what is and will be. Alignment in tentacular worlding must be a seriously tangled affair!

Intent on the crucial refusal of self-certainty and preexisting god tricks, which I passionately share, Latour turns to a resource—relentless reliance on the material-semiotic trope of trials of strength—that, I think, makes it unnecessarily hard to tell his and our needed new story. He defines war as the absence of a referee so that trials of strength must determine the legitimate authority. Humans in History and the Earthbound in the Anthropocene are engaged in trials of strength where there is no Referee who/which can establish what is/was/will be. History vs. Gaiastories are at stake. Those trials—the war of the Earthbound with the Humans—would not be conducted with rockets and bombs; they would be conducted with every other imaginable resource and with no god trick from above to decide life and death, truth and error. But still, we are in the story of the hero and the first beautiful words and weapons, not in the story of the carrier bag. Anything not decided in the presence of the Authority is war; Science (singular and capitalized) is the Authority; the Authority conducts police actions. In contrast, sciences (always rooted in practices) are war. Therefore, in Latour's passionate speculative fabulation, such war is our only hope for real politics. The past is as much the contested zone as the present or future.

Latour's thinking and stories need a specific kind of enemies. He draws on Carl Schmitt's "political theology," which is a theory of peace through war, with the enemy as *hostis*, with all its tones of host, hostage, guest, and worthy enemy. Only with such an enemy, Schmitt and Latour hold, is there respect and a chance to be less, not more, deadly in conflict. Those who operate within the categories of Authority and of belief are notoriously prone to exterminationist and genocidal combat (it's hard to deny that!). They are lost without a preestablished Referee. The *hostis* demands much better. But all the action remains within the narrative vise grip of trials of strength, of mortal combat, within which the knowledge of how to murder each other remains well entrenched. Latour makes clear that he does not *want* this story, but he does not propose another. The only real possibility for peace lies in the tale of the respected enemy, the *hostis*, and trials of strength. "But when you are at war, it is only through the throes of the encounters that the authority you have or don't have will be decided *depending whether you win or lose*" (Latour 2013b; also Schmitt 2003).[29]

Schmitt's enemies do not allow the story to change in its marrow; the Earthbound need a more tentacular, less binary life story. Latour's Gaiastories deserve better companions in storytelling than Schmitt. The question of whom to think-with is immensely material. I do not think Latour's dilemma can be resolved in the terms of the Anthropocene. His Earthbound will have to trek into the Chthulucene to entangle with the ongoing, snaky, unheroic, tentacular, dreadful ones, the ones who craft material-semiotic netbags of little use in trials of strength but which are capable of bringing home and sharing the means of living and dying well, perhaps even the means of ecological recuperation for human and more-than-human critters alike.

Shaping her thinking about the times called Anthropocene and "multifaced Gaia" (Stengers's term) in companionable friction with Latour, Isabelle Stengers does not ask that we recompose ourselves to become able, perhaps, to "face Gaia." But like Latour and even more like Le Guin, one of her most generative SF writers, Stengers is adamant about changing the story. Focusing on intrusion rather than composition, Stengers calls Gaia a fearful and devastating power that intrudes on our categories of thought, that intrudes on thinking itself.[30] Earth/Gaia is maker and destroyer, not resource to be exploited or ward to be protected or nursing mother promising nourishment. Gaia is not a person but a complex systemic phenomenon that composes a living planet. Gaia's intrusion into our affairs is a radically materialist event that collects up multitudes. This intrusion threatens not life on earth itself—microbes will adapt, to put it mildly—but threatens the livability of earth for vast kinds, species, assemblages, and individuals in an "event" already underway called the Sixth Great Extinction.[31]

Stengers, like Latour, evokes the name of Gaia in the way James Lovelock and Lynn Margulis did, to name complex nonlinear couplings between processes that compose and sustain entwined but nonadditive subsystems as a partially cohering systemic whole (Lovelock and Margulis 1974; Lovelock 1967).[32] In this hypothesis, Gaia is autopoietic—self-forming, boundary maintaining, contingent, dynamic, and stable under some conditions but not others. Gaia is not reducible to the sum of its parts, but achieves finite systemic coherence in the face of perturbations within parameters that are themselves responsive to dynamic systemic processes. Gaia does not and could not care about human or other biological beings' intentions or desires or needs, but Gaia puts into question our very existence, we who have provoked its brutal mutation that threatens both human and nonhuman livable presents and futures. Gaia is not about a list of questions waiting for rational policies;[33] Gaia is an intrusive event that undoes thinking as usual. "She is what specifically questions the tales and refrains of modern history. There is only one real mystery at stake, here: it is the answer we, meaning those who belong to this history, may be able to create as we face the consequences of what we have provoked."[34]

So, what have we provoked? It is past time to turn directly to the time-space-global thing called Anthropocene.[35] The term seems to have been coined in the early 1980s by University of Michigan ecologist Eugene Stoermer (d. 2012), an expert in fresh water diatoms. He introduced the term to refer to growing evidence for the transformative effects of human activities on the earth. The name Anthropocene made a dramatic star appearance in globalizing discourses in 2000 when the Dutch Nobel Prize-winning atmospheric chemist Paul Crutzen joined Stoermer to propose that human activities had been of such a kind and magnitude as to merit the use of a new geological term for a new epoch, superseding the Holocene, which dated from the end of the last ice age, or the end of the Pleistocene, about twelve thousand years ago. Anthropogenic changes signaled by the mid-eighteenth-century steam engine and planet-changing exploding use of coal were evident in the airs, waters, and rocks (Crutzen and Stoermer 2000; Crutzen 2002; Zalasiewicz et al. 2008).[36] Evidence was mounting that the acidification and warming of the oceans are rapidly decomposing coral reef ecosystems, resulting in huge ghostly white skeletons of bleached and dead or dying coral. That a symbiotic system—coral, with its watery world-making associations of cnidarians and zooanthellae with many other critters too—indicated such a global transformation will come back into our story.

But for now, notice that the Anthropocene obtained purchase in popular and scientific discourse in the context of ubiquitous urgent efforts to find ways of talking about, theorizing, modeling, and managing a Big Thing called Globalization. Climate-change modeling is a powerful positive feedback loop provoking change-of-state in systems of political and ecological discourses.[37] That Paul Crutzen was both a Nobel laureate and an atmospheric chemist mattered. By 2008, many scientists around the world had adopted the not-yet official but increasingly indispensible term;[38] and myriad research projects, performances, installations, and conferences in the arts, social sciences, and humanities found the term mandatory in their naming and thinking, not least for facing both accelerating extinctions across all biological taxa and also multispecies, including human, immiseration across the expanse of Terra. Fossil-burning human beings seem intent on making as many new fossils as possible as fast as possible. They will be read in the strata of the rocks on the land and under the waters by the geologists of the very near future, if not already. The festival of Burning Man, indeed![39]

The scale of burning ambitions of fossil-making man—of this Anthropos whose hot projects for accelerating extinctions merits a name for a geological epoch—is hard to comprehend. Leaving aside all the other accelerating extractions of minerals, plant and animal flesh, human homelands, and so on, surely, we want to say, the pace of development of renewable energy technologies and of political and technical carbon pollution-abatement measures, in the face of palpable and costly ecosystem collapses and spreading political disorders, will mitigate, if not eliminate, the burden of planet-warming excess carbon from burning still more fossil fuels. Not so. Even casual acquaintance with the daily news erodes such hopes, but the trouble is worse than what even a close reader of IPCC documents and the press will find. In "The Third Carbon Age," Michael Klare (2013), a professor of peace and world security studies at Hampshire College, lays out strong evidence against the idea that the old age of coal, replaced by the recent age of oil, will be replaced by the age of renewables.[40] He details the large and growing global national and corporate investments in renewables; clearly, there is big profit and power advantages to be had in this sector. And at the same time, every imaginable, and many unimaginable, technologies and strategic measures are being pursued by all the big global players to extract every last calorie of fossil carbon, at whatever depth and in whatever formations of sand, mud, or rock, and with whatever horrors of travel to distribution and use points, to burn before someone else gets at that calorie and burns it first in the great prick story of the first and the last beautiful words and weapons.[41] In what he calls the Age of Unconventional Oil and Gas, hydro-fracking is the tip of the (melting) iceberg. Melting of the polar seas, terrible for polar bears and for coastal peoples, is very good for big competitive military, exploration, drilling, and tanker shipping across the northern passages. Who needs an icebreaker when you can count on melting ice?

A complex systems engineer named Brad Werner addressed a session at the meetings of the American Geophysical Union in San Francisco in 2012. His point was quite simple: scientifically speaking, global capitalism "has made the depletion of resources so rapid, convenient and barrier-free that that 'earth-human systems' are becoming dangerously unstable in response." Therefore, he argued, the only scientific thing to do is: Revolt! Movements, not just individuals, are critical. What is required is action and thinking that do not fit within the dominant capitalist culture; and, said Werner, this is not a matter of opinion, but of geophysical dynamics. The reporter who covered this session summed up Werner's address: "He is saying that his research shows that our entire economic paradigm is a threat to ecological stability" (Klein 2013). Werner is not the first or the last researcher and maker of matters of concern to argue this point, but his clarity is bracing. Revolt! Think we must; we must think. Actually think, not like Eichmann the Thoughtless. Of course, the devil is in the details— how to revolt? How to matter and not just want to matter?

But at least one thing is crystal clear. No matter how much he might be caught in the generic masculine universal and how much he only looks up, the Anthropos did not do this fracking thing and he should not name this double-death-loving epoch. The Anthropos is not Burning Man after all. But because the word is already well entrenched and seems less controversial to many important players compared to the Capitalocene, I know that we will continue to need the term Anthropocene. I will use it too, sparingly; what and whom the Anthropocene collects in its refurbished netbag might prove potent for living in the ruins and even for modest Terran recuperation. Still, if we could only have one word for these SF times, surely it must be the Capitalocene.[42] Species Man did not shape the conditions for the Third Carbon Age. The story of Species Man as the agent of the Anthropocene is an almost laughable rerun of the great phallic humanizing and modernizing Adventure, where man, made in the image of a vanished god, takes on super powers in his secular-sacred ascent, only to end in tragic detumescence, once again. Autopoietic, self-making man came down once again, this time in tragic system failure, turning biodiverse ecosystems into flipped-out deserts of slimy mats and stinging jellyfish. Neither did technological determinism produce the Third Carbon Age. Coal and the steam engine did not determine the story, and besides the dates are all wrong, not because one has to go back to the last ice age, but because one has to at least include the great market and commodity reworldings of the long sixteenth and seventeenth centuries of the current era, even if we think (wrongly) that we can remain Euro-centered in thinking about "globalizing" transformations shaping the Capitalocene.[43] One must surely tell of the networks of sugar, precious metals, plantations, indigenous genocides, and slavery, with their labor innovations and relocations and recompositions of critters and things sweeping up both human and nonhuman workers of all kinds. The infectious industrial revolution of England mattered hugely, but it is only one player in planet-transforming, historically situated, new enough, world-ing relations. The relocation of peoples, microbes, plants, and animals; the leveling of vast forests; and the violent mining of metals preceded the

Icon for the Capitalocene and the Third Age of Carbon[44] Sea ice clearing from the Northwest Passage, 2012. NASA Visible Earth image by Jesse Allen, 2015, using data from the Land Atmosphere Near Real-time Capability for EOS (LANCE). National Snow and Ice Data Center. Public domain.

steam engine; but that is not a warrant for wringing one's hands about the perfidy of the Anthropos, or of Species Man, or of Man the Hunter.

The systemic stories of the linked metabolisms, articulations, or co-productions (pick your metaphor) of economies and ecologies, of histories and human and nonhuman critters, must be relentlessly opportunistic and contingent. They must also be relentlessly relational, sympoietic, and consequential.[45] They are Terran, not cosmic or blissed or cursed into outer space. The Capitalocene is Terran; it does not have to be the last biodiverse geological epoch that includes our species too. There are so many good stories yet to tell, so many netbags yet to string, and not just by human beings.

As a provocation, let me summarize my objections to the Anthropocene as a tool, story, or epoch to think with: (1) The myth system associated with the Anthropos is a set up, and the stories end badly. More to the point, they end in double death; they are not about ongoingness. It is hard to tell a good story with such a bad actor. (2) Species Man does not make history. (3) Man plus Tool does not make history. History is the sort of story human exceptionalists tell. (4) History must give way to geostories, to Gaiastories, to sym-chthonic stories; Terrans do webbed, braided, and tentacular living and dying in sympoietic multispecies string figures; they do not do History. (5) The human social apparatus of the Anthropocene tends to be top heavy and bureaucracy prone. Revolt needs other forms of action and other stories for solace, inspiration, and effectiveness. (6) Despite its reliance on agile computer modeling and autopoietic systems theories, the Anthropocene relies too much on what should be an "unthinkable" theory of relations, namely the old one of bounded individualism—preexisting units in competition relations that take up all the air in the atmosphere (except, apparently, carbon dioxide). (7) The sciences of the Anthropocene are too much contained within systems theories of autopoiesis and within evolutionary theories called the Modern Synthesis, which for all their extraordinary importance have proven unable to think well about sympoiesis, symbiosis, symbiogenesis, development, webbed ecologies, and microbes. That's a lot of trouble for adequate evolutionary theory.[46]

I am aligned with feminist environmentalist Eileen Crist when she writes against the managerial, technocratic, market-and-profit besotted, modernizing, and humanist business-as-usual commitments of so much Anthropocene discourse. This discourse is not simply wrong-headed and wrong-hearted in itself; it also saps our capacity for imagining and caring for other worlds, both those that exist precariously now (including those called wilderness, for all the contaminated history of that term in racist settler colonialism), as well as those we need to bring into being in alliance with other critters, for still possible recuperating pasts, presents, and futures. "Scarcity's deepening persistence, and the suffering it is auguring for all life, is an artifact of human exceptionalism at every level," Crist writes. Instead, a humanity with more earthly integrity "invites the *priority* of our pulling back and scaling down, of welcoming limitations of our numbers, economies, and habitats for the sake of a higher, more inclusive freedom and quality of life" (this volume, 29).

If Humans live in History and the Earthbound take up their task within the Anthropocene, too many Posthumans (and posthumanists, another gathering altogether) seem to have emigrated to the Anthropocene for my taste. Perhaps my human and nonhuman people are the dreadful Chthonic ones who snake within the tissues of Terrapolis.[47]

Note that in so far as the Capitalocene is told in the idiom of fundamentalist Marxism, with all its trappings of Modernity, Progress, and History, that term is subject to the same or fiercer criticisms. The stories of both the Anthropocene and the Capitalocene teeter constantly on the brink of becoming much Too Big. Marx did better than that, as did Darwin. We can inherit their bravery and capacity to tell big enough stories without determinism, teleology, and plan.[48]

Historically situated relational worldings make a mockery both of the binary division of nature and society and of our enslavement to Progress and its evil twin Modernization. The Capitalocene was relationally made, and not by a secular godlike anthropos, a law of history, the machine Itself, or a demon called modernity. The Capitalocene must be relationally unmade in order to compose in material-semiotic SF patterns and stories something more livable, something Ursula Le Guin could be proud of. Shocked anew by our—billions of earth habitants', including yours and mine—ongoing daily assent in practice to this thing called capitalism, Philippe Pignarre and Isabelle Stengers note that denunciation has been singularly ineffective, or capitalism would have long ago vanished from the earth. A kind of dark bewitched commitment to the lure of Progress lashes us to endless infernal alternatives, as if we had no other ways to reworld, reimagine, relive, and reconnect with each other, in multispecies well being. Note that this explication does not excuse us from doing many important things better, quite the opposite. Pignarre and Stengers affirm on-the-ground collectives capable of inventing new practices of imagination, resistance, revolt, repair and mourning, and of living and dying well. They remind us that the established disorder is not necessary; another world is not only urgently needed, it is possible, but not if we are ensorcelled in despair, cynicism, or optimism, and the belief/disbelief discourse of Progress.[49] Many Marxist critical and cultural theorists, at their best, would agree.[50] So would the tentacular ones.

Gaia figures the Anthropocene. Arising from Chaos,[51] Gaia was and is a powerful intrusive force, in no one's pocket, no one's hope for salvation, capable of provoking the late twentieth century's best autopoietic complex systems thinking that led to recognizing the devastation caused by anthropogenic processes of the last few centuries, a necessary counter to the Euclidean figures and stories of Man.[52] Brazilian anthropologists and philosophers Eduardo Viveiros de Castro and Déborah Danowski exorcise lingering notions that Gaia is confined to the ancient Greeks and subsequent Eurocultures in their refiguring of the urgencies of our times in the post-Eurocentric conference on "The Thousand Names of Gaia."[53] Names, not faces, not morphs of the same, something else, a thousand somethings else, still telling of linked ongoing generative and destructive

OCTOPI WALL STREET

Invertebrates are 97% of animal diversity!

Brought to you by Oregon Institute of Marine Biology, University of Oregon

Symchthonic Revolt! Artwork by Marley Jarvis, Laurel Hiebert, Kira Treibergs 2011; design by Laurel Hiebert and Kira Treibergs. Oregon Institute of Marine Biology. With permission.[54]

worlding and reworlding in this age of the earth. We need another figure, a thousand names of something else, to erupt out of the Anthropocene into another, big enough story. Bitten in a California redwood forest by spidery *Pimoa cthulu*, I want to propose snaky Medusa and the many unfinished worldings of her antecedents, affiliates, and descendants. Perhaps Medusa, the only mortal Gorgon, can bring us into the holobiomes of Terrapolis and heighten our chances for dashing the twenty-first-century ships of the Heros on a living coral reef instead of allowing them to suck the last drop of fossil flesh out of dead rock.

This terracotta figure of Potnia Theron, the Mistress of the Animals, depicts a winged goddess wearing a split skirt and touching a bird with each hand. She is a vivid reminder of the breadth, width, and temporal reach into pasts and futures of chthonic powers in Mediterranean and Near Eastern worlds and beyond.[55] Potnia Theron is rooted in Minoan and then Mycenean cultures and infuses Greek stories of the Gorgons (especially the only mortal Gorgon, Medusa) and of Artemis. A kind of far-traveling Ur-Medusa, the Lady of the Beasts is a potent link between Crete and India. The winged figure is also called Potnia Melissa, Mistress

Icon for the Chthulucene. Potnia Theron with a Gorgon Face. Type of Potnia Theron, Kameiros, Rhodes, circa 600 BCE, terracotta, 13 in. diameter, British Museum, excavated by Auguste Salzmann and Sir Alfred Bilotti; purchased 1860. Photo by Marie-Lan Nguyen, ©2007. Licensed under Creative Commons Attribution 2.5 Generic.[56]

of the Bees, draped with all their buzzing-stinging-honeyed gifts. Note the acoustic, tactile, and gustatory senses elicited by the Mistress and her sympoietic, more-than-human flesh. The snakes and bees are more like stinging tentacular feelers than like binocular eyes, although these critters see too, in compound-eyed insectile and many-armed optics.

In many incarnations around the world, the winged bee goddesses are very old, and they are much needed now.[57] Potnia Theron/Melissa's snaky locks and Gorgon face tangle her with a diverse kinship of chthonic earthly forces that travel richly in space and time. The Greek word Gorgon translates as dreadful, but perhaps that is an astralized, patriarchal hearing of much more awe-ful stories and enactments of generation, destruction, and tenacious, ongoing Terran finitude. Potnia Theron/Melissa/Medusa give faciality a profound makeover, and that is a blow to modern humanist (including technohumanist) figurations of the forward-looking, sky-gazing Anthropos. Recall that the Greek *chthonios* means of, in, or under the earth and the seas—a rich Terran muddle for SF, science fact, science fiction, and speculative fabulation. The chthonic ones are precisely not sky gods, not a foundation for the Olympiad, not friends to the Anthropocene or Capitalocene, and definitely not finished. The Earthbound can take heart—as well as action.

The Gorgons are powerful winged chthonic entities without a proper genealogy; their reach is lateral and tentacular; they have no settled lineage and no reliable kind (genre, gender), although they are figured and storied as female. In old versions, the Gorgons twine with the Erinyes (Furies), chthonic underworld powers who avenge crimes against the natural order. In the winged domains, the bird-bodied Harpies carry out these vital functions.[58] Now, look again at the birds of Potnia Theron and ask what they do. Are the Harpies their cousins? Around 700 BCE Hesiod imagined the Gorgons as sea demons and gave them sea deities for parents. I read Hesiod's *Theogony* as laboring to stabilize a very bumptious queer family. The Gorgons erupt more than emerge; they are intrusive in a sense akin to what Stengers understands by Gaia.

The Gorgons turned men who looked into their living, venomous, snake-encrusted faces into stone. I wonder what might have happened if those men had known how to politely greet the dreadful chthonic ones. I wonder if such manners can still be learned, if there is time to learn now, or if the stratigraphy of the rocks will only register the ends and end of a stony Anthropos.[59]

Because the deities of the Olympiad identified her as a particularly dangerous enemy to the sky gods' succession and authority, mortal Medusa is especially interesting for my efforts to propose the Chthulucene as one of the big enough stories for staying with the trouble of our ongoing epoch. I resignify and twist the stories, but no more than the Greeks themselves constantly did.[60] The hero Perseus was dispatched to kill Medusa; and with the help of Athena, head-born favorite daughter of Zeus, he cut off the Gorgon's head and gave it to his accomplice, this virgin goddess of wisdom and war. Putting Medusa's severed head face-forward on her shield, the Aegis, Athena, as usual, played traitor to the Earthbound; we expect no better from motherless mind children. But great good came of this murder-for-hire, for from Medusa's dead body came the winged horse Pegasus. Feminists have a special friendship with horses. Who says these

Day Octopus, *Octopus cyanea*. ©OceanwideImages.com, image for Tentacles: The Astounding Lives of Octopuses, Squids, and Cuttlefish, Monterey Bay Aquarium Exhibit, 2014.

stories do not still move us materially?[61] And from the blood dripping from Medusa's severed head came the rocky corals of the western seas, remembered today in the taxonomic names of the Gorgonians, the coral-like sea fans and sea whips, composed in symbioses of tentacular animal cnidarians and photosynthetic algal-like beings called zooanthellae.[62]

With the corals, we turn definitively away from heady facial representations, no matter how snaky. Even Potnia Theron, Potnia Melissa, and Medusa cannot alone spin out the needed tentacularities. In the tasks of thinking, figuring, and storytelling, the spider of my first pages *Pimoa cthulu* allies with the decidedly non-vertebrate critters of the seas. Corals align with octopuses, squids, and cuttlefish. Octopuses are called spiders of the seas, not only for their tentacularity, but also for their predatory habits.[63] The tentacular chthonic ones have to eat; they are at table, cum panis, companion species of Terra. They are good figures for the luring, beckoning, gorgeous, finite, dangerous precarities of the Chthulucene. This Chthulucene is neither sacred nor secular; this earthly worlding is thoroughly Terran, muddled, and mortal.

All of these stories are a lure to proposing the Chthulucene as a needed third story, a third netbag for collecting up what is crucial for ongoing, for staying with the trouble.[64] The chthonic ones are not confined to a vanished past. They are a buzzing, stinging, sucking swarm now, and human beings are not in a separate compost pile. We are humus, not homo, not anthropos; we are compost, not posthuman. As a suffix, the word *kainos*, "-cene," signals new, recently made, fresh, epochs of the thick present. To sympoietically renew the biodiverse powers of Terra—that is the sympoietic work and play of the Chthulucene. Specifically, unlike either the Anthropocene or the Capitalocene, the Chthulucene is made up of ongoing multispecies stories and practices of becoming-with in times that remain at stake, in precarious times, in which the world is not finished and the sky has not fallen—yet. We are at stake to each other. Unlike the dominant dramas of Anthropocene and Capitalocene discourse, human beings are not the only important actors in the Chthulucene, with all other beings able simply to react. The order is rather reversed: human beings are with and of the earth, and the other biotic and abiotic powers of this earth are the main story.

However, the doings of situated, actual human beings matter. It matters which ways of living and dying we cast our lot with rather than others. It matters not just to human beings, but also to those many critters across taxa which and whom we have subjected to exterminations, extinctions, genocides, and prospects of futurelessness. Like it or not, we are in the string figure game of caring for and with precarious world-ings made terribly more precarious by fossil-burning man making new fossils as rapidly as possible in Anthropocene and Capitalocene orgies. Diverse human and nonhuman players are necessary in every fiber of the tissues of the urgently needed Chthulucene story. The chief actors are not restricted to the too-big players in the too-big stories of Capitalism and the Anthropos, both of which invite odd apocalyptic panics and even odder disengaged denunciations rather than attentive practices of thought, love, rage, and care.

Both the Anthropocene and the Capitalocene lend themselves too readily to cynicism, defeatism, and self-certain and self-fulfilling predictions, like the "game over, too late" discourse I hear all around me these days, in both expert and popular discourses, in which both technotheocratic geoengineering fixes and wallowing in despair seem to co-infect any possible common imagination. Encountering the sheer not-us, more-than-human worlding of the coral reefs, with their requirements for ongoing living and dying of their myriad critters, is also to encounter the knowledge that at least 250 million human beings today depend directly on the ongoing integrity of these holobiomes for their own ongoing living and dying well. Diverse corals and diverse people and peoples are at stake to and with each other. Flourishing will be cultivated as a multispecies response-ability without the arrogance of the sky gods and their minions, or else biodiverse Terra will flip out into something very slimy, like any overstressed complex adaptive system at the end of its abilities to absorb insult after insult.

Corals helped bring the Earthbound into consciousness of the Anthropocene in the first place. From the start, uses of the term Anthropocene emphasized human-induced warming and acidification of the oceans from fossil-fuel generated CO_2 emissions. Warming and acidification were known stressors that sicken and bleach coral reefs, killing the photosynthesizing zooanthellae and so ultimately their cnidarian symbionts and all of the other critters belonging to myriad taxa whose worlding depends on intact reef systems (Rosenberg and Falkovitz 2004).[65] Corals of the seas and lichens of the land also bring us into consciousness of the Capitalocene, in which deep-sea mining and drilling in oceans and fracking and pipeline construction across delicate lichen-covered northern landscapes are fundamental to accelerating nationalist, transnationalist, and corporate unworlding.

But coral and lichen symbionts also bring us richly into the storied tissues of the thickly present Chthulucene, where it remains possible—just barely—to play a much better SF game, in non-arrogant collaboration with all those in the muddle. Sympoietically, we are all lichens now. We can be scraped off the rocks by the Furies, who still erupt to avenge crimes against the earth; or we can join in the metabolic transformations between and among rocks and critters for living and dying well. "'Do you realize, the phytolinguist will say to the aesthetic critic, 'that [once upon a time] they couldn't even read Eggplant?' And they will smile at our ignorance, as they pick up their rucksacks and hike on up to read the newly deciphered lyrics of the lichen on the north face of Pike's Peak'" (Le Guin 1988, 175).

Attending to these ongoing matters returns me to the question that began this essay. What happens when human exceptionalism and bounded individualism become unthinkable in the best sciences across the disciplines and interdisciplines? Seriously unthinkable: not available to think with. Why is it that the epochal name of the Anthropos imposed itself at just the time when understandings and knowledge practices about and within symbiogenesis and sympoietics are wildly and wonderfully available and generative in all the humusities, including non-colonizing and decolonizing arts, sciences, and politics? What if the doleful doings of the Anthropocene and the unworldings of the Capitalocene are the last gasps of the sky gods, not guarantors of the finished future, game over? It matters which thoughts think thoughts. We must think!

The unfinished Chthulucene must collect up the trash of the Anthropocene, the exterminism of the Capitalocene, and chipping and shredding and layering like a mad gardener, make a much hotter compost pile for still possible pasts, presents, and futures.

Notes

1   First published in a shorter version in French in *Gestes spéculatifs*, edited by Isabelle Stengers, 2015. A longer version will appear in Haraway (2016).

2   This is Scott Gilbert's rallying call: http://cstms.berkeley.edu/baysts/ai1ec_event/we-are-all-lichens-now-scott-gilbert-philosophy-colloquium/?instance_id. See Gilbert et al. 2012.

3   These sentences are on the rear cover of Stengers et al. (2014). From Virginia Woolf's *Three Guineas*, "think we must" is the urgency relayed to feminist collective thinking-with by Puig de la Bellacasa (2013).

4   For the keynote lecture "Staying with the Trouble: Sympoiesis, String Figures, Multispecies Muddles, go to http://new.livestream.com/aict/DonnaHaraway. Research-Creation Think Tank, Knowing and Knots, University of Alberta, Edmonton, Canada, March 23–25, 2014.

5   "The brand of holist ecological philosophy that emphasizes that 'everything is connected to everything,' will not help us here. Rather, everything is connected to *something*, which is connected to something else. While we may all *ultimately* be connected to one another, the specificity and proximity of connections matters—*who we are bound up with and in what ways*. Life and death happen inside these relationships. And so, we need to understand how particular human communities, as well as those of other living beings, are entangled, and how these entanglements are implicated in the production of both extinctions and their accompanying patterns of amplified death" (van Dooren 2014, 60).

6   Two indispensible books by my colleague-sibling from thirty-plus years in the History of Consciousness Department at the University of California Santa Cruz guide my writing (Clifford 1997, 2013).

7   Chthonic derives from ancient Greek khthonios, *of the earth*, and from khthōn, *earth*. Greek mythology depicts the chthonic as the underworld, beneath the earth; but the chthonic ones are much older (and younger) than those Greeks. Sumeria is a riverine civilizational scene of emergence of great chthonic tales, including possibly the great circular snake eating its own tail, the polysemous uroborus (figure of the continuity of life, an Egyptian figure as early as 1600 BCE; Sumerian SF worlding dates to 3500 BCE or before). The chthonic will

accrue many resonances throughout my essay (see Jacobsen 1976). Gildas Hamel, scholar of ancient Middle Eastern worlds at UC Santa Cruz, in lectures, conversations, and e-mails gave me "the abyssal and elemental forces before they were astralized by chief gods and their tame committees." Cthulhu (note spelling), luxuriating in the science fiction of H.P. Lovecraft, plays little role for me, although it/he did play a role for the scientist who named my spider demon familiar. For the monstrous male elder god (Cthulhu), see Lovecraft (2009).

I take the liberty of rescuing my spider from Lovecraft for other stories, and mark the liberation with the more common spelling of chthonic ones. My spider *Pimoa cthulhu* has the Lovecraftian spelling in its Linnaean name, but I insist that the savvy arachnid is really aligned with non-Lovecraftian chthonic powers! Lovecraft's underworld of dreadful chthonic serpents were terrible only in the patriarchal mode. The Chthulucence has other terrors—more dangerous and generative in worlds where gender does not reign. Undulating and dark eros, tangled snakes, ongoing tentacular forces coiling through the twenty-first century CE. Consider: Old English oearth, German erde, Greek Gaia, Roman terra, Dutch aarde; Old English w(e)oruld ("affairs of life," "a long period of time," "the known life" or "life on earth" as opposed to the "afterlife"), from a Germanic compound meaning "age of the human race" (wer); Old Norse heimr, literally "abode." Then consider Turkish dünya and go to *dunyā* (دُنْيا) (the temporal world), an Arabic word that was passed to many other languages, such as Persian, Dari, Pashto, Bengali, Punjabi, Urdu, Hindi, Kurdish, Nepali, Turkish, Arumanian and North Caucasian languages. *Dunyā* is also a loanword in Malay and Indonesian, as well as in Greek δουνιας—so many words, so many roots, so many pathways, so many micorrhizial symbioses, even if we restrict ourselves only to Indo-European tangles. There are so many kin who might better have named this time of the Anthropocene that is at stake now. The anthropos is too much of a parochial fellow; he is both too big and too small for the needed stories.

The Goshute of eastern Nevada and western Utah are Shoshone peoples. The name Goshute or Gosiute, derived from Kutsipiuti (Gutsipiuti), means "desert people." There are currently two bands of the Goshute Nation. See http://www.goshutetribe.com/, http://www.utahindians.org/archives/goshute.html. Like all the peoples of the U.S. Southwest, the Goshute are embroiled in the ecologies, economies, and politics of nuclear mining, war, and waste processing and storage. Their relatives have lived in these deserts for more than a thousand years; and, living and dead, they are indigenous to the ongoing Chthulucene, tangled in the grip of the colonial and imperial Anthropocene and Capitalocene. For a claymation video of "Frog Races Coyote," constructed from archives of several Shoshoni-language storytellers by the Gosiute/Shoshoni Project of the University of Utah, see http://stream.utah.edu/m/dp/frame.php?f=72b1a0fc6341cb41542. Frogs think-with frogs; frog wins the race around the lake with coyote; frog is a kind of SF GECo, Le Groupe d'Études Constructivistes, the homeworld for thinking-with for Isabelle Stengers, Maria Puig de la Bellacasa, Benedikte Zitouni, Émilie Hache, and others shaped in Brussels to practice SF as "think we must; we must think" (http://phi.ulb.ac.be/

domaine_02.php). The frog and coyote story is taught today in the Utah Indian Curriculum Guide, http://utahindians.org/Curriculum/pdf/4thgoshute.pdf. Listening to and learning a Shoshoni language today in public schools and on the internet is very much part of Indigenous America *not* disappearing, but traveling in tongues to unexpected places to reopen questions of ongoingness, accountability, and lived storying. It pleases me that GECo in English suggests gecko, an unblinking social chirping group of lizards, the most biodiverse of all their kind, with thousands of species worldwide, who moisten their eyes with their tongues, ready to track their life lines with unique grasping toe pads. Gēkok is an Indonesian-Malay word that found its way, with many other loans, into Euro sciences and popular culture. Wayfarers for a Habitable Planet!

8   Eva Hayward proposes the term tentacularity; her trans-thinking and doing in spidery and coralline worlds entwine with my writing in SF patterns (2010a, 2010b, 2012).

9   Katie King aligns Hayward's "fingery eyes" and "tentacularity" with "networked reenactments" or "transknowledges." "Working out in a multiverse of articulating disciplines, interdisciplines, and multidisciplinarities, such transdisciplinary inspection actually *enjoys* the many flavors of details, offerings, passions, languages, things. . . . One index for the evaluation of transdisciplinary work is how well it learns and models *how* to be affected or moved, how well it *opens up* unexpected elements of one's own embodiments in lively and re-sensitizing worlds" (King 2011, 19). See also King's summer 2012 "platform/paper": http://sfonline.barnard.edu/feminist-media-theory/a-naturalcultural-collection-of-affections-transdisciplinary-stories-of-transmedia-ecologies-learning/. Think we must.

10   Muddle, Old Dutch for muddying the waters. I use muddle as a theoretical trope and soothing wallow to trouble the trope of visual clarity as the only sense and affect for mortal thinking. Muddles team with company. Empty spaces and clear vision are bad fictions for thinking, not worthy of SF or of contemporary biology. My speculative feminist courage has been fed by Puig de la Bellacasa (2009).

For a gorgeous animated model of a densely packed living neuron, where proteins muddle on their herky-jerky way to making cells work, see "Protein Packing: Inner Life of a Cell," Harvard University, Video by XVIVO Scientific Animation, in Carl Zimmer, April 10, 2014, http://www.nytimes.com/2014/04/10/science/watch-proteins-do-the-jitterbug.html?_r=0, 2014.

11   Baila Goldenthal (1925–2011) painted an extraordinary series of four cat's cradle oil-on-wood panels in 1995–96 and an oil-on-canvas in 2008. For her and for me, cat's cradle is an open-ended practice of continuous weaving (see her Weavers Series, 1989–94). "The techniques of under-painting and glazing invoke historical time; the enigma of the game itself reflects the complexity of human relationships." http://www.bailagoldenthal.com/painting/cats_cradle/cats_cradle.html. Goldenthal relates to cat's cradle games as a metaphor for the game of life, and the intensely present, moving hands invite kinship with other tentacular beings. Her 2008 Cat's Cradle/String Theory is the cover image for *Nuclear Abolition Forum*, no. 2, 2013, issue on "Moving Beyond Nuclear

Deterrence to a Nuclear Weapons Free World." Metamorphosis, fragility, temporality, disintegration, revelation—these are everywhere in her work. A student of the Kabbalah and of South Asian Indian culture and philosophy, Goldenthal worked in oils, bronze, leaded glass, paper, photography, printmaking, film, and ceramics. She accomplished powerful work in sculpture and in two-dimensional formats. http://www.bailagoldenthal.com/resume.html.

12 The pile was made irresistible by Puig de la Bellacasa (2014).

13 Art-science activism infuses this essay. In the struggle for multispecies environmental justice in the face of coal company mountain top removal in her homeworld in West Virginia, with her wife Annie Sprinkle (environmental activist, radical adult film director and performer, former sex worker), UC Santa Cruz artist Beth Stephens made the "sexiest nature documentary ever," *Goodbye to Gauley Mountain: An Ecosexual Love Story* (http://goodbyegauleymountain. org/). The quote is from McSpadden's review (2013). In love and rage (Emma Goldman), think we must (Virginia Woolf) for a habitable planet.

14 Throughout this essay I use the Latinate words Terran and Terra, even while I swim in Greek names and stories, including the material-semiotic story of Gaia and Bruno Latour's "gaiastories/geostories." Terra is especially legible in SF, but Gaia is important in SF too. My favorite is John Varley's Gaea Trilogy, *Titan* (1979), *Wizard* (1980), and *Demon* (1984). Varley's Gaea is an old woman, who/which is a living being in the shape of a 1,300 km diameter Stanford torus, inhabited by many different species, in orbit around the planet Saturn. Latour's Earthbound and Stengers's intrusive Gaia would recognize Varley's irascible, unpredictable Gaea. Gaia is more legible in systems theories than Terra, as well as in "new age" cultures. Gaia comes into her/its own in the Anthropocene, but Terra sounds a more earthy tone for me. However, Terra and Gaia are not in opposition, nor are the Earthbound who are given to us in loving, risk-taking, powerful writing by Bruno Latour in opposition to Terrans. Rather, Gaians and Terrans are in a queer planet-wide litter of chthonic ones who must be remembered urgently. It is in that sense that I hear together Isabelle Stengers's "cosmopolitics" and my verbally miscegenated "terrapolis." We are making string figures together.

15 Allied to this kind of argument is Karen Barad's *Meeting the Universe Halfway* (2007). Outside the odd thing named the West, there are myriad histories, philosophies, and practices—some civilizational, some urban, some neither—that propose living and dying in other knots and patterns that do not presume isolated, much less binary, unities and polarities that then need to be brought into connection. Variously and dangerously configured relationality is just what is.

An American evolutionary biologist, David Barash, writes compellingly about convergences (not identities and not resources than can be hijacked to cure Western ills) between ecological sciences and various Buddhist streams, schools, and traditions that emphasize connectedness. Barash emphasizes that ways of living, dying, acting, and nurturing response-ability are embedded in these matters (2012). What if Western evolutionary and ecological sciences had been developed from the start within Buddhist instead of Protestant ways of worlding?

Based on his extensive study of Chinese knowledges and sciences, Joseph Needham asked a similar question many years ago about embryology and biochemistry (2013). Needham's organicism and Marxism are both crucial for this story, something to remember in thinking about how to configure what I will explore in this essay under the sign Capitalocene. On Needham, see Haraway (2004). What happens if we cultivate response-ability for the Capitalocene inside the netbags of sympoiesis, Buddhism, ecological evolutionary developmental biology (EcoEvoDevo), Marxism, Stengerian cosmopolitics, and other strong pulls against the modernizing foolishness of some analyses of capitalism?

16 See Dempster (1988, 27–32) for a concise comparison of autopoietic and sympoietic systems. Table 1, p.30, is instructive:

AUTOPOIETIC SYSTEMS	SYMPOIETIC SYSTEMS
Defining Characteristics	**Defining Characteristics**
self-produced boundaries	lacking boundaries
organizationally closed	organizationally ajar
external structural coupling	internal and external structural coupling
Characteristic Tendencies	**Characteristic Tendencies**
autonomous units	complex amorphous entities
central control	distributed control
'packaged,' same information	distributed, different information
reproduction by copy	amorphous reproduction
evolution between systems	evolution within system
growth/development oriented	evolutionary orientation
homeostatic balance	balance by dynamic tension
steady state	potentially dramatic, surprising change
finite temporal trajectories	potentially infinite temporal trajectories
predictable	unpredictable
Examples	**Examples**
Cells, organisms	Ecosystems, cultural systems

Note that in 1998 Dempster thought that biology supported the conceptualization of organisms as units, and only ecosystems and cultures are sympoietic. I argue, on biological grounds, that we can no longer think like that. I also think that dynamic boundaries are crucial to both sorts of systems.

Katie King told me about the Dempster thesis as we tried to sort out our overlapping but not identical pleasures and resistances to autopoiesis and sympoiesis. Katie King, "Pulling Together," http://pullingtogeth.blogspot.com/p/slides.html, Utrecht, June 2014, and "Toward a feminist boundary object-oriented ontology . . . or should it be a boundary object-oriented feminism? These are both queer methods," paper for Queer Method, University of Pennsylvania, October 31, 2013; http://fembooo.blogspot.com:

"Recursions, sometimes unfolding, sometimes I speculate enfoldings, 'made through one another,' transdisciplinary demonstrations of themselves: boundary objects matter, and boundary objects help us question with, rather than assume, ourselves amid apparatus in boundary-making practices. A boundary object-oriented feminism works to orient these methods as the various 'we' we are." In King's and my terms, this is SF.

17 I set aside the strict humanism and the specific kind of thinking subject of Arendt's project, as well as her insistence on the essential solitude of thinking. Thinking-with in the SF compost pile of this essay is not an enemy to the profound secular self-examination of Arendt's historically situated human figure, but that is an argument for another day.

18 Arendt characterized thinking as "training one's mind to going visiting": "This distancing of some things and bridging of others is part of the dialogue of understanding, for whose purposes direct experience establishes too close contact and mere knowledge erects artificial barriers" (Arendt 1977, 241, quoted in Hartouni 2012, 75).

19 Title of a conference that Anna Tsing and coworkers organized at the University of California Santa Cruz, May 8–10, 2014: *Anthropocene: Arts of Living on a Damaged Planet.*

20 Van Dooren's colleague Deborah Bird Rose is everywhere in this thinking, especially in her treatment of the undoing of the tissues of ongoingness, the killing of generations, which she called "double death" (Rose 2004). See also Rose and van Dooren (2011), and van Dooren and Rose (2012). The Extinction Studies Group is a rich sympoietic gathering: http://extinctionstudies.org/people/.

21 This writing is in SF exchange with Vinciane Despret's thinking about learning to be affected (2004).

22 Also crucial to grasping thinking and semiotics outside the premises of modernist humanist doctrines, see Kohn (2013).

23 Le Guin's essay shaped my thinking about narrative in evolutionary theory and of the figure of woman the gatherer (see Haraway 1989). Le Guin learned about the carrier bag theory of evolution from Elizabeth Fisher (1975) in that period of large, brave, speculative, worldly stories that burned in feminist theory in the 1970s and 1980s. Like speculative fabulation, speculative feminism was, and is, an SF practice.

24 For a science fiction game with Le Guin and Octavia Butler, see Haraway (2013b).

25 For introduction and elucidation of the "god trick" in science and politics, see Haraway (1988).

26 Latour's proportionality here is bracing. Humans: business as usual :: the Earthbound: total subversion.

27 Latour's "Why Has Critique Run Out of Steam?" (2004) is a major landmark in our collective understanding of the corrosive, self-certain, and self-contained traps of nothing-but-critique. Cultivating response-ability requires much more from us. It requires the risk of being for some worlds rather than others and helping to compose those worlds with others. In multistranded SF

worlding, Maria Puig de la Bellacasa re-composts Latour's "matters of concern" to ferment an even richer soil in her "Matters of Care in Technoscience" (2011).

28 To understand how the modernizing category of "belief" works in the United States in law, politics, and pedagogy, including religion and social science, see Harding 2014. The figure of the never properly belonging, always leaving and returning "Prodigal Daughter" further unpacks the enabling and disabling operations of "belief" in deVries (2014). Tying knowledge practices to professions of belief in both religion and science is perhaps the single most difficult habit of thought to dislodge for Moderns, at least in the United States. Where belief is exacted, the Inquisition is never far behind. SF in the muddle of Terra/Gaia cannot exact belief, but can shape committed thinking companions. The figure for thinking-with in this ecology of practices is not so much "decision" as sympoietic "care" and "discernment." The Prodigal Daughter remains a wayfarer, much more promising for pathways in troubled times than the paved road toward the feast prepared for the returning, forever-after obedient Prodigal Son and legitimate heir.

29 For a full exposition of his reliance on Schmitt's *hostis* and political theology, see Latour (2013a, Lecture Five): "If Humans are at war with It [Gaia], what about those whom I have proposed to call the Earthbound? Can they be '*artisans of peace*'?" Such artisans are what Latour works to nourish here and elsewhere.

His question deserves more space, but a few words about *hostis* are necessary. Latour and I both ate the "host" in the sacrificial Eucharistic feast, and so we know what it means to be in the material-semiotic world where sign and signifier have imploded in meaningful flesh. Neither of us fit very well in secular Protestant semiotics, dominant in the University and in Science, and that shapes our approaches to science studies and much else. But note that the "host" that we ate—our communion—is firmly ensconced in the story of the acceptable sacrifice to the Father. Latour and I ate too much and too little when we consumed this host and refused (and still refuse) to disavow it. I have a case of permanent raging indigestion, even as I hold fast to the joy and the implosion of metaphor and world. I need to know more about Latour's digestive comforts and discomforts because I suspect they are at the root of our different lures for changing the story for the Earthbound. In the sacrificial Eucharistic worlding, there are strong kin ties, etymologically and historically, to the host of Schmitt, where we find the guest, hostage, one held in surety for another, generator and collector of debt, host as the one who feeds the traveller as guest, stranger to be respected even if killed, hostiles, host as an array armed for combat in the field of battle (a trial of strength). Not vermin, not trash, not *inimicus*, but those co-producing the engagement of war and so perhaps a new peace rather than extermination. But host has other tones too, ones that lead a little way to the chthonic and tentacular ones in the carrier bag story, where Latour and I may yet luckily be gathered and transformed by some old hag collecting dinner. We might be allowed to stay as guests, as companion species, especially if we are on the menu. The host is the habitat for the parasite, the condition of life and ongoingness for the parasite; this host is in the dangerous world-making contact zones of symbiogenesis and sympoiesis, where newly cobbled together, good-enough orders may or may not emerge from the ever so promiscuous and opportunistic associations of host and parasite. Perhaps Gaia's abyssal gut, habitat for chthonic powers, is the muddle for SF, where ongoingness remains at stake. This is the world that evokes the epigraph of this paper, "we are all lichens."

But not so fast! First we have to wrestle with the ill-named Anthropocene. I am not against all trials of strength; after all, I love women's basketball. I just think trials of strength are the old story. Overvalued, they are a bit like the never-ending task of cleaning the toilet—necessary but radically insufficient. On the other hand, there are excellent composting toilets.... We can outsource some trials of strength to the ever-eager microbes to make more time and space for SF in other muddles.

30 Gaia intrudes in this text from p. 48 on. Stengers discusses the "intrusion of Gaia" in numerous interviews, essays, and lectures. Discomfort with the ever more inescapable label of the Anthropocene, in and out of sciences, politics, and culture, pervades Stengers's thinking, as well as that of many other engaged writers, including Latour, even as we struggle for another word. See Isabelle Stengers in conversation with Davis and Turpin (2013).

Stengers's thinking about Gaia and the Lovelock-Margulis development of the Gaia hypothesis was from the start entwined with her work with Ilya Prigogine, which understood that strong linear coupling in complex systems theory entailed the possibility of radical global system change, including collapse (Prigogine and Stengers 1984). The relation of Gaia to Chaos is an old one in science and philosophy. What I want to do is knot that emergence sympoietically into a worlding of ongoing chthonic powers, which is the material-semiotic time-space of the Chthulucene rather than Anthropocene or Capitalocene. This is part of what Stengers means when she says that her intrusive Gaia was "ticklish" from the start. "Her 'autopoietic' functioning is not her truth but what 'we' [human beings] have to face, and are able to read from our computer models, the face she turns on 'us'" (Stengers e-mail to Haraway, May 9, 2014).

31 Scientists estimate that this extinction "event," the first to occur during the time of our species, could, as previous great extinction events have, but much more rapidly, eliminate 50 to 95 percent of existing biodiversity. Sober estimates anticipate half of existing species of birds could disappear by 2100. By any measure, that is a lot of double death. For a popular exposition, see http://newswatch.nationalgeographic.com/2012/03/28/the-sixth-great-extinction-a-silent-extermination/. For a bibliography on the Sixth Great Extinction, see http://www.izilwane.org/the-sixth-great-extinction1.html. For a report by an award-winning science writer, see Kolbert (2014). Reports from the Convention on Biological Diversity are more cautious about predictions and discuss the practical and theoretical difficulties of obtaining reliable knowledge, but they are not less sobering, e.g., https://www.cbd.int/gbo1/chap-01-02.shtml.

32 For a lecture by Lynn Margulis explaining the Gaia Hypothesis to National Aeronautic and Space Administration (NASA) employees in 1984, go to https://

archive.org/details/gaia_hypothesis. Autopoiesis was crucial to Margulis's transformative theory of symbiogenesis; but I think if she were alive to take up the question, Margulis would often prefer the terminology and figural-conceptual powers of sympoiesis. I suggest that Gaia is a system mistaken for autopoietic that is really sympoietic, a common error that M. Beth Dempster identified in her master's thesis (1998). Gaia's story needs an intrusive makeover to knot with a host of other promising sympoietic tentacular ones for making rich compost, for going on. Gaia or Ge is much older and wilder than Hesiod (Greek poet around the time of Homer, circa 750 to 650 BCE), but Hesiod cleaned her/it up in the *Theogony* in his story-setting way: after Chaos, "wide-bosomed" Gaia (Earth) arose to be the everlasting seat of the immortals who possess Olympus above (*Theogony* 116–18, translated by Glenn W. Most, Loeb Classical Library), and the depths of Tartarus below (*Theogony* 119). The chthonic ones reply, Nonsense! Gaia is one of theirs, an ongoing tentacular threat to the astralized ones of the Olympiad, not their ground and foundation, with their ensuing generations of gods all arrayed in proper genealogies. Hesiod's is the old prick tale, already setting up canons in the eighth century BCE.

33 Although I cannot help but think more rational environmental and socialnatural policies of all sorts would help!

34 Isabelle Stengers, from English compilation sent by e-mail January 14, 2014.

35 I use "thing" in two senses that rub against each other: 1) the collection of entities brought together in the Parliament of Things that Bruno Latour called our attention to, and 2) something hard to classify, unsortable, and probably with a bad smell.

36 Much earlier dates for the emergence of the Anthropocene are sometimes proposed, but most scientists and environmentalists tend to emphasize global anthropogenic effects from the late eighteenth century on. A more profound human exceptionalism (the deepest divide of nature and culture) accompanies proposals of the earliest dates, coextensive with *Homo sapiens* on the planet hunting big now-extinct prey and then inventing agriculture and domestication of animals. Zalasiewicz et al. argue that adoption of the term Anthropocene as a geological epoch by the relevant national and international scientific bodies will turn on stratigraphic signatures (2008). Perhaps, but the resonances of the Anthropocene are much more disseminated than that.

37 For a powerful ethnographic encounter in the 1990s with climate change modeling, see Tsing (2005). Tsing asks, "What makes global knowledge possible?" She replies, "erasing collaborations." But Tsing does not stop with this historically situated critique. Instead she, like Latour and Stengers, takes us to the really important question: "Might it be possible to attend to nature's collaborative origins without losing the advantages of its global reach?" (ibid., 95). "How might scholars take on the challenge of freeing critical imaginations from the specter of neoliberal conquest—singular, universal, global? Attention to the frictions of contingent articulation can help us describe the effectiveness, and the fragility, of emergent capitalist—and globalist—forms. In this shifting heterogeneity there are new sources of hope, and, of course, new nightmares" (ibid., 77). At her first climate modeling conference in 1995,

Tsing had an epiphany: "*The global scale takes precedence—because it is the scale of the model*" (ibid., 103, italics in original). But this and related properties have a particular effect: they bring negotiators to an international, heterogeneous table, maybe not heterogeneous enough, but far from full of identical units and players. "The embedding of smaller scales into the global; the enlargement of models to include everything; the policy-driven construction of the models: Together these features make it possible for the models to bring diplomats to the negotiating table" (ibid., 105). That is not to be despised.

The reports of the Intergovernmental Panel on Climate Change (http://www.ipcc.ch/) in 2014 are necessary documents and excellent illustrations of Tsing's accounts. "*Climate Change 2014: Mitigation of Climate Change*": http://report.mitigation2014.org/spm/ipcc_wg3_ar5_summary-for-policymakers_approved.pdf and *Climate Change 2014: Impacts, Adaptation, and Vulnerability: Summary for Policy Makers*, http://ipcc-wg2.gov/AR5/images/uploads/IPCC_WG2AR5_SPM_Approved.pdf.

Tsing's stakes in her tracking of the relentless ethnographic specificities of far-flung chains of intimate dealings and livings are to hold in productive, non-utopian friction the scale-making power of the things climate-change models do with the life and death messiness of place- and travel-based worldings, which always make even our best and most necessary universals very lumpy. She seeks and describes multiple situated worldings and multiple sorts of translations to engage globalism. "Attention to friction opens up the possibility of an ethnographic account of global interconnection" (p. 6). Appreciation of what she calls "weediness" is indispensible: "To be aware of the necessity for careful coalitions with those whose knowledges and pleasures come from other sources is the beginning of nonimperialist environmentalism" (p. 170). The *hostis* will not make an appearance in this string figuring, but mushrooms as guides for living in the ruins most certainly will.

38 The Anthropocene Working Group, which was established in 2008 to report to the International Union of Geological Sciences and the International Commission on Stratigraphy on whether or not to name a new epoch in the geological time line, will issue its final report in 2016. See *Newsletter of the Anthropocene Working Group*, vol. 4, June 2013, http://quaternary.stratigraphy.org/workinggroups/anthropo/anthropoceneNI4a.pdf.

39 Attended by tens of thousands of human people (and an unknown number of dogs), Burning Man is an annual weeklong festival of art and (commercial) anarchism held in the Black Rock Desert of Nevada since 1990 and on San Francisco's Baker Beach from 1986 to 1990. The event's origins tie to San Francisco artists' celebrations of the summer solstice. "The event is described as an experiment in community, art, radical self-expression, and radical self-reliance" (http://en.wikipedia.org/wiki/Burning_Man). The globalizing extravaganzas of the Anthropocene are not the drug- and art-laced worlding of Burning Man, but the iconography of the immense fiery "man" ignited during the festival is irresistible. The first burning effigies on the beach in San Francisco were of a nine-foot-tall wooden Man and a smaller wooden dog. By 1988 the Man was forty feet tall and dogless. Relocated to a dry lakebed in

Nevada, the Man topped out in 2011 at more than one hundred feet. This is America; supersized is the name of the game. http://en.wikipedia.org/wiki/File:BurningMan-picture.jpg.

"Anthropos" (ἄνθρωπος) is an ambiguous word with contested etymologies. What Anthropos never figures is the rich generative home of a multispecies earth. The Online Etymology Dictionary states that it comes from the Greek *aner*, "man", "as opposed to a woman, a god, or a boy." Just what I suspected! Or, "Anthropos sometimes is explained as a compound of *aner* and *ops* (genitive *opos*) 'eye, face;' so literally 'he who has the face of a man.'" Or, sometimes, the shape of a man. Biblical scholars find it hard to make the Greek ανθρωπος include women, and it complicates translations in fascinating ways. http://www.bible-researcher.com/anthropos.html Other sources give the meaning of the compound as "that which is below, hence earthly, human," or, the "upward looking one," and so below, lamentably on earth. Unlike the animals, man as anthropos "looks up at what he sees." http://www.science-bbs.com/114-lang/0e74f4484bff3fe0.htm The Anthropos is NOT Latour's Earthbound.

It is safe to say that Eugene Stoermer and Paul Crutzen were not much vexed by these ambiguities. Still, thank the heavens, looking up, their human eyes were firmly on the earth's atmospheric carbon burden. Or, also, swimming in too hot seas with the tentacular ones, their eyes were the optic-haptic fingery eyes of marine critters in diseased and dying coral symbioses. See Hayward (2010a).

40 "According to the International Energy Agency (IEA), an inter-governmental research organization based in Paris, cumulative worldwide investment in new fossil-fuel extraction and processing will total an estimated $22.87 trillion between 2012 and 2035, while investment in renewables, hydropower, and nuclear energy will amount to only $7.32 trillion" (Klare 2013). Nuclear, after Fukushima! Not to mention that none of these calculations prioritizes a much lighter, smaller, more modest human presence on earth, with all its critters. Even in its "sustainability" discourses, the Capitalocene cannot tolerate a multispecies world of the Earthbound. For the switch in Big Energy's growth strategies to nations with the weakest environmental controls, see Klare (2014).

41 Heavy tar sand pollution must break the hearts and shatter the gills of every Terran, Gaian, and Earthbound critter. The toxic lakes of waste water from tar sand oil extraction in northern Alberta, Canada, shape a kind of new Great Lakes region, with more giant "ponds" added daily. Current area covered by these lakes is about 50 percent greater than the area covered by the world city of Vancouver. Tar sands operations return almost none of the vast quantities of water they use to natural cycles. Earthbound peoples trying to establish growing things at the edges of these alarmingly colored waters filled with extraction tailings say that successional processes for re-establishing sympoietic biodiverse ecosystems, if they prove possible at all, will be an affair of decades and centuries. http://www.theglobeandmail.com/news/national/rebuilding-land-destroyed-by-oil-sands-may-not-restore-it-researchers-say/article552879/. Only Venezuela and Saudi Arabia have more oil reserves than Alberta. All that said, the Earthbound, the Terrans, do not cede either the

present or the future; the sky is lowering, but has not yet fallen, yet. http://www.pembina.org/oil-sands/solutions First Nation, Métis, and Aboriginal peoples are crucial players in every aspect of this unfinished story. http://tarsandssolutions.org/tar-sands/human-rights.

42 Capitalocene is one of those words like sympoiesis; if you think you invented it, just look around and notice how many other people are inventing the term at the same time. That certainly happened to me, and after I got over a small fit of individualist pique at being asked whom I got the term Capitalocene from—hadn't I coined the word? ("Coin"!) And why do other scholars almost always ask women which male writers their ideas are indebted to?—I recognized that not only was I part of a cat's cradle game of invention, as always, but that Jason W. Moore had already written beautiful and compelling arguments to think with, and my interlocutor both knew Moore's work and was relaying it to me. "Capitalocene" was first proposed by then-graduate student Andreas Malm at Lund University. In an urgent historical conjuncture, words-to-think-with pop out all at once from many bubbling cauldrons because we all feel the need for better netbags to collect up the stuff crying out for attention. Despite its problems, the term Anthropocene was and is embraced because it collects up many matters of fact, concern, and care; and I hope Capitalocene will roll off myriad tongues soon. In particular, see the work of Moore (2014a, 2014b, 2015a).

43 To get over flu-like bouts of Eurocentrism while thinking about the history of pathways and centers of globalization over the last few centuries, see Flynn and Giráldez (2012). For analysis attentive to the differences and frictions among colonialisms, imperialisms, globalizing trade formations, and capitalism, see Ho 2004, 2006.

44 Note a report from the Soufan Group, 2014: "The *Guardian* estimates that the Arctic contains 30% of the world's undiscovered natural gas and 15% of its oil." "In late February, Russia announced it would form a strategic military command to protect its Arctic interests." "Russia, Canada, Norway, Denmark, and the US all make some claim to international waters and the continental shelf in the Arctic Ocean." "[A Northwest Passage] route could provide the Russians with a great deal of leverage on the international stage over China or any other nation dependent on sea commerce between Asia and Europe." The province of Alberta in Canada ranks third in the world after Saudi Arabia and Venezuela for proven global crude reserves. Almost all of Alberta's oil is in the tar sands in the north of the province, site of the great new petrotoxic lakes of North America (http://www.energy.alberta.ca/oilsands/791.asp). The Capitalocene in action! See the Indigenous Environmental Network Canadian Indigenous Tar Sands Campaign (http://www.ienearth.org/what-we-do/tar-sands/). Over twenty corporations operate in the tar sands in the home area of many indigenous peoples, including the First Nation Mikisew Cree, Athabasca Chipewyan, Fort McMurray, Fort McKay Cree, Beaver Lake Cree, Chipewyan Prairie, and also the Métis.

45 Moore puts it this way: "This means that capital and power—and countless other strategic relations—do not act upon nature but develop through the web of life. 'Nature' is here offered as the relation of the whole. Humans live as

a specifically endowed (but not special) environment-making species within Nature. Second, capitalism in 1800 was no Athena, bursting forth, fully grown and armed, from the head of a carboniferous Zeus. Civilizations do not form through Big Bang events. They emerge through cascading transformations and bifurcations of human activity in the web of life. . . . [For example,] the long 17th century forest clearances of the Vistula Basin and Brazil's Atlantic Rainforest occurred on a scale, and at a speed, between five and ten times greater than anything seen in medieval Europe" (Moore 2014a).

46 Units (genes, cells, organisms, populations, species) and relations described mathematically in competition equations are the story formats of the Modern Synthesis. Evolutionary momentum, always verging on modernist notions of progress, is a constant theme. By contrast, see Hustak and Myers (2012), for one of the key writings for tracking the inflection of the curve of knowledge and affect to a deeply sympoietic evolutionary theory. The sensual attractions of wasps and orchids, situated in rereadings of Darwin, form the core of this beautiful paper. Hustak and Myers write, "Involutionary momentum helps us to get a feel for affective push and pull among bodies, including the affinities, ruptures, enmeshments, and repulsions among organisms constantly inventing new ways to live with and alongside one another. . . . Rather, the orchid and its bee-pollinators are mutually constituted through a reciprocal capture from which neither plant nor insect can be disentangled. It is in conversation with this "wasp-orchid" that we track the involutionary momentum that ingathers plants and insects in acts of pollination and communication." For the innovative sweep of the reworking of biological theory, along with Gilbert et al. (2012), see McFall-Ngai et al. (2013): 3229–36.

47 For a serious mathematical joke-exposition of Terrapolis, see Haraway (2011, 2010). "Terrapolis is rich in world, inoculated against post-humanism but rich in com-post, inoculated against human exceptionalism but rich in humus, ripe for multispecies storytelling. This Terrapolis is not the home world for the human as *homo*, that ever parabolic, re- and de-tumescing, phallic self-image of the same; but for the human that is transmogrified in etymological Indo-European sleight of tongue into *guman*, that worker of and in the soil" (Haraway 2010, 20–22).

48 I owe the insistence on "big enough stories" to James Clifford: "I think of these as 'big enough' histories, able to account for a lot, but not for everything—and without guarantees of political virtue" (2013, 201). Rejecting one big synthetic account or theory, Clifford works to craft a realism that "works with open-ended (because their linear historical time is ontologically unfinished) 'big-enough stories,' sites of contact, struggle, and dialogue" (ibid., 85–86).

49 Pignarre and Stengers (2005). Latour and Stengers are deeply allied in their fierce rejection of discourses of denunciation. They have both patiently taught me to understand and relearn in this matter. I love a good denunciation! It is a hard habit to unlearn.

50 It is possible to read Horkheimer and Adorno's *Dialectic of Enlightenment* (1972) as an allied critique of Progress and Modernization, even though their resolute secularism gets in their own way. It is very hard for a secularist to really

listen to the squids, bacteria, and angry old women of Terra/Gaia. The most likely Western Marxist allies, besides Marx, for nurturing the Chthulucene in the belly of the Capitalocene are Antonio Gramsci and Stuart Hall.

51 Hesiod's *Theogony* in achingly beautiful language tells of Gaia/Earth arising out of Chaos to be the seat of the Olympian immortals above and of Tartarus in the depths below. She/it is very old and polymorphic and exceeds Greek tellings, but just how remains controversial and speculative. At the very least, Gaia is not restricted to the job of holding up the Olympians! The important and unorthodox scholar-archaeologist Marija Gimbutas claims that Gaia as Mother Earth is a later form of a pre-Indo-European, Neolithic Great Mother. In 2004, filmmaker Donna Reed and neopagan author and activist Starhawk released a collaborative documentary film about the life and work of Gimbutas, *Signs Out of Time*; for the hour-long YouTube version, see https://www.youtube.com/watch?v=whfGbPFAy4w (see also Gimbutas 1999).

52 To understand what is at stake in "non-Euclidean" storytelling, go to Le Guin (1985, 1989b).

53 "The Thousand Names of Gaia: From the Anthropocene to the Age of the Earth," International Colloquium, Rio de Janeiro, September 15–19, 2014.

54 For the fascinating history of cephalopods figuring the depredations of Big Capital in the United States (for example, the early twentieth-century John D. Rockefeller/Standard Oil octopus strangling workers, farmers, and citizens in general with its many huge tentacles), see Gilson (2011). Resignification of octopuses and squids as chthonic allies is excellent news. We have been there before.

55 The bee was one of Potnia Theron's emblems, and she is also called Potnia Melissa, Mistress of the Bees. Modern Wiccans re-member these chthonic beings in ritual and poetry.

56 Links between Potnia Theron and the Gorgon/Medusa continued in temple architecture and building adornment well after 600 BCE, giving evidence of the tenacious hold of the chthonic powers in practice, imagination, and ritual, for example, from the fifth through the third centuries BCE on the Italian peninsula. The dread-ful Gorgon figure faces outward, defending against exterior dangers, and the no less awe-ful Potnia Theron faces inward, nurturing the webs of living (see Busby 2007). The Christian Mary, Virgin-Mother of God, who herself erupted in the Near East and Mediterranean worlds, took on attributes of these and other chthonic powers in her travels around the world. Unfortunately, Mary's iconography shows her ringed by stars and crushing the head of the snake (for example, in the Miraculous Medal dating from an early nineteenth-century apparition of the Virgin), rather than allying herself with earth powers. The "lady surrounded by stars" is a Christian Scriptural apocalyptic figure for the end of time. That is a bad idea. Throughout my childhood, I wore a gold chain with the Miraculous Medal. Finally and luckily, it was her residual chthonic infections that took hold in me, turning me from both the secular and also the sacred, and toward humus and compost.

57 The Hebrew word Deborah means bee, and she was the only female judge mentioned in the Bible. She was a warrior and counselor in pre-monarchic

Israel. The *Song of Deborah* may date to the twelfth century BCE. Deborah was a military hero and ally of Jael, one of the 4Js in Joanna Russ's formative feminist science fiction novel *The Female Man* (1975).

On May 2, 2014, the Reverend Billy and the Church of Stop Shopping exorcised the robobee from the Micro Robotics Laboratories at Harvard. The robobee is a high-tech drone bee that is intended to replace overworked and poisoned biological pollinating bees as they become more and more diseased and endangered (http://www.revbilly.com/chatter/blog/2014/02/robobee-lab-at-harvard-exorcised-monsanto-devils-confronted). Honeybeealujah, old stories live! Or, as Brad Werner put it at the American Geophysical Union Meetings, Revolt! Do we hear the buzzing yet? It is time to sting. It is time for a chthonic swarm. It is time to take care of the bees.

58 Theoi Greek Mythology, "Erinyes 1," http://www.theoi.com/Khthonios/Erinyes.html.

59 Martha Kenney pointed out to me that the story of the Ood, in the long-running British science fiction TV series *Doctor Who*, shows how the squid-faced ones became deadly to humanity only after they were mutilated, cut off from their sym-chthonic hive mind, and enslaved. The humanoid empathic Ood have sinuous tentacles over the lower portion of their multifolded alien faces; and in their proper bodies they carry their hindbrains in their hands, communicating with each other telepathically through these vulnerable, living, exterior organs (organons). Humans (definitely not the Earthbound) cut off the hindbrains and replaced them with a technological communication-translator sphere, so that the isolated Ood could only communicate through their enslavers, who forced them into hostilities. I resist thinking the Ood techno-communicators are a future release of the iPhone, but it is tempting when I watch the faces of twenty-first-century Humans on the streets, or even at the dinner table, apparently connected only to their devices. I am saved from this ungenerous fantasy by the SF fact that in the episode "The Planet of the Ood," the tentacular ones were freed by the actions of Ood Sigma and restored to their non-singular selves. *Doctor Who* is a much better story cycle for going-on-with than *Star Trek*.

For the importance of reworking fables in sciences and other knowledge practices, see Kenney (2013). Kenney explores different genres of fable, which situate what she calls unstable "wild facts" in relation to proposing and testing the strength of knowledge claims. She investigates strategies for navigating uncertain terrain, where the productive tensions between fact and fiction in actual practices are necessary.

60 "Medousa and Gorgones." http://www.theoi.com/Pontios/Gorgones.html.

61 Suzy McKee Charnas's Holdfast Chronicles, beginning with *Walk to the End of the World* (1974), is great SF for thinking about feminists and their horses. The sex is exciting if very incorrect, and the politics are bracing.

62 Eva Hayward first drew my attention to the emergence of Pegasus from Medusa's body and of coral from drops of her blood. "If coral teaches us about the reciprocal nature of life, then how do we stay obligated to environments—many of which we made unlivable—that now sicken us? ... Perhaps Earth will follow Venus, becoming uninhabitable due to rampaging greenhouse effect. Or,

maybe, we will rebuild reefs or construct alternate homes for the oceans refugees. Whatever the conditions of our future, we remain obligate partners with oceans" (Hayward 2012b). For the Hyperbolic Coral Reef Project pioneered by Margaret and Christine Wertheim at their Los Angeles-based Institute for Figuring, see http://crochetcoralreef.org/. By 2013, this art-science-activist project had brought together more than seven thousand active collaborators in twenty-seven countries in solidarity with vulnerable coral reefs and their human and more-than-human critters.

63 Go see the ongoing exhibit Tentacles: The Astounding Lives of Octopuses, Squids, and Cuttlefish at the Monterey Bay Aquarium. To understand, see Detienne and Vernant (1978), with thanks to Chris Connery for this reference in which cuttlefish, octopuses, and squids play a large role. Polymorphy, the capacity to make a net or mesh of bonds, and cunning intelligence are the traits the Greek writers foregrounded. "Cuttlefish and octopuses are pure *áporai* and the impenetrable pathless night they secrete is the most perfect image of their *metis*" (ibid., 38). Chapter 5, "The Orphic Metis and the Cuttle-fish of Thetis" is the most interesting for the Chthulucene's own themes of ongoing looping, becoming-with, and polymorphism. "The suppleness of molluscs, which appear as a mass of tentacles (*polúplokoi*), makes their bodies an interlaced network, a living knot of mobile animated bonds" (ibid., 159). For Detienne and Vernant's Greeks, the polymorphic and supple cuttlefish are close to the primordial multisexual deities of the sea—ambiguous, mobile and ever changing, sinuous and undulating, presiding over coming-to-be, pulsating with waves of intense color, cryptic, secreting clouds of darkness, adept at getting out of difficulties, and having tentacles where proper men would have beards.

64 See Haraway and Kenney (2015).

65 The hypothesis that bacteria trigger coral bleaching, rather than thermal stress and acidification alone, remains controversial but has lost ground. See "Is There a Case for Bacterial Bleaching Hypothesis? *Octagonia patagonia/ Vibrio shiloi* Revisited," 2008, http://archive-org.com/page/1334998/2013-02-06/ http://www.climateshifts.org/?p=123. Another *Vibrio* bacterium is the infectious agent in human cholera. Still another *Vibrio* critter infects the newly hatched Hawaiian bobtail squid and provides the necessary developmental signal for these little cephalopods to make their light organ on their ventral surface, which luminescent bacteria will inhabit, so that the squid can look like a starry sky to its prey below on dark nights. *Vibrio*, motile and flagellated, are talented communicators, for good and for ill, depending on point of view. "*Vibrio fischeri, Photobacterium phosphorem*, and *Vibrio harveyi* are notable for their ability to communicate. Both *V. fischeri* and *Ph. phosphoreum* are symbiotes of other marine organisms (typically jellyfish, fish, or squid), and produce light via bioluminescence through the mechanism of quorum sensing. *V. harveyi* is a pathogen of several aquatic animals, and is notable as a cause of luminous vibriosis in shrimps (prawns)" (http://en.wikipedia.org/wiki/ Vibrio#Non-cholera_Vibrio_infections). See McFall-Ngai (2014). It could be said that bacteria and other microbes invented biocommunication, the innovation critical to all subsequent semioses, including human language.

PART II
Histories of the Capitalocene

THREE

The Rise of Cheap Nature

Jason W. Moore[1]

We live at a crossroads in the history of our species—and of planetary life. What comes next is unknowable with any certainty. But it is not looking good.

Environmentalist theory and research tells us, today, just how bad it is. Mass extinction. Climate change. Ocean acidification. To these planetary shifts, one can add countless regional stories—runaway toxic disasters on land and at sea; cancer clusters; frequent and severe droughts. Our collective sense of "environmental consequences" has never been greater.

But *consequences* of what? Of humanity as a whole? Of population? Of industrial civilization? Of the West? Of capitalism? How we answer the question today will shape the conditions of life on Earth—for millennia to come.

Once we begin to ask this question—What drives today's disastrous state of affairs?—we move from the consequences of environment-making to its conditions and causes. And once we begin to ask questions about human-initiated environment-making, a new set of connections appears. These are the connections between environment-making and relations of inequality, power, wealth, and work. We begin to ask new questions about the relationship between environmental change and whose work is valued—and whose lives matter. Class, race, gender, sexuality, nation—and much, much more—can be understood in terms of their relationship within the whole of nature, and how that nature has been radically remade over the past five centuries. Such questions unsettle the idea of Nature and Humanity in the uppercase: ecologies without humans, and human relations without ecologies. Far from merely a philosophical difference, the uppercase Nature and Humanity that dominate Anthropocene stories do something unintentional—but deeply violent. For the story of Humanity and Nature conceals a dirty secret of modern world history. That secret is how capitalism was built on excluding most *humans* from Humanity— indigenous peoples, enslaved Africans, nearly all women, and even many white-skinned men (Slavs, Jews, the Irish). From the perspective of imperial administrators, merchants, planters, and *conquistadores*, these humans were not Human at all. They were regarded as part of Nature, along with trees and soils and rivers—and treated accordingly.

To register the bloody history of this Human/Nature binary is a moral protest. It is also an analytical protest. For capitalism does not thrive on violence and inequality alone. It is a prodigiously creative and productive system too—at least until recently. The symbolic, material, and bodily violence of this audacious separation—Humanity and Nature—performed a special kind of "work" for the modern world. Backed by imperial power and capitalist rationality, it mobilized the unpaid work and energy of humans— especially women, especially the enslaved—in service to transforming landscapes with a singular purpose: the endless accumulation of capital.

Some of us have begun to call this way of thinking *world-ecological* (Moore 2015a).[2] World-ecology does not refer to the "ecology of the world." Our *ecology* is not the ecology of Nature—with uppercase *N*—but the ecology of the *oikeios*: that creative, generative, and multilayered relation of life-making, of species and environments. Species make environments; environments make species. The philosophical point shapes the historical method: human activity *is* environment-making. And in this observation, nature moves from noun ("the environment") to verb (environment-making). Human organizations *are* environment-making processes and projects; in turn the web of life shapes human organization. This is the *double internality* of historical change—humanity inside nature, nature inside humanity. (With *humanity* differentiated, not reduced to a formless, abstract homogeneity.) World-ecology is not alone in making the broad philosophical argument. But it is distinctive in arguing for the translation of these philosophical positions into methodological premises, narrative strategies, and theoretical frames. In these frames, specific human organizations—such as capitalism—are revealed as producers and products of the web of life.

Such questions have led us to a set of problems very different from the usual environmentalist critique, with its easy metaphors of Humanity's "footprint" upon Nature (e.g., Wackernagel and Rees 1996). Enfolding cause, condition, and consequence in thinking the fate of the planet—and of humans on it—leads us to explore different stories. These are not so simple as Humanity's fall from Eden, as narratives of catastrophe and collapse would have it (e.g., Diamond 2004). But if they are not so simple, I think we may also find more hopeful stories of how *some* humans have remade the planet, and of how *most* humans might work with other species to co-produce a planet not only more habitable—but more just.

Anthropocene Problems, Capitalocene Vistas

The Anthropocene is one of those ideas—like "globalization" in the 1990s—that worms its way out of academia and captures the popular imagination. It is subject to a bewildering spectrum of arguments, advanced by scholars across the Two Cultures. Geologists, cultural theorists, ecologists, literary analysts, historians, geographers, and anthropologists—everyone wants to get in on the game.

From the outset, then, it is good to be clear about the Anthropocene's Two Lives. One is the Anthropocene as a broader conversation that transcends the university. In this life, the Anthropocene has opened some measure of public space for dialogue around humanity's place in the web of life (but see Crist, "On the Poverty of Our Nomenclature" in this volume). This is the Anthropocene as a cultural phenomenon, gracing the cover of the *Economist* (2011a, 2011b) and winning the attention of the *New York Times* editors (2011). This wider conversation has been productive in scholarly circles as well, creating opportunities for scholars across the human and physical sciences to discuss humanity's role in making planetary natures.

As an analytic, the Anthropocene operates a bit differently. Among earth system scientists, there is an ongoing search for—and debate about— "golden spikes" in the stratigraphic record.[3] Here the method hews closely to a broadly conceived "natural history." Which golden spike inaugurates the "Age of Man" remains hotly debated.[4]

Here the Anthropocene perspective engages the really big questions of historical change: How do humans make natures, how do natures make humans, and how does that relation shape the long run of human history?

These are questions that the Anthropocene can pose, but cannot answer. Why? Because the perspective retains—even as it seeks to transcend—the binary of Humanity and Nature. It is a binary seemingly inscribed in the intellectual DNA of the Anthropocene project. This binary animates gripping—but ill-conceived—questions: "Are humans overwhelming the great forces of nature?" (Steffen et al. 2007). More problematic, the Anthropocene's cultural success sometimes feeds a casual dismissal of conceptual and historical criticisms. For Clive Hamilton, "this discussion [Anthropocene or Capitalocene] is a *diversion*. Will Steffen . . . understands the social roots of this geological epoch. Paul Crutzen, the inventor of this concept, *immediately linked to the burning of fossil fuels and English capitalism*" (Lindgaard 2015, emphasis added). Worse still, Hamilton asks, "Do we really believe a word is so powerful that it has the capacity to change people's ideas about the causes of climate change? It is not plausible." These are curious words coming from an advocate of the Anthropocene! Here we see a dangerous closure. That closure is not only a dismissive polemic aimed at closure rather than dialogue—echoed even by the radical magazine *Monthly Review* (e.g., Angus 2015). It reveals a profound, and I am tempted to say willful, misunderstanding of the alternative: the Capitalocene.

For the Capitalocene—"Age of Capital"—is not an argument about replacing one word with another. The Capitalocene argument says three things that the Anthropocene perspective does not—*and cannot*. First, it insists that the history of capitalism is a relation of capital, power, and nature as an organic whole. It is world-ecological (Moore 2015a). It is a multispecies affair. Capitalism is neither a purely economic nor social system, but "a historically situated complex of metabolisms and assemblages" (Haraway et al. 2015, 21). Second, the history of capitalism cannot be reduced to the burning of fossil fuels, in England or anywhere else. It is a history of the relations of power and re/production premised on the cash nexus. Those relations enfolded coal and other energy sources from the sixteenth century; they allowed for successive waves of global conquest and the worldwide appropriations of Cheap Nature. Third, the Capitalocene argument challenges the Eurocentric—and frankly false— view of capitalism as emerging in England during the eighteenth century.

As Hamilton's riposte to the Capitalocene reveals, the dominant Anthropocene argument assumes a standard narrative. It says that the origins of modern world are to be found in England, right around the dawn of the nineteenth century.[5] The motive force behind this epochal shift? Coal and steam. The driving force behind coal and steam? Not class. Not capital. Not imperialism. Not even culture. But . . . you guessed it, the *Anthropos*: humanity as an undifferentiated whole.

The Anthropocene makes for an easy story. Easy, because it does not challenge the naturalized inequalities, alienation, and violence inscribed in modernity's strategic relations of power and production. It is an easy story to tell because it does not ask us to think about these relations *at all*. It reduces the mosaic of human activity in the web of life to an abstract, homogenous humanity. It removes inequality, commodification, imperialism, patriarchy, and much more from the problem of humanity-in-nature. If sometimes acknowledged, at best these relations exist in the Anthropocene discourse as after-the-fact supplements.

We have noted two major dimensions of the Anthropocene analytic today. One is a strict emphasis on geophysical change and its proximate drivers. The second is an argument about history, and therefore about the present as history. There is frequent slippage between the two. In this latter, the dominant Anthropocene argument goes beyond the domain of earth-system science, reaching into the very heart of historical analysis: the dialectically bound questions of historical agency and periodization.

The Anthropocene argument takes biogeological questions and facts— turning on the presence of variously significant stratigraphic signals (Zalasiewicz et al. 2008, 2011)—as an adequate basis for historical periodization. Two subtle but powerful methodological decisions underpin this approach. In the first instance, empirical focus is narrowed to the consequences of human activity. In this, the Anthropocene argument embodies the *consequentialist bias* of Green Thought across the Two Cultures. It makes the case for humanity's domination of the earth almost entirely through a significant catalogue of biospheric changes. The drivers of such changes are typically reduced to very broad "black box" descriptive categories: industrialization, urbanization, population, and so forth (Steffen et al. 2011a, 2011b). The second methodological choice turns on the construction of humanity as "collective" actor (e.g., Zalasiewicz et al. 2011; Crist, "On the Poverty of Our Nomenclature" in this volume). This choice erases the historical-geographical patterns of differentiation and coherence in the interests of narrative simplicity. This erasure, and the elevation of the *Anthropos* as a collective actor, has encouraged several important mis-recognitions: (1) a neo-Malthusian view of population (see especially Crutzen 2002; Fischer-Kowalski et al. 2014; Ellis et al. 2010), ignoring the modern world-system's actually existing patterns of family formation and population movement (e.g., Seccombe 1992, 1995; Massey et al. 1999); (2) a view of historical change dominated by technology-resource complexes; (3) a concept of scarcity abstracted from relations of capital, class, and empire; and (4) assigning responsibility for global change to humanity as a whole, rather than to the forces of capital and empire that have given modern world history its coherence (see also Hartley's essay "Anthropocene, Capitalocene, and the Problem of Culture," in this volume).

If we boil down the Anthropocene's historical perspective, we can identify two principal narrative strategies. First, consequences determine periodization. Second, the *Anthropos* drives these consequences. The two frames stem from a philosophical position that we may call Cartesian dualism (Moore 2015a). As with Descartes, the separation of humans from the rest of nature—"Are humans overwhelming the great forces of nature?" (Steffen et al. 2007)—appears as a self-evident reality. In its simplest form, this philosophy locates human activity in one box, the rest of nature in another. To be sure, these two acting units interact and influence each other. But the differences between and within each acting unit are not mutually constitutive, such that changes in one imply changes in the other—although such relations are empirically acknowledged from time to time (Steffen et al. 2011a 845–46). This dualism leads Anthropocene advocates to construct the historical period since 1800 on an arithmetic basis: "human activity plus significant biospheric change = the Anthropocene."

This perspective obscures the actually existing *relations* through which women and men make history within the web of life. To be sure, some radicals have sought to recuperate the Anthropocene argument as crystallizing "capitalism WITH nature" (Swyngedouw 2013, 16). But I find it difficult to square such recuperations with the Anthropocene's fundamentally bourgeois character: above all, its erasure of capitalism's historical specificity and the attendant implication that capitalism's socio-ecological contradictions are the responsibility of all humans.

Anthropocene Questions, Capitalocene Answers

The dominant Anthropocene argument therefore poses a question that it cannot answer: *How* have humans become a "geological force"? (Were we not *already* a geological force?) Anthropocene advocates do of course respond to the question. But they are responses, not explanations in any reasonable sense. Most of these responses focus on demography and technology, though additional factors are often recognized—consumerism, trade liberalization, investment flows, and so forth. These imply, but do not engage directly, questions of power, work, and capital. The identification of multiple "trajectories" of the Anthropocene describes a lot but explains very little.

The Anthropocene argument cannot explain *how* the present crisis is unfolding for a basic reason: it is captive to the very thought-structures that created the present crisis. At the core of these thought-structures is Cartesian dualism. The term is one of my possible shorthands. This dualism owes its name to René Descartes's famous argument about the separation of mind and body. Descartes surely does not deserve all blame. He personified a much broader scientific and especially philosophical movement that encouraged

> a strict and total division not only between mental and bodily activity, but between mind and nature and between human and animal. As mind becomes pure thought—pure *res cogitans* or thinking substance, mental, incorporeal, without location, bodiless—body as its dualised other becomes pure matter, pure *res extensa*, materiality as lack. As mind and nature become substances utterly different in kind and mutually exclusive, the dualist division of realms is accomplished and the possibility of continuity is destroyed from both ends. The intentional, psychological level of description is thus stripped from the body and strictly isolated in a separate mechanism of the mind. The body, deprived of such a level of description and hence of any capacity for agency, becomes an empty mechanism which has no agency or intentionality within itself, but is driven from outside by the mind. The body and nature become the dualised other of the mind. (Plumwood 1993, 115)

To be sure, humans had long recognized a difference between "first" and "second" natures, and between body and spirit (Cicero 1933). *However*, capitalism was the first civilization to organize itself on this basis. For early modern materialism, the point was not only to interpret the world but to control it: "to make ourselves as it were the masters and possessors of nature" (Descartes 2006, 51). This sensibility was a key organizing principle for an emergent capitalist civilization.

Thus Cartesian dualism is a problem not merely because it is philosophically problematic, but because it is *practically* bound up with a way of thinking the world—ontologically (what is?) and epistemologically (how do we know?)—that took shape between the fifteenth and eighteenth centuries.

These centuries saw the rise of capitalism. Most people—and most scholars—still think about capitalism as matter of "economics." Markets, prices, money, and all that—not necessarily the most exciting thing to think about. What if, instead of thinking capitalism = economics, we asked if "capitalism" was about something much more profound? One alternative is to think about the rise of capitalism as a new way of organizing nature, and therefore a new way of organizing the relations between work, reproduction, and the conditions of life. Markets, prices, and money are still important in this frame. But the alternative allows us to start looking at how every market, every price, and every movement and accumulation of money was bundled with extra-human nature—and human work too, much of it unpaid.

Instead of capitalism as world-economy, then, we would start to look at capitalism as *world-ecology*. From this angle of vision, three entwined historical processes were fundamental. One was what Marx called primitive accumulation (1977, Part VIII). This entailed a range of processes that made humans dependent on the cash nexus for their survival. Social scientists call this "proletarianization," and it assumed the widest range of forms. It was nearly always partial ("semi-proletarianization"). It is about the transformation of human activity into labor-power, something to be "exchanged" in the commodity system—sometimes called "the labor market." Even if one thinks that human activity is somehow independent of nature, there is no avoiding one fact: proletarianization was rooted in the governance of nature and the replacement of custom and common by the dictatorship of the commodity. Sometimes peasants who were forced off the land found their way to the towns. Sometimes they were dispossessed and kept on the land, reduced to cottagers and forced into agricultural wage work—or neoserfdom as in Poland—to acquire what their small plots could not provide. And sometimes proletarians did not look *proletarian* at all—African slaves in Brazilian and Caribbean sugar plantations were a good example (Mintz 1978). Like wage-workers in seventeenth-century England or Peru, slaves also depended upon the cash nexus to survive.

Proletarianization was never principally *economic*; it was a product of new forms of territorial power that emerged after 1450. Here is our second process. The old territorial power—the overlapping jurisdictions and personalized authority of medieval Europe—had crumbled in the long feudal crisis (ca. 1315–1453). West-central Europe's ruling classes had tried to restore feudal labor systems—and failed. The most dynamic of the new states owed their dynamism to an alliance with merchant capitalists who were far more than merchants. It was the alliance of the Iberian crowns with Genoese capitalists that, quite literally, made the space that made capitalism possible. In its early centuries, capitalism was trans-Atlantic or it was nothing (Moore 2003a, 2003b, 2007). The new empires—but also the internal transformations of the Low Countries and England—were made possible by power of a new type. At its core was the generalization of private property. For a new *praxis* of modern private property emerged in these centuries. Its "strategic goal" was the separation of the peasantry from nonmarket access to land: arable and grazing land, forests, wetlands, and all the rest (Sevilla-Buitrago 2015). This was the fundamental condition of proletarianization, and like proletarianization, these enclosures and dispossessions were enormously varied. So too were the states and empires that pursued this strategic goal. Their "central function" was "the internal maintenance and external defence of a private property regime" (Teschke 2006, 51; see also Parenti's essay "Environment-Making in the Capitalocene," in this volume). And may we add that these states and empires were equally central to the *expanded, globalizing, reproduction* of that property regime?

Our third great historical process turned on new ways of knowing the world. These were purely symbolic, but they were far more than symbolic. The ongoing condition of turning human activity into labor-power, and land into property, was a symbolic-knowledge regime premised on separation—*on alienation*. Let us think of the new knowledge regime as a series of "scientific revolutions" in the broadest sense of the term. This regime made it possible to launch and sustain a process that threatens us all today: putting the whole of nature to work for capital. The job of "science" was to make nature legible to capital accumulation—transforming it into units of Nature and counterpoised to the forces of capital and empire. The job of "the economy" was to channel this alienation through the cash nexus. The job of "the state" was to enforce that cash nexus. To be sure, that "separation from nature" was illusory: humans could never escape nature. But the terms of the relation *did* change. And those changing terms of Humanity/Nature—a complex and protracted process— bundled the symbolic and material. It was a *world-praxis* of remaking the world in the image of capital.

To say *praxis* invokes an ongoing process of capital's self-reflection and capacity for innovation—symbolically and materially. For no civilization has been so adept at overcoming its limits. The new knowledge regime prized dualism, separation, mathematization, the aggregation of units. Its innovations, clustered into scientific revolutions, were at once producers and products of the previous two transformations—of labor (proletarianization) and land (property). At the core of the new thought-structures was a mode of distinction that presumed separation. The most fundamental of these separations was Humanity/Nature. Some people became Humans, who were members of something called Civilization, or Society, or both—as in Adam Smith's "civilised society" ([1776] 1937, 14). From the beginning of capitalism, however, most humans were either excluded from Humanity—indigenous Americans, for example—or were designated as *only partly* Human, as were virtually all European women. As with property, the symbolic boundaries between who was—and who was not—part of Nature (or Society) tended to shift and vary; they were often blurry; and they were flexible. But a boundary there was, and much of the early history of modern race and gender turns on the struggles over that line. (Is it so different today?)

That boundary—the Nature/Society divide that the Anthropocene affirms and that many of us now question—was fundamental to the rise of capitalism. For it allowed nature to become Nature—environments without Humans. But note the uppercase *H*: Nature was full of humans treated as Nature. And what did this mean? It meant that the web of life could be reduced to a series of external objects—mapped, explored, sur-veyed, calculated for what Nature could do for the accumulation of capital. And the substance of that value? Human labor productivity—but not all *humanly productive work*—measured without regard for its cultural, bio-physical, and cooperative dimensions. This was human work as abstracted, averaged, deprived of all meaning but for one: value as the average labor-time making the average commodity.

For this to occur, not only did new conceptions of nature—as exter-nal Nature—take shape, but new conceptions of time and space. For good reason, Mumford tells us that the "key machine" of modernity is not the steam engine but the mechanical clock, the physical expression of an earth-shaking idea: linear time (1934, 14). The clock, Marx underlines, was the "first automatic machine applied to practical purposes" (1979, 68). Nor did this early modern revolution of abstraction stop with labor and time. Successive cartographic revolutions, beginning in the fifteenth century, made possible an extraordinary new apprehension of geography. In the new cartography, geography was cleansed of its troubling particularities and meanings. It became "space as pure quantity" (Biggs 1999, 377). It became abstract space—and therefore, abstract Nature.

Here we can begin to see the thought-structures of modernity as more than "superstructures." To turn work into labor-power and land into private property was to transform nature into Nature. In equal measure, this transformation produced Society as something outside of Nature, the better that Society could turn Nature into a set of discrete units, into a repertoire of calculable objects and factors of production. Marx tells us, famously, that the relations of capital and labor "drip with blood and dirt" (1977, 926). Does not also the dualism of Society and Nature? We do well to grasp Society and Nature not merely as false, but also as *real* abstractions with real force in the world. In highlighting Cartesian dualism as a key source of the problem—unconsciously embraced by the Anthropocene argument—we are seeking to make sense of three great thought-procedures that have shaped the modern world: (1) the imposition of "an ontological status upon entities (substances) as opposed to relationships (that is to say energy, matter, people, ideas and so on became things)"; (2) the centrality of "a logic of either/or (rather than both/and)"; and (3) the "idea of a purposive control over nature through applied science" (Watts 2005, 150–51; Glacken 1967, 427).

These thought-procedures dominate Anthropocene thinking in all sorts of ways—not least in their embrace of technical fixes such as geoengineering (see Altvater's essay in this volume). The point I wish to emphasize, however, concerns the fundamentally substantialist and arithmetic character of the Anthropocene perspective. Anthropocene thinking remains firmly rooted in a model that "*aggregate[s]* socio-economic and Earth system trends" (Steffen et al. 2015, 8). The model is descriptively powerful, yielding powerful visual representations of the "Great Acceleration" (*New Scientist* 2008). Descriptively powerful, perhaps—but analytically anemic. Nature and Society are taken as unproblematic; the concepts are confused for actually existing historical processes, in which capitalism is actively shaped by the web of life—and vice versa. In sum, the perspective *integrates* factors without synthesizing them. Absent is the actual whole of power, capital, and nature entwined in modern world history. More problematic still: the adding up of Nature and Society makes claims for wholeness that undermine efforts to forge a new, post-Cartesian synthesis of humanity-in-nature.

Challenging the Industrial Revolution Myth: From "Work" *And* "Energy" to Work/Energy

The Industrial Revolution is the lodestar of Green Thought. No narrative in modern social thought is so powerful as the idea that *It*—capitalism, industrial civilization, and all the rest—all began with coal and steam. Marxist Greens have scarcely altered the story—even if they prefer to speak of capitalism rather than industry. Enzensberger crystallized the Green perspective in his landmark 1974 essay: "the industrial societies of this earth are producing ecological contradictions, which must in the foreseeable future lead to their collapse" (1974, 4). The Marxist position is more nuanced and historical: fossil fuels enabled the "generalization" of capitalist relations and forces of production (Huber 2009; Malm 2013). Both perspectives are grounded in a substantialist rather than relational view of capitalism and nature. In this narrative, fossil fuels become the spark that ignites the circuit of capital and unleashes the dynamism of modern economic growth. From this naturally follows "the destruction of nature on a planetary scale" (Deléage 1989).

What does this narrative get wrong? Quite a lot, it turns out. Even if we take a conventional approach to environmental history, the fossil capital narrative ignores the epochal revolution in landscape change that occurred between 1450 and 1750. But if we go further—and given the pressing realities of biospheric change today, we need to go further—we can see that the rise of capitalism in the long sixteenth century was premised a fundamentally new law of environment-making. Capitalism's "law of value" was, it turns out, a law of Cheap Nature. It was "cheap" in a specific sense, deploying the capacities of capital, empire, and science to appropriate the unpaid work/energy of global natures within reach of capitalist power.

The concept of work/energy looms large in this argument (Moore 2015a). It allows us to pierce the Cartesian fog that surrounds the unity of human and extra-human work. Marx's observation that large-scale industry is a mechanism for turning "blood into capital" was no mere polemic. It was a means of highlighting the ways that the capital relation transforms the work/energy of *all* natures into a frankly weird crystallization of wealth and power: value. Work/energy helps us to rethink capitalism as a set of relations through which the "capacity to do work"—by human and extra-human natures—is transformed into value, understood as socially necessary labor-time (abstract social labor). "Work/energy" (or *potential* work/energy) may be capitalized—as in commodified labor-power via the cash nexus—or it may be appropriated via noneconomic means, as in the work of a river, waterfall, forest, or some forms of social reproduction. My thinking about work/energy finds inspiration from White's view of

> energy as the capacity to do work. Work, in turn, is the product of a force acting on a body and the distance the body is moved in the direction of that force. Push a large rock and you are expending energy and doing work; the amount of each depends on how large the rock and how far you push it. The weight and flow of water produce the energy that allows rivers to do the work of moving rock and soil: the greater the volume of water in the river and the steeper the gradient of its bed, the greater its potential energy. (1995, 6)

White's sketch is focused on the geophysical work/energy implied in the historical geography of a river (the Columbia, in this instance). Work/energy is also about organic life: from photosynthesis to hunting prey to bearing children. What bears emphasis is *how* capitalism incorporates work/energy into its re/production of wealth, life, and power. The work/energy alternative sees metabolism through the double internality: flows of power and capital in nature, flows of nature in capital and power. Metabolism, in this perspective, is nearly always better understood as a matter of shifts rather than rifts (Moore 2015a, 75–90).

Capitalism's metabolism of work/energy is crucial because it sharpens our focus on how human work unfolds through the *oikeios*: the pulsing, renewing, and sometimes-exhaustible relation of planetary life. The genius of capitalism—and a morbid genius at that—has been to find ways, through culture, science, and the state, to appropriate streams of work/energy for free or low cost. We find—has it not been right in front of our eyes all along?—that great "economic" revolutions, propelling labor productivity within the commodity system, are always accompanied by "new" imperialisms, "new" sciences, "new" forms of state power. Capitalism has always flourished as archipelagos of commodified relations within oceans of uncommodified life-activity, living and (in the case of fossil fuels) dead.

Let's begin with the gist of the Industrial Revolution story. This story tells us that capitalism—or Humanity, in the Anthropocene narrative—begins its journey to "overwhelm" planetary nature sometime around 1800. This narrative is shaped by a peculiar kind of past/present binary: the whole of history, at least since the Neolithic Revolution, is cast into the dustbin of the "preindustrial." Most scholars are well aware that civilizations transformed environments in significant ways well before the nineteenth century. But, or so the story goes, the really significant changes occurred after this point.

This conventional story misses something significant. In the three centuries after 1450, there occurred the greatest landscape revolution in human history. "Greatest" in three senses: speed, scale, and scope. This revolution was centered in the Atlantic world, itself a creation of early capitalism. For the first time in human history, a durable transoceanic division of labor underpinned the accumulation of wealth. Because that wealth was *capital*, it was premised on a kind of wealth very different from medieval Europe's. Early capitalism's defining innovation was its inversion of the age-old primacy of land productivity. Increasingly, labor productivity within a very narrow zone—the production and exchange of commodities—dominated. At first, that dominance was uneven and tentative—but it was nonetheless decisive. It posited a rule of civilizational reproduction—labor productivity within commodity production—that allowed territorial and capitalist agencies to do something quite novel. They put the whole of nature—at least, those human and extra-human natures within their grasp—in service to advancing labor productivity. Long before economists coined the term, nature became a factor of production: Nature.

Let's be clear on the nature/Nature distinction: most humans were part of Nature, and this designation worked through the new divisions of labor. An African slave was not part of Society in the new capitalist order, but part of Nature—giving a post-Cartesian twist to Patterson's characterization of slavery as "social death" (1982). Most *human* work was not labor-power and therefore most humans within capital's gravitational pull were not, or not really, Humans. This meant that the realm of Nature—as ontological formation and world-praxis—encompassed virtually all peoples of color, most women, and most people with white skin living in semicolonial regions (e.g., Ireland, Poland, etc.)

To put most humans into the category of Nature rather than Humanity was to enable an audacious act of global bookkeeping. On the one hand, the decisive thing was work reproduced—directly or indirectly—through the cash nexus. This included a great deal more people in early modern capitalism than scholars usually acknowledge, a point to which we return later in the essay. On the other hand, the volume of work reproduced through the cash nexus depended upon a much greater volume of work outside that nexus—but within reach of capitalist power. Hence, the appropriation of "women, nature, and colonies" is the fundamental condition of the exploitation of labor-power in the commodity system (Mies 1986, 77). This is the disproportionality at the heart of capitalism between "paid work," reproduced through the cash nexus, and "unpaid work," reproduced outside the circuit of capital but indispensable to its expanded reproduction. Every act of producing surplus value, then, depends upon a disproportionately greater act of appropriating the unpaid work of human and extra-human natures.

Once we recognize this disproportionality—between work reproduced inside and outside the cash nexus—the question of work becomes central to our thinking about nature. Because capitalism is a system driven by competition in the productive sphere—which implies rising labor productivity, and more throughput per hour of necessary labor time—it must appropriate ever-larger spheres of uncapitalized nature. The whole system works, as ecological economists have long underscored, because capital pays for only one set of costs, and works strenuously to keep all other costs off the books. Centrally, these are the costs of reproducing labor-power, food, energy, and raw materials.

Technology, then, works through this disproportionality. It works not only to advance labor productivity but to appropriate a rising physical mass of unpaid work/energy from manifold natures. We see this at work in the long history of capitalist mechanization. Sixteenth-century sugar mills, eighteenth-century steam engines, the Fordist assembly lines—all were premised, at every turn, on the appropriation of Cheap Natures. The plantation system was built on Cheap land and labor; steam engines developed at the pitheads of coal mines; the Fordist assembly lines were worthless without Cheap oil, steel, and coal. The bonanza of Cheap fossil fuels allowed capital to smooth out its greatest problem before 1830—the recurrent "underproduction" of food, energy, and raw materials owing to advancing labor productivity in industrial centers (Marx 1967, III, 111–21; Moore 2015a). But since the 1970s, the possibilities for securing Cheap Natures have narrowed. This progressive closure—of capitalism's Cheap Nature frontiers—has set in motion a new tendency, widely discussed in terms of neoliberalism, the reassertion of market rule, and sharply rising inequality between rich and poor. Often viewed as a triumph, what we have in fact seen is the exhaustion of a centuries-long model of appropriating unpaid work/energy outside the cash nexus. Now, increasingly, firms must *capitalize* rather than appropriate: think of factory-farmed animals (CAFOs) or tree plantations or aquaculture since the 1970s. Such capitalization, essentially rationalizing primary production through the cash nexus, brings middle-run benefits (rising labor productivity) but also rising costs of production. Increasingly, the costs of socio-ecological reproduction start to show up "on the books."

The upshot is that the nonlinearity of the Anthropocene's "Great Acceleration" cannot be explained through technology or population or even "the economy" as such. The organization of work—inside and outside the cash nexus, in all its gendered, semicolonial, and racialized forms—must be at the center of our explanations, and our politics. The question of work and the question of nature will be intimately joined in the politics of the twenty-first century. Indeed, they already are.

The Capitalocene: A Relational View

If we think about work in these more expansive terms, a different view of history comes into focus. We retain our awareness of "environmental" consequences—nearly always imposed on those creatures, humans included, *doing the work*. But we are no longer captive to a view of history premised on consequences. If indeed capitalism is defined by its commitment to endless accumulation, then our starting point—and point of return—must be work. What Marx understood better than most Marxists is that capitalism "works" because it organizes *work* as a multispecies process (Marx 1977, 238 and passim; Moore 2015a; Hribal 2003; Haraway 2008). Far from undermining Marx's conceptualization of value, however, the post-Cartesian critique reinforces it. Many species—and biological and geological processes—perform work for capital that *cannot* be "valued" in a system that values only paid work. The nonlinearity of the Great Acceleration is the logical outcome of a "law of value" premised on advancing labor productivity within a very narrow zone: paid work. As labor productivity advances, there is a geometric uptake of manifold natures, resulting in abrupt and rapid shifts in environment-making. Such a work-centered perspective roots the historical geography of endless accumulation in systems of power, knowledge, and technology that pursue the infinite expansion of work/energy—human and extra-human, paid and unpaid.

Here then is a line in the sand between Anthropocene and Capitalocene arguments. In taking the centrality of work as central to our thinking about capitalism—ontologically (how it is defined) and epistemologically (how we know it and its history)—we have a relational view of work, power, and re/production since 1492. From this angle of vision, a very different view of the Anthropocene problem comes into focus: how the origins of a new pattern of environment-making began in the Atlantic world during the "long" sixteenth century.

The difference speaks to divergent historical interpretations—and also to differences in political strategy. To locate modernity's origins through the steam engine and the coal pit is to prioritize shutting down the steam engines and the coal pits, and their twenty-first century incarnations. To locate the origins of the modern world with the rise of capitalism after 1450, with its audacious strategies of global conquest, endless commodification, and relentless rationalization, is to prioritize a much different politics—one that pursues the fundamental transformation of the relations of power, knowledge, and capital that have made the modern world. Shut down a coal plant, and you can slow global warming for a day; shut down the relations that made the coal plant, and you can stop it for good.

The erasure of capitalism's early modern origins, and the extraordinary reshaping of global natures long before the steam engine, is therefore of some significance—analytically, and politically. Ask any historian and she will tell you: how one periodizes history decisively shapes the interpretation of events, and one's choice of decisive relations. Start the clock in 1784, with James Watt's rotary steam engine (Crutzen 2002), and we have a very different view of history—and a very different view of modernity—than we do if we begin with the English or Dutch agricultural revolutions, with Columbus and the conquest of the Americas, with the first signs of an epochal transition in landscape transformation after 1450. Are we really living in the *Anthropocene*, with its return to a curiously Anglocentric vista of humanity, and its reliance on well-worn notions of resource- and technological-determinism? Or are we living in the *Capitalocene*, the historical era shaped by relations privileging the endless accumulation of capital?

The Capitalocene argument posits capitalism as a situated and multispecies world-ecology of capital, power, and re/production. As such it pushes back—strongly—against the Anthropocene's love affair with Two Century model of modernity: *industrial* society, *industrial* civilization, *industrial* capitalism. The model has obscured something hidden in plain sight: the remarkable remaking of land and labor beginning in the long sixteenth century, ca. 1450–1640, the subject of an extraordinary postwar historiography.[6] Only occasionally did these historians frame

94

their analyses in terms of capitalism; but there was no question that the early modern transformations of economies and landscapes were closely bound.[7] Since the 1970s, for all their distinctive geographical emphases and interpretive differences, the view of *early* modernity as *real* modernity has persisted.[8] For some, this ongoing "revolt of the early modernists" (van Zanden 2002) did not go nearly so far enough: the decisive period begins sometime just after the turn of the millennium (van Zanden 2009; Levine 2001; Arrighi 1994; Mielants 2007).[9] Yet Green Thought has been slow—*very* slow—to think outside the Two Century box. Industrialization still often appears as a *deus ex machina* dropped onto the world-historical stage by coal and steam power.

On the terrain staked out by the Anthropocene argument, we might consider how the definite relations of early capitalism—co-produced in the web of life—transformed coal from a rock in the ground into a fossil fuel. Let us be clear that the call for the relationality of humanity-in-nature does not deny the materiality of resources. Far from it! The world-ecology alternative argues that resources are relational and therefore historical. Geology is a "basic fact"; it becomes a "historical fact" through the co-produced character of resource production, unfolding through the human/extra-human nexus: the *oikeios* (quotation from Carr 1962; Moore 2015a, 33–50; Harvey 1974).

Geology, in other words, becomes *geohistory* through definite relations of power and production; these definite relations are geographical, which is to say they are not relations between humans alone. (Any geographical point of view unfolds from the premise that human activity is always ontologically coincident with its geographical conditions and consequences.) In the case of coal, we might note the revolution in English coal production began not in the eighteenth century but in the first half of the *sixteenth* century. English coal production rose from 50,000 tons (1530), to 210,000 tons (1560) to 1.5 million tons by 1630. By this point, most of England's important coalfields were being exploited. Production continued to surge, doubling to 2.9 million tons of coal by the 1680s. If the Anthropocene begins not in 1800 but in the long sixteenth century, we begin to ask much different questions about the drivers of world-ecological crisis in the twenty-first century. English coal's rapid ascent after 1530 directs our attention to the relations of primitive accumulation and agrarian class structure, to the formation of the modern world market, to new forms of commodity-centered landscape change, to new machineries of state power. This line of argument only appears to return to "social relations" because the legacy of Cartesian thought continues to tell us that state formation, class structure, commodification, and world markets are purely about relations between humans . . . *which they are not*. These too—states, classes, commodity production and exchange—are bundles of human and extra-human nature. They are processes and projects that reconfigure the relations of humanity-in-nature, within large and small geographies alike.

The Origins of Ecological Crisis: From Geological History to Geohistory

Capitalism in 1800 was no Athena, bursting forth, fully grown and armed, from the head of a carboniferous Zeus. Civilizations do not form through Big Bang events. They emerge through cascading transformations and bifurcations of human activity in the web of life. This cascade finds its origin in the chaos that followed the epochal crisis of feudal civilization after the Black Death (1347–53), followed by the emergence of a "vast but weak" capitalism in the long sixteenth century (Braudel 1961). If we are to put our finger on a new era of human relations with the rest of nature it was in these centuries, centered geographically in the expansive commodity-centered relations of the early modern Atlantic. At the risk of putting too fine a point on the matter: the rise of capitalism after 1450 marked a turning point in the history of humanity's relation with the rest of nature. It was greater than any watershed since the rise of agriculture and the first cities. And in relational terms, it was even *greater than the rise of the steam engine*.

The rise of capitalism after 1450 marked an epochal shift in the scale, speed, and scope of landscape transformation across the geographical expanse of early capitalism. The long seventeenth-century forest clearances of the Vistula Basin and Brazil's Atlantic Rainforest occurred on a scale, and at a speed, between five and ten times greater than anything seen in medieval Europe (Moore 2007, 2010b; Darby 1956; Williams 2003). Feudal Europe had taken centuries to deforest large expanses of western and central Europe. After 1450, however, comparable deforestation occurred in decades, not centuries. To take but one example, in medieval Picardy (northeastern France), it took two hundred years to clear twelve thousand hectares of forest, beginning in the twelfth century (Fossier 1968, 315). Four centuries later, in northeastern Brazil at the height of the sugar boom in the 1650s, twelve thousand hectares of forest would be cleared in a single year (Moore 2007, chap. 6). These are precious clues to an epochal transition in the relations of power, wealth, and nature that occurred over the course of the long medieval crisis and the epochal shift that commenced after 1450.

Whereas the Anthropocene argument begins with biospheric consequences and moves toward social history, another approach is plausible, even desirable. An unconventional ordering of crises would begin with the relations between (and among) humans and the rest of nature, and thence move toward geological and biophysical change. These consequences, in turn, constitute new conditions for successive eras of capitalist restructuring across the *longue durée*. Relations of power and production, themselves co-produced within nature, enfold and unfold consequences. The modern world-system becomes, in this approach, a *capitalist world-ecology*: a civilization that joins the accumulation of capital, the pursuit of power, and the production of nature as an organic whole. This means that capital and power—and countless other strategic relations—do not act *upon* nature, but develop *through* the web of life. Crises are turning points of world-historical processes—accumulation, imperialism, industrialization, and so forth—that are neither social nor environmental as conventionally understood. Rather, these processes are bundles of human and extra-human natures, materially practiced and symbolically enabled.

The Origins of Cheap Nature

The capitalist world-ecology began in the long sixteenth century. Nearly everyone seems to have missed the geography of global environmental transformation as the decisive clue to all other moments of transition. The environmentalists looked for the modern machine and found it: the steam engine and all the rest. The Marxists looked for the "right" class structure—wage-workers, bourgeois property relations, and all that—and they too found what they were looking for. The economists looked for something that looked like modern markets and institutional mechanisms favoring a "modern economy." All these were very important. And all overlooked something very important: a new pattern of environment-making.

Humans had transformed environments from the very beginning. From the rise of civilization, humans had been making large-scale environmental change. A lot—maybe most—of that environment-making could be characterized negative. Nor did humans require civilization to transform environments on an epochal scale: witness the ecocide of

97

North America's Pleistocene megafauna. Medieval Europe transformed Continental ecology, deforesting vast regions, in the five centuries after 800 CE—and the confluence of regional ecology, demography, and feudal class structure was central to the demise of feudalism as the climate turned wetter and colder after 1250.

These environmental histories played out over hundreds—sometimes thousands—of years. After 1450, human-initiated transformations would be measured in decades. In the centuries between 1450 and 1750, we find a new era of human relations with the rest of nature: the Age of Capital. Its epicenters were the seats of imperial power and centers of financial might. Its tentacles wrapped around ecosystems—humans included!—from the Baltic to Brazil, from Scandinavia to Southeast Asia. The Capitalocene accelerated environmental transformation beyond anything known before—sometimes, as with forest clearance, moving at speeds an order of magnitude greater than the medieval pattern. There were, to be sure, certain technological shifts that facilitated this landscape revolution— some of which I detail below. Alongside new technologies, there was a new *technics*—a new repertoire of science, power, and machinery—that aimed a "discovering" and appropriating new Cheap Natures (Mumford 1934; Moore 2015). Above all, there were new ways of mapping and calculating the world (Moore 2015a, 193–220). Perhaps most fundamental, however, was a shift—scarcely detectable to contemporaries—in what was *valued*.

All civilizations have laws of value—broadly patterned priorities for what is valuable and what is not. The decisive shift between the Black Death and the conquest of the Americas was precisely this: value shifted from land productivity under conditions of seigneurial power to labor productivity under the hegemony of the modern world market, "the very basis and living atmosphere of the capitalist mode of production" (Marx 1981, 205). What difference could this make to our understanding of biospheric crisis in the twenty-first century? Quite a big one. The shift from land to labor productivity as the decisive metric of wealth implied an entirely novel approach to the relation between human activity and the web of life. For the first time, the forces of nature were deployed to advance the productivity of human work—but only *some* human work. Human work within a porous sphere of commodity production and exchange— sometimes (misleadingly) called "the economy"—was to be valued. All other activity was devalued, and appropriated in service to advancing labor productivity in a narrow zone of commodification. Thus: the birth

of Nature, which implied and necessitated the birth of Society, both dripping with blood and dirt, the necessary ontological counterpoint to the
separation of the producers from the means of production.

The condition of the rise of capitalism, in other words, was the creation of Cheap Nature. But Cheap is not free. Cheap is here understood
as work/energy and biophysical utility produced with minimal labor-
power, and directly implicated in commodity production and exchange.
That labor-power was partly the segment of the population who worked
for wages, rapidly growing after 1500. But proletarianization assumes
manifold forms. Viewed from the standpoint of reproduction—that is, to
the degree that social reproduction depends upon the cash nexus—the
proletarian relation reached much farther, even in this long sixteenth
century. It included that wider layer of the population within capitalism that depended on capital flows—directly or indirectly—for daily life
and intergenerational reproduction. This layer included the fast-grow-
ing urban population of western Europe and Latin America—expanding
much faster in the period 1550–1700 than in 1700–1850 (de Vries 1984).
It included the slave population of the Americas, whose modest demographic weight in 1700—around three hundred thousand souls—belied its
centrality to capital accumulation through the sugar frontier (Blackburn
1998, 3; Moore 2007). And toward the end of the seventeenth century, it
reached deep into the countrysides of western Europe through proto-
industrialization, centering on textiles and taking advantage of women's
work and the seasonal agricultural cycle, in turn propelling (semi) proletarian population growth (Seccombe 1992).

The first accomplishment of this new law of value—a law of Cheap
Nature—was therefore to create Cheap Labor. The number of slaves disem-
barked each decade in the Americas—mostly to grow sugar, modernity's
original cash crop—increased a staggering 1,065 percent between 1560
and 1710.[10] Slave prices still tended to rise, a tribute to capitalism's devastation of *human* nature, but from a base much lower than the wage bill
for European proletarians. Meanwhile, most Europeans were not doing
so great, either:

> In Languedoc . . . a "grain wage" lost half its value between 1480 [and]
> 1600. In Lyon, . . . the buying power of a "wheat wage" dropped to half
> its original value between 1500 and 1597. A Modena "bread wage"
> was devalued 50 percent between 1530 and 1590, while a Florence

wage slumped 60 percent between 1520 and 1600. In Vienna, wages lost more than half their value against a standard breadbasket of goods between 1510 and 1590; in Valencia, a similar decline occurred between 1500 and 1600. In southern England, a builder's wage fell to half its original value against a bundle of subsistence commodities between 1500–10 and 1610–19. . . . Women's wages declined even further than men's. . . . When one considers . . . that the labouring poor had not been very far above the subsistence floor in 1500, the subsequent decline in awful to contemplate. The underlying cause is readily apparent: a deteriorating ratio of land to labour-power, swelling the ranks of the nearly landless, driving real wages down as the village poor became increasingly dependent on wage income to stay alive. (Seccombe 1992, 161)

This Cheap Labor was hardly created out of thin air. It was an expression of the class struggle. But a class struggle over what? Over the terms of what would be—and what would not be—valued. And over the terms of who and what counted—and who and what did not count—as Nature.

Labor-power mattered little without a productivity revolution. Of course, we are told by the Anthropocene advocates—and not a few Marxists—that early capitalism was not *really* modern, and not really capitalist. Why? Because early capitalism was technologically inert, and unable to sustain the long-run advance of labor productivity. This was, we are told, the era of *merchant* capitalism—a preindustrial era.

Was early capitalism really preindustrial? The proposition is hard to sustain. Labor productivity surged in one key commodity sector after another. In printing, labor productivity advanced two-hundred-fold in the century after 1450, with twenty million printed books in circulation by 1500. In the sugar colonies, new mill technology successively boosted productivity across the early modern centuries; meanwhile sugar refineries in European cities such as Amsterdam were the only industrial establishments comparable to nineteenth-century factories. In iron-making, large blast furnaces allowed output per worker to increase fivefold between 1450 and 1650, clearing and transforming forests at every step. In shipping, led by the firms in the Dutch Republic, productivity increased fourfold. Meanwhile, a new ship*building* regime, also led by the Dutch, tripled labor productivity. It combined Smithian specialization (simplified tasks), the standardization of parts, organizational innovation (integrated supply systems), and technical change (sawmills to displace costly skilled labor). Everywhere, but especially in northwestern Europe, the use of iron tools in agriculture expanded. In the central European copper-silver metals complex, the *saigerprozess* smelting technique revolutionized mining and metallurgy after 1450. New rod-engines, allowing for effective drainage, allowed for a second great wave of European mining after 1540. In the New World, the mercury-amalgamation process boosted silver production rapidly after the 1560s, especially in Peru. Back in Europe, the quick diffusion of the "Saxony Wheel" in textile manufacturing tripled labor productivity, amplified yet further by the diffusion of fulling and napping mills in the fifteenth and sixteenth centuries. Across Europe, but especially in the west, the number of water mills doubled in the three centuries after 1450, tripling aggregate horsepower.[11]

What do these transformations suggest? Any adequate explanation must recognize that there was a transition from control of land as a direct relation of surplus appropriation to control of land as a condition for rising labor productivity within commodity production. This transition was of course tremendously uneven and messy. Hence, where peasant cultivation persisted across early modern Europe, the rupture with medieval rhythms of landscape transformation was often subtle and gradual—*except where, as in seventeenth-century Poland, peasants were directly pushed toward sylvan zones by cash-crop cultivation* (Moore 2010b).

Wherever primary commodity production penetrated, however, the tempo of landscape transformation accelerated. Why should this be? Part of the answer is the pace of technical change, which did indeed quicken—and the diffusion of techniques even more so—in the "first" sixteenth century (1450–1557). But I do not think this was enough to compel such an epochal shift in landscape transformation. More decisive was the inversion of the labor-land relation and the ascendance of labor productivity as metric of wealth, unfolding on the basis of appropriating Cheap Natures.

For Cheap Labor and productive labor required one thing if profitability was to be advanced, and the accumulation of capital was to quicken: Cheap energy, food, and raw materials. Cheap thermal energy to smelt the metals, process the sugarcane, and make glass, beer, bricks, and everything else demanded by the world market. Cheap food to keep the price of labor-power from rising, or at least from rising too fast. And Cheap raw materials—timber for shipbuilding, potash for dyeing textiles, iron for everything—to maintain a virtuous circle of expanding commodity production. In sum, the whole of nature had to be put to work—in a radically alienating and dynamic way—for capitalism to survive.

This entrained a landscape revolution unprecedented in human history. Its first condition was the conquest of the Atlantic. Between 1535 and 1680, the capitalist world-ecology more than doubled in size, conquering some four million square kilometers between 1535 and 1680 (Chaunu 1959, 148). This appropriation of the New World was "the fundamental structure of the first modernity" (Dussel 1998, 11). These conquests incorporated not only vast expanses of potentially Cheap Nature, but also the labor-power to activate it. By 1500, Spain alone had "colonized more than 2 million square kilometers (an area greater than the whole of Europe of the center) and more than 25 million (a low figure) indigenous peoples, *many of whom were integrated into a system of work that produces value (in Marx's strict sense)* for the Europe of the center" (Dussel 1998, 11–12, emphasis added).

The impressive figures were complemented by capital's new thirst for the Cheap Nature within Europe. In the Low Countries, an agricultural revolution allowed three-quarters of Holland's labor force to work outside of agriculture. It was a "revolution" because—like the English agricultural revolution that followed—it advanced labor productivity and expelled labor from the countryside (van Bavel 2001, 2010). By the end of the sixteenth century, wheat yields peaked, reaching a level not exceeded until the late nineteenth century (Bieleman 2010, 49). The Dutch agricultural revolution was not merely an affair of new techniques and specializations in garden, dairy, and industrial input crops (such as hemp, hops, and madder), but fundamentally a revolution in the *built environment* of the town-country division of labor. The fifteenth century saw the emergence of a windmill landscape, while land reclamation through complex material and organizational systems of water control—*polders*—dominated the century after 1540 (Kaijser 2002; Grigg 1980, 151). A complex "system of dikes, dams, sluices, and drainage canals" remade the countryside, whose maritime regions were committed to an "extreme market dependence" by the sixteenth century (TeBrake 2002, 477; de Vries and van der Woude 1997). Meanwhile, dozens of new harbors were built—not only in Amsterdam, but across the northern Netherlands (de Vries and van der Woude 1997, 34). Urbanization accelerated, and so did proletarianization—in the countryside as much as the city. By the mid-sixteenth century, wage-work occupied as much as half of the economically active population (van Bavel 2010). Meanwhile, this built environment implied expansionary movements within the northern Netherlands as well as beyond (as we shall see momentarily). By the turn of the eighteenth century, the inland regions of the eastern Netherlands been transformed into "virtually treeless landscapes" (Groenewoudt 2012, 61).

Agricultural revolutions are world-historical events. The condition for labor productivity revolutions in one region is the expansion of "accumulation by appropriation" on a much larger scale (Moore 2015a). As Dutch farmers retrenched from cereal cultivation into higher-profit lines, grain imports filled the shortfall. These were drawn initially, and always in part, from Flanders, northern France, and the Rhineland. By 1470, however, a line had been crossed. Imports from the Baltic—primarily an expansive Prussian-Polish zone—grew rapidly: fivefold between 1470 and 1500; another fivefold by 1560. This was "enough to feed 15–20 percent of the population of the entire Burgundian Netherlands, and a far greater proportion of the coastal and urban populations" (de Vries and van der Woude 1997, 198).

Poland became an agricultural district of the Dutch Republic. By the early seventeenth century, the Polish Crown was exporting one-third of its net rye production (Slicher van Bath 1977, 88). Such large export shares in low productivity agriculture are fraught with danger. Output was sustained "by deviating from the fundamental principles of rotation in tilling the soil" (Szcygielski 1967, 97). Yields fell—sharply. The physical surplus fell by as much as *half* between the 1550s and 1700 (Topolski 1962; de Maddalena 1974; DuPlessis 1997, 82). It was a "catastrophic" decline (Szcygielski 1969, 86). It was also uneven. Declining labor productivity and cereal yield could be attenuated, even reversed in some regions, through a large-scale—*and rapid*—movement of forest clearance.

Deforestation was also driven by the rising demands of industrial capital in northwestern Europe. The case of potash, used for cloth bleaching, is breathtaking. In the last quarter of the sixteenth century, English potash imports required the "unpaid work" of 12,000 hectares of (cleared) forest, *every year*. Potash, the most profitable export sector (Zins 1972, 269), encouraged renewed frontier movements through the Baltic. The hinterlands around Konigsberg and Riga were subjected to the same dynamic as in Poland. Danzig, at least through the 1630s, remained dominant—the city's potash exports required the *annual* clearing of 135,000 hectares in that decade alone.[12] Even as the potash commodity frontier moved north and east along the Baltic coast over the next two centuries, the "devastation of the forests" registered in the Baltic's declining ash exports (North 1996, 9–14; also Moore 2010b). (Baltic shortfalls would be made good—and then some—by North American suppliers in the eighteenth century [Roberts 1972].) My sense is that we are looking at a deforestation of the Vistula Basin on the order of a million hectares (10,000 square kilometers), and possibly twice as much, between 1500 and 1650.

In central Europe, a mining and metallurgical revolution supplied the emergent capitalist order with a physical basis for money (silver) and manufacturing (iron and copper). Forests—and more importantly, forest commons—were rapidly transformed. Central European mining and metallurgical reached its zenith in the half century after 1470. This region produced the lion's share of early capitalism's basic raw materials: copper, lead, and iron. More significantly, new mining and metallurgical techniques—underpinning as prodigious an industrialization as any that came after—allowed for a revolutionary increase in silver production. Here we can glimpse the origins of Cheap Money within Cheap Nature. Production of all metals soared, by fivefold or greater, between the 1450s and 1530s (Nef 1964). Across central Europe, the new metallurgical capitalism scoured the countryside for fuel, effecting widespread pollution and deforestation:

> The woods and groves are cut down, for there is need of an endless amount of wood for timbers, machines, and the smelting of metals. And when the woods and groves are felled, then are exterminated the beasts and birds, very many of which furnish a pleasant and agreeable food for man. . . . When the ores are washed, the water which has been used poisons the brooks and streams, and either destroys the fish or drives them away. (Agricola [1556] 1950, 8)

As mining boomed and forests retreated, forest enclosures advanced. By 1524, the radical priest Thomas Müntzer decried these enclosures, through which "every creature should be transformed into property—the fishes in the water, the birds of the air, the plants of the earth: the creatures too should become free" (quoted in Marx 1972, 49). In 1450, "there were still extensive forests, so there were few conflicts between peasants and forest overlords. . . . By 1525 the situation was *entirely changed*" (Blickle 1981, 73, emphasis added). The German Peasant War of 1525—as much a proletarian as a peasant revolt—registered not only a mighty protest against the lords' enclosure of forests, but the stark realities of rapid changes in land and labor.

Meanwhile, a different kind of agricultural revolution was unfolding in the Atlantic. Here was the rise of the sugar plantation complex. Sugar was modernity's original cash crop. No crop in modern world history was at the root of more misery and devastation than sugar. For sugar not only devoured forests and exhausted soils—it was an apparatus of mass killing in the form of African slavery. On the island of Madeira, located off the western coast of north Africa, the first sugar boom—and the first signs of the modern sugar-slave nexus—emerged. The boom began in the 1470s, quickly ousting Mediterranean producers from their privileged position. In the two decades after 1489, sugar production soared—and labor productivity with it.[13] So did deforestation. As an economic activity, sugar was closer to the iron smelter than the wheat farm. By 1510, 160 square kilometers of forest, nearly one-quarter of the island and over half its accessible forest, had been cleared. Output plummeted; scarcely any sugar would be grown in ensuing centuries (Moore 2009, 2010c). Madeira's crisis was followed quickly by sugar's advance to São Tomé (1540s–1590s) and the first modern, large-scale plantation system, which deforested one-third of the island by 1600 and encouraged large-scale slave revolts.

Northeastern Brazil had, in any event, already displaced São Tomé at the commanding heights of the world sugar economy by 1570. Brazil's sugar boom drove the first great wave of clearing Brazil's Atlantic rainforest, which unfolded at an unprecedented pace. In an era when agricultural output growth can typically be measured in fractions of a percentage point, Brazilian sugar output grew 3 percent every year between 1570 and 1640 (Moore 2007, 257). That it remained profitable owed everything to Cheap Labor and Cheap Energy. The logic of labor management was gruesome: "extract as much labor at as little cost as possible" (Schwartz 1970, 317). It is difficult to convey the sheer lethality of the sugar/slave regime. Nearly 240,000 Africa slaves arrived in northeastern Brazil in the half century after 1600—not counting those who died in the Middle Passage— sustaining a population of just over sixty thousand slaves by 1650 (Moore 2011c). Brazil's Atlantic rainforest did not fare any better. Sugar's cultivation and fuelwood demands *alone* required the clearance some 5,000 square kilometers of forest by 1650 (Dean 1995; Moore 2007, 2009). As if this was not enough, sugar's demographic vortex advanced slaving frontiers within Africa. By 1700, "the human resources of the [Angolan] coast were exhausted," pushing the "hunt for men" ever deeper into the interior (Godinho 2005, 320; Wolf 1982, 195–231). Every great commodity expansion, it seems, requires new streams of Cheap Labor—by market coercion if possible, by bloody coercion if necessary.

As Brazil's sugar boom unfolded, a different commodity revolution remade Andean life. Potosí emerged as the world's leading silver producer after 1545. The rise of Peruvian silver was a curious brew—imperial conquest, geological good fortune, and declining production in the old central European centers, afflicted by rapid deforestation, declining ore quality, and escalating labor unrest. But the flood of *produced*—rather than simply plundered—silver began to falter in the 1560s. On the heels of deepening fiscal crisis, the Spanish Crown moved quickly, inaugurating one of early modernity's most audacious moments of producing Cheap Nature. As ever, the question of work was central. The arrival of a new Viceroy, Francisco de Toledo, in 1569 was followed by a far-ranging transformation. A new method of extracting silver, mercury amalgamation, was instituted. Labor organization in mining and processing moved from arms-length sharecropping to more direct forms of labor control. A radical process of agrarian restructuring—centering on the *reducciones* (village resettlement) and the *mita* (a labor draft)—was launched to ensure a steady supply of Cheap labor-power for the mines. Three million Andeans would work in the mines before the mita's abolition in 1819—a dramatic undercount when one considers that *mitayo* were customarily accompanied by family. This kept labor costs low in the face of the rising labor demands of pit mining. The mita was not only a system of forced wage labor—but of forcible resettlement. Starting in 1571, some 1.5 million Andeans—a population equal to contemporary Portugal!—was forced to settle into reducciones, Spanish-style towns designed to facilitate colonial control and steady Cheap Labor. Meanwhile, vast hydraulic infrastructures were built to power the mills that ground ore preparatory to amalgamation. Potosí's "lakes" would eventually contain thirty-two reservoirs covering 65 square kilometers (Moore 2010d). Output was quickly restored. Potosí's silver output increased nearly 600 percent between 1575 and 1590 (Bakewell 1987, 242). Spain's fiscal crisis was—temporarily—resolved; more importantly, it fed the rise of Dutch capitalism.

The changes upon life and land were immediately apparent to contemporaries:

> Even though today, because of all the work done on the mountain,
> there is no sign that it had ever had a forest, when it was discovered

it was fully covered with trees they call quínoa, whose wood they used to build the first houses of this settlement. . . . On this mountain, there was also a great amount of hunting of vicuñas, guanacos and viscachas, animals very similar to the rabbits of Spain in their fur and meat, but with a long tail. There were also deer, and today not even weeds grow on the mountain, not even in the most fertile soils where trees could have grown. This is the most frightening, because now the mountain is covered with loose gravel, with little or no fertile land, crossed with sterile mineralized outcroppings. (*Descripción de la Villa y Minas de Potosí* 1603, 114–15)

Returning to Europe, shortfalls from Poland's agricultural decline were quickly made good by the English agricultural revolution. By 1700, England had become Europe's breadbasket. Between 1700 and 1753, England's grain exports increased 511 percent, six times faster than aggregate exports.[14] By midcentury, however, English agriculture stagnated, as nitrogen reserves were depleted (Moore 2015b; Overton 1996). Exports collapsed (Davis 1954). Rapid gains in agricultural productivity after 1600 stalled by 1750 (Broadberry et al. 2011). The problem was capitalist and world-ecological: a problem of how humans have "mixed their labor with the earth" (Williams 1972). The problem of agricultural productivity in late eighteenth-century England—marked by runaway food price inflation and a net per capita reduction in food consumption—was one of the soil mixed with labor. The era's best practices allowed for a revival of agricultural productivity, but only at the cost of faltering labor productivity. On this the English bourgeoisie could not compromise as the manufacturing expansion gathered steam. Pulling labor out of industry would have reversed the very processes of proletarianization that had propelled the urban-industrial expansion over the previous century (Moore 2015b)!

England's iron consumption, which continued growing rapidly in the eighteenth century, increasingly resorted to the world market to satisfy the rising demand. The island's forests had been rapidly appropriated during the seventeenth-century expansion, such that pig iron output in 1620 would not be exceeded until 1740. Imports were sourced from across the North Sea, where iron devoured the forests with such speed that even Sweden's sylvan abundance was threatened (King 2005; Brinley 1993; Fouquet 2008, 59–60; Mathias 1969, 450; Hildebrand 1992). But all was not market demand—empire mattered, too. The stagnation of English iron output after 1620 also stimulated a colonial movement of appropriation into Ireland. The Emerald Isle's forest cover contracted from 12.5 percent to just 2 percent, such that little iron would be produced after the seventeenth century (Kane 1844, 3; Kinahan 1886–87; McCracken 1971, 15, 51, and *passim*).

British developments were, however, only part of a broader global story. Before Britain became the workshop of the world, the Dutch ruled the roost. The Dutch Republic, the great superpower of the seventeenth century, transformed environments across the globe. The Dutch energy regime, centered on the extraction of domestic peat as cheap fuel, peaked in the seventeenth century. From this point, decline was swift: easily tapped zones were quickly exhausted and costs increased. Peat output declined sharply after 1750 (de Zeeuw 1978). In Southeast Asia, the Dutch imposed a new colonial regime between the 1650s and 1670s. Seeking a monopoly over the clove trade, the Dutch organized the large-scale removal of "unauthorized" clove trees, the large-scale relocation of indigenous populations from the interior into new administrative units suitable for labor drafts, and established new shipyards outside the Batavian core on the island of Java (Boxer 1965, 111–12; Boomgaard 1992a; Peluso 1992, 36–430). From the early seventeenth century, wetlands across the Atlantic world were reclaimed, often by Dutch engineers, from England to Pernambuco and Suriname, Rome to Göteborg.

The great burst of Iberian and Italian expansion during the "first" sixteenth century (ca. 1450–1557) produced a relative, but widespread, exhaustion of Mediterranean forests. This began earlier for the Italians and Portuguese, somewhat later for Spain. For these powers, deforestation weighed heavily on their capacity to supply quality shipbuilding timber, so fundamental to the commercial and military struggles of the time (Wing 2012; Moore 2010b). Spain relocated its shipbuilding to Cuba, where one-third of the fleet was built by 1700 (Parry 1966; Funes Monzote 2008). Portugal expanded its shipyards in Salvador da Bahia (Brazil) and Goa (India) (Morton 1978; Huei 2008). The Iberian relocation was followed in the eighteenth century by the emergence of major shipbuilding centers and significant frontiers for timber, potash, and naval stores in North America.

The relentless geographical expansion of forest products and shipbuilding frontiers was bound up with a "Great Hunt" (Richards 2003). One key moment was the launching of increasingly vast fleets of herring, cod, and whaling vessels that devoured the North Atlantic's sources of maritime protein (Perlin 1989; Poulsen 2008; Richards 2003). Another was the transcontinental search for furs in Siberia and North America. While fur trading had only a modest economic weight in world accumulation, its steady advance (and serialized exhaustion of fur-bearing animals) across North America encouraged significant infrastructures of colonial power—and the spread of new diseases—by the mid-eighteenth century.

Great frontier movements continued across the Atlantic world in the eighteenth century, reshaping food, energy, and labor relations. Steadily rising sugar demand and the exhaustion of Bahia's sugar complex by the mid-seventeenth century favored successive sugar revolutions in the West Indies. Sugar transformed Barbados, Jamaica, and St. Domingue (the island of Hispaniola) into agro-export platforms over the next century, leaving a trail of African graves and denuded landscapes in its wake. The resurgence of Mexican silver production in the eighteenth century led to the deforestation of already-thin Mexican forests. And, perhaps most significantly, the epoch-making "Columbian exchange," as Old World diseases, animals, and crops flowed into the Americas, and New World crops, such as potatoes and maize, flowed into the Old World (Crosby 1972; Watts 1992; Moore 2015a, 169–92; Studnicki-Gizbert and Schecter 2010; Richards 2003; Wolf 1982).

The Making of the Capitalist World-Ecology
These transformations tell us that something epochal was in play—much earlier than usually supposed. Let me advance two propositions concerning this early modern landscape revolution. First, these transformations represented an early modern revolution in labor productivity. In this new era of Cheap Nature, the advance of commodification was tightly connected to a revolution in strategies of global appropriation. Crucially, this labor productivity revolution in the zone of commodification was made possible by a revolution in the *technics* of global appropriation—*including* appropriation within Europe. This was manifested not only in the immediate practices and structures of European imperialism. More fundamentally, the "new" imperialism of early modernity was impossible without a new way of seeing and ordering reality. One could conquer the globe only if one could see it. Here the early forms of external nature, abstract space, and abstract time enabled capitalists and empires to construct global webs of exploitation and appropriation, calculation and credit, property and

profit, on an unprecedented scale. The early modern labor productivity revolution turned, in short, on the possibility of opening and appropriating vast frontiers of Cheap Nature (Moore 2015a, 193–219). The fact that early capitalism relied on global expansion as the principal means of advancing labor productivity and facilitating world accumulation reveals the remarkable precocity of early capitalism, not its premodern character. This precocity allowed early capitalism to defy the premodern pattern of boom and bust: there would be no systemwide reversal of commodification after 1450, not even during the "crisis" of the seventeenth century. Why? In sum, because early capitalism's *technics*—its crystallization of tools and power, knowledge and production—were *specifically organized* to treat the appropriation of global nature in pursuit of the endless accumulation of capital. As long as there were frontiers of Cheap Nature, the problems of capitalism could be fixed with new technologies and now forms of power premised on the Great Frontier.

The rise of capitalism launched a new way of organizing nature. For the first time, a civilization mobilized a metric of wealth premised on labor rather than land productivity. This was the originary moment of today's fast-fading Cheap Nature. This transition from land to labor productivity during the early modern era explains much of the revolutionary pace of early modern landscape transformation. The soils and forests of northeastern Brazil, Scandinavia, and Poland were appropriated (and exhausted) in the long seventeenth century. Human nature too was freely appropriated (and exhausted), as New World sugar frontiers and African slaving frontiers moved in tandem. Far from being abolished after the eighteenth century, these frontier-led appropriations were amplified by the long fossil boom. Fossil fuels were a new frontier—subterranean "Americas" with seemingly unlimited supplies of Cheap Nature. These frontiers of unpaid work/energy have always been pivotal to the new "tools of empire" and metropolitan productive capacities that destabilized (and appropriated the labor of) peasant formations from South Asia to southern Italy. In light of this history, we may well ask: Is capitalism today capable of appropriating nature's free gifts on a scale sufficient to launch a new phase of accumulation, or are we witnessing the exhaustion of a Cheap Nature strategy that has underwritten capital accumulation since the sixteenth century?

The question confounds the usual Green critique. Two words crystallize its essence: "environmental degradation." Scholars have used the term a whopping 183,000 times since 1990. The key issue has been, What does humanity—or for radicals, capitalism—do *to* the environment? The most celebrated Green concepts of our times—the Anthropocene and the ecological footprint—embody this sensibility. Their popularity is often justified—even by radicals—for enhancing popular awareness of capitalism's place in the web of life. For Samir Amin, the ecological footprint concept represents the development of a "major strand in radical social thinking about construction of the future" (2009). For McKenzie Wark, the Anthropocene may be understood as a "series of metabolic rifts," through which the "soil depletes, the climate alters, the gyre widens" (2015, 4). The difficulty emerges when one considers that the Green critique has dozens of ways to talk about what capitalism *does to* nature, but hardly any way to talk about how nature *works for* capitalism.

A radical and emancipatory alternative does not deny the degradation of nature. Far from it! But a politics of nature premised on degradation rather than work renders the radical vision vulnerable to a powerful critique. This says, in effect, that pristine nature has never really existed; that we are living through another of many eras of environmental change that can be resolved through technological innovation (Lynas 2011; Shellenberger and Nordhaus 2011). The counterargument for the Capitalocene—an ugly word for an ugly system—understands the degradation of nature as a specific expression of capitalism's organization of work. "Work" takes many forms in this conception; it is a multispecies and manifold geo-ecological process. This allows us to think of technology as rooted in the natures co-produced by capitalism. It allows us to see that capitalism has thrived by mobilizing the work of nature as a whole; and to mobilize human work in configurations of "paid" and "unpaid" work by capturing the work/energies of the biosphere.

The long history of industrial, agricultural, scientific, and technological revolutions may be read in this light. I do not mean to suggest that this is the whole story—it isn't. But I don't think we can arrive at something approximating an adequate interpretation without seeing how paid and unpaid work—and their cognate processes of accumulation by capitalization and appropriation—have reworked planetary geographies. For this line of thought pinpoints how capitalism's *specific* degradation of nature occurs through its *specific* mobilization of the "forces of nature" as "forces of production." Now, one clarification is immediately necessary, because we are still in the thought-habit of seeing Nature (environments without humans) whenever one says nature (the web of life). The extraordinary *longue durée* remaking of global nature as a force of production has regularly assigned the majority of humanity—at least the majority of humans within capitalism's reach—to the status of Nature. There was always contradiction and ambiguity in such assignments, but it is clear that successive racialized and gendered "social" orders over the past five centuries have relied heavily upon the Nature/Society binary. These have been about many things—but not least, they have facilitated the accumulation of capital through manifold gendered and racialized surpluses of unpaid work.

William Kapp, one of the founders of ecological economics, famously characterized the modern economy as a system of "unpaid costs" (1950). Today we know this all too well—heavy metals in children's bloodstreams and Arctic ice, massive garbage patches in the oceans, agro-toxic overload in our soil and water, never mind that small matter of climate change. But capitalism is more than a system of unpaid costs; it is a system of *unpaid work*.

The genius of capitalism—from the global conquests that commenced in 1492—has been to treat the work of nature as a "free gift." From the beginning, Europe's great empires set out deploying science in its widest sense—mapping the world, collecting and organizing biogeographical knowledge, establishing new administrative technologies—to make the whole of nature work on the cheap. These were conquests that made plunder "work" for capitalism in a way that went beyond brute force and domination. But it is hard to sustain a civilization on the basis of plunder. By itself, plunder is too episodic; too violent; and over the long run, too costly. The Spaniards discovered this quickly in the sixteenth century—the mines of Potosí, the great silver mountain, would only yield their riches through new systems of colonial control, technology, and work. They also discovered that the great divide of "Nature" and "Society" could be very useful for rendering not only land, but labor, cheap: the Spaniards referred to Peru's indigenous peoples as *naturales*. Not all humans were part of Humanity, the better that they could deliver Cheap Nature.

That long history has been reproduced over the past four decades: the earth is now ringed by over two thousand satellites enabling the unprecedented surveillance and mapping of planetary space; the human genome was mapped; biopiracy and biotechnology have proceeded. But today is different from the 1970s, for two big, and closely related, reasons. First, the potential sources of Cheap Nature are fewer than ever before. The non-revolution in agricultural biotechnology shows this well (Moore 2010e). For all the claims that biotech will somehow feed the world, there has been no revolution in agricultural productivity—indeed, agricultural productivity growth has *slowed* steadily since the mid-1980s. So too, the non-revolution in energy. After the opening of modest oil frontiers in the 1970s—in Alaska, the Gulf of Mexico, West Africa, the North Sea—no major sources of *cheap* energy have appeared. Indeed, the world energy history of the past decade has been marked by the opening of frontiers that are the very opposite of those which have sustained capitalism. These are not low-cost frontiers of production, but very *high-cost* frontiers, especially in North America's "unconventional" oil sector. Nor does Cheap Labor seem to be here to stay. The rise of China as the workshop of the world in the 1990s and 2000s occurred, in part, because of massive Cheap Labor flowing into the cities from the countryside. But this—like all Cheap Nature frontiers—was a one-shot deal. Even in China, wages are rising in the cities—rapidly—and the countryside no longer offers an easy reservoir of Cheap labor-power (Moore 2015a, 221–40).

Conclusion

The origins of capitalism as a system of Cheap Nature are fundamental to thinking through the reality—and politics—of the present crisis. Let me be clear that we are dealing with capitalism as world-ecology, as a double internality of humanity-in-nature—not as a closed system that interacts with the rest of nature. The point is important, as even friendly critics of the Capitalocene concept have characterized it in dualist terms. With capitalism we are dealing with an emergent pattern of symbolic innovation and material transformation in which the value of labor-power, the rise of world-money, and the endless transformation of the earth form an evolving historical whole.

The problem today is the end of the Capitalocene, not the march of the Anthropocene. The reality is not one of humanity "overwhelming the great forces of nature" (Steffen et al. 2007), but rather the exhaustion of its Cheap Nature strategy. (This is the small kernel of truth in the otherwise absurd discourse on ecosystem services.) That process of getting Nature to work for very low expenditures of money and energy is the history of capitalism's great commodity frontiers, and with it, of capitalism's long waves of accumulation.

The appropriation of frontier land and labor—Cheap Nature—has been the indispensable condition for great waves of capital accumulation, from Dutch hegemony in the seventeenth century to the rise of neoliberalism in the 1970s and 1980s (Moore 2010b, 2012, 2015). Capitalism has been able to outrun the rising costs of production by co-producing manifold Cheap Nature strategies, locating, creating, mapping, and quantifying natures external to capitalism but within reach of its power. Today there is nowhere to run. Much of what we have seen global capitalism achieve over the past decade has been a shifting of costs—from one capitalist to another, and especially from capital to the vast majority. And there has been another vector of cost-shifting, which has been accelerating in recent years: from the present to the future. This is true, as widely recognized, for future generations. But it is also true for the accumulation of capital, which has always been a series of bets on future income. The real basis of that future income has always been Cheap Nature. Hence: financialization and the polarization of income and wealth—the 1 percent and the 99 percent—are the predictable results of the end of Cheap Nature. That "end" of Cheap Nature may not bring liberation, but it cannot sustain capitalism. Popular strategies for liberation will succeed or fail on our capacity to forge a different ontology of nature, humanity, and justice—one that asks not merely how to redistribute wealth, but how to remake our place in nature in a way that promises emancipation for all life.

Notes

1   Special thanks to Diana C. Gildea, and also to Henry Bernstein, Jay Bolthouse, Holly Jean Buck, Christopher Cox, Sharae Deckard, Joshua Eichen, Ben Marley, Michael Niblett, Roberto José Ortiz, Christian Parenti, Andy Pragacz, Stephen Shapiro, Richard Walker, and Tony Weis for conversations and correspondence on the themes explored in this essay.
2   See references in the Introduction.
3   "Today, one typically looks for a 'marker' level where the strata above and below are recognizably different (usually because they contain different types of fossils) and then selects the place in the world that best shows that level. That point then is chosen to represent, formally, the beginning of a geological time unit. Its title is grand—it is a Global Stratigraphic Section and Point, but more popularly it is known as a '*golden spike*'; it is the standard reference level for a geological time boundary" (Zalasiewicz et al. 2010, 2229, emphasis added).
4   The argument over the periodization of the Anthropocene rages on. Some archaeologists now argue for converting most or all of the Holocene into the Anthropocene, either from the megafauna extinctions at the dawn of the Holocene, or the origins of agriculture, ca. 11,000 BP (summarized in

Balter 2013; see Smith et al. 2010; Ruddiman 2005, 2013; Gowdy and Krall 2013). Still others argue for an Anthropocene ca. 2,000 years BP (e.g., Certini and Scalenghe 2011). While other still argue for a post–1945/1960 periodization (Zalasiewicz et al. 2008). Recently, Lewis and Maslin (2015) proposed a different date with a different kind of spike: an *orbis* spike ("global" spike). The result is a date strikingly close to what I am proposing: 1610.

5   See Crutzen and Stoermer 2000; Crutzen 2002; Steffen, Crutzen, and McNeill 2007; Steffen et al. 2011a, 2011b, 2015; Chakrabarty 2009; *The Economist*, 2011a, 2011b.

6   See my critique and reconstruction (Moore 2003a, 2003b). The field of economic history—prior to the cliometric revolution of the 1970s—was the most consistently environmentally aware field of world social science in the first three-quarters of the twentieth century.

7   See, for example, Braudel 1972; Galeano 1973; Kellenbenz 1974, 1976; Kriedte 1983; Nef 1964; Malowist 2009; Prado 1967; Wallerstein 1974; Brenner 1976; Sella 1974; de Vries 1974, 1976; Cipolla 1976.

8   For example, de Vries and van der Woude 1997; de Vries 2001; Brenner 2001; Crosby 1997; DuPlessis 1997; Jones 1987; Landes 1998; Seccombe 1992; Mokyr 1990, 57–80; Moore 2007, 2010a, 2010b; Nef 1964; Prak 2001; van Zanden 1993.

9   Much of this literature is often extraordinarily Eurocentric—Landes, Jones, and van Zanden especially.

10 Calculated from Eltis, 2015.

11 This paragraph draws on a vast historiography. For references, see Moore (2015a).

12 The calculations for this account draw, respectively, on Zins (1972, 268) for English imports; on North's (1996) estimate of potash weight to timber volume, biased in favor of very high conversation rates of wood to ash and ash to potash (for much higher estimates, see Kunnas 2007); and on my generous estimate of 200m^3/hectare as the maximal harvestable volume one could extract from a hectare of European forest (Moore 2007, ch. 2).

13 Output grew 4.42 percent annually, and labor productivity 2.18 percent annually, between 1489 and 1509 (calculated from Moore 2010d, 12).

14 Calculated from Davis (1954, 302).

FOUR

Accumulating Extinction
Planetary Catastrophism in the Necrocene

Justin McBrien

Capital was born from extinction, and from capital, extinction has flowed.

Capital does not just rob the soil and worker, as Marx observes, it necrotizes the entire planet. Here is a "metabolic rift" (Foster 2000)— between earth and labor—driven by the contradictions of endless accumulation. That accumulation is not only productive; it is necrotic, unfolding a slow violence, occupying and producing overlapping historical, biological, and geological temporalities. Capital is the Sixth Extinction personified: it feasts on the dead, and in doing so, devours all life. The deep time of past cataclysm becomes the deep time of future catastrophe; the residue of life in hydrocarbons becomes the residue of capital in petrochemical plastics.[1] Capitalism leaves in its wake the disappearance of species, languages, cultures, and peoples. It seeks the planned obsolescence of all life. Extinction lies at the heart of capitalist accumulation.

Today's debate about planetary crisis has yielded the concepts of the Anthropocene and the Capitalocene. Both recognize extinction but have yet to grasp its ontological significance—for humanity or for capitalism. What I wish to propose is that we recognize the Necrocene—or "New Death"—as a fundamental biogeological moment of our era: the Capitalocene. The Necrocene reframes the history of capitalism's expansion through the process of *becoming extinction*.

The accumulation of capital is the accumulation potential extinction—a potential increasingly activated in recent decades. This *becoming extinction* is not simply the biological process of species extinction. It is also the extinguishing of cultures and languages, either through force or assimilation; it is the extermination of peoples, either through labor or deliberate murder; it is the extinction of the earth in the depletion fossil fuels, rare earth minerals, even the chemical element helium; it is ocean acidification and eutrophication, deforestation and desertification, melting ice sheets and rising sea levels; the great Pacific garbage patch and nuclear waste entombment; McDonalds and Monsanto.

Here the process of *Necrosis* is central. Unlike apoptosis, the process of programmed cell death beneficial to the organism, Necrosis is born of traumatic injury. Necrosis proceeds by autolysis, a form of self-digestion in which a cell destroys itself through its own enzymes action. Capitalism is the reciprocal transmutation of life into death and death into capital. Necrosis is capital's mode of apoptosis, reproducing the means of production by its destruction. It is both saprophytic and parasitic: it feeds on live and dead nature the same; it seeks to render them indistinguishable. From the standpoint of the Necrocene, capital appears as a *species*, an opportunistic detritus feeder producing mass extinction in the present through the exploitation of past extinctions. The more capitalism exerts its planetary power through the intensification of surplus extraction from Cheap Natures (Moore 2015a),[2] the more it necrotizes the world-ecology it has created.

The Necrocene is the Capitalocene's shadow double, the future past of its necromancy, its monstrous sublime and uncanny paradox. Extinction is the both the immediate success and ultimate failure of the real subsumption of the earth by capital; the ecology of capital is constructed through attempted erasure of existing ecologies—ecologies that include humans. Nothing embodies the reciprocal conditioning between the Capitalocene and the Necrocene more than fossil fuels. Even if the Cheap Natures of charcoal fueled capital's monstrous appetite long before fossil fuels became a general form of energy use, early modern deforestation quickly induced a shift from "shallow" to "deep" time. By the nineteenth century, world accumulation came to depend upon fossil fuels—the appropriation of the deep-time decay of life. Here the Necrocene, but an embryonic omen at the start of the Capitalocene, becomes actualized in capital's novel conscription of deep time.

The argument for the Necrocene flows from a view of capitalism as world-ecology, in which capital accumulation is understood as fundamentally embedded in, and shaped by, the web of life (see Moore 2015a; also Parenti and Hartley's essays in this volume). The Necrocene highlights the relation between capital accumulation and negative-value. That latter encompasses those forms of nature that are directly hostile to capital accumulation, and which cannot be overcome through capital's productivist logic. Questions of waste and toxicity loom large in Moore's account, including of course the rising concentration of greenhouse gases in the atmosphere. But waste and toxification are only part of the reality suggested by the "rise of negative-value" (Moore 2015b). Extinction must be conceptualized in relation to the *longue durée* of capitalism.

We have, it seems, reached a historical tipping point of negative-value accumulation. The nonlinear reproduction of negative-value has clearly become an urgent problem—for capital as well as for planetary life. The "entwinement" of climate change and capital has produced a new contradiction in negative-value: "processes of extracting nature's 'free gifts' (including human labor) and toxifying the biosphere (including humans) have now reached a breaking point." While negative-value accumulation might become more apparent with capital's increasingly frantic efforts to appropriate surplus value and restore Cheap Nature, its history is rooted in the origins of capitalism (Moore 2015b, 5). The Necrocene, coterminous with the Capitalocene, is the slow emergence of the crisis of negative-value accumulation.

The Necrocene concept traces the relation between the material unfolding of extinction through capital and the history of its scientific inquiry. That is why extinction must be examined through exhumation of dead matter: as an object of knowledge, the fossils that led to the discovery of extinction and the concept of catastrophism, and the decayed biomass of hydrocarbons whose use precipitates actual ecological catastrophe. Dead matter is our link to the seeming oblivion of deep time. Through its inspection, we can learn something about our own future catastrophes. The earth is wracked by punctuated cataclysms—subterranean, extraterrestrial, and biological—a press-pulse of species extirpations and radiations (Arens and West 2008). Today we look for analogies for our present epoch in strange hyphenated names: the contemporary mass extinction found in the Permian-Triassic "Great Dying"; the explosive rise of CO_2 ppm in the Paleocene-Eocene Thermal Maximum; life's geological agency in the Great Oxygenation Event of 2.5 billion years ago, when cyanobacterial photosynthesis triggered perhaps life's first "climate catastrophe."[3]

In what follows, we make sense of the Necrocene in four stages. I begin with the "Columbian exchange" that accompanied the conquest of the Americas after 1492 (Crosby 1972). Pangea was restored through the intercontinental and transoceanic exchanges of crops, humans, animals—and commodities. The decimation of indigenous populations made for another "discovery": the idea of extinction. Extinction became a problem of knowledge. Second, the reorganization of capital through scientific management and fossil fuel extraction made extinction an apparent problem: one that needed "stewardship." Capitalism's dialectic of accumulation and extinction coevolved with a conceptualization of knowledge of "risk" and "environment." Capitalism did not ignore environmental risk; it made it the central problem of its survival. Third, the post-World War II "Great Acceleration" witnessed the convergence of financial, actuarial, military strategic, and environmental risk around biosecurity. These emerged primarily from the problems of nuclear warfare and the environmental consequences of nuclear testing. Finally, biosecurity disappeared into catastrophic nihilism and the embrace of necrosis; the "survival economy" of neoliberalism as the Donner Party. The belief in our alienation from nature became embodied in the perspective of the human being as the monstrous all-powerful offspring *of nature*. The problem of extinction was rendered intrinsic to human nature rather than to capital.[4] The history of environmentalism is the history of capitalism realizing its own principle of *becoming extinction* through the conceptual system of planetary catastrophism. *This in turn produced a being toward extinction as a permanent characteristic.*

The "Anthropocene" displaces the origins of the contemporary crisis onto the human being *as species* rather than *as capital*. It reinforces what capital wants to believe of itself: that human "nature," not capital, has precipitated today's planetary instability. The Anthropocene says "humanity" put the earth under its power, that it could either save or destroy it—yet it also says the unintended consequences of this power only accelerate our powerlessness over earth's inevitable revenge. We have mistaken who "we" are (as some kind of undifferentiated human mass) from what "we" perform through capital. We have mistaken a historical condition of our economic organization for an innate aspect of the human being. Planetary Catastrophism has become the ideology of capitalism, and in this catastrophism begets catastrophe. The more capital attempts the real subsumption of the earth, the more the earth subsumes it. In the Necrocene, capitalism's farce runs concurrent with its tragedy.

We have finally inverted Benjamin's "Angel of History" (2006). No longer do we blindly fly along, face turned toward the past in horror as the wreckage builds and builds; now we hurl forward, ignorant of the past, eyes fixed on catastrophe upon catastrophe piling up ahead.

Birth and Burial of Catastrophe

Capital might think itself a pioneer species, but the best term for it would be a *disaster taxon*, a species that does not merely fill vacant niches after ecological catastrophes, but creates catastrophes in order to do so.[5] Its history begins with the "unification of the globe by disease" (Ladurie 1981). The demographic collapse of the Amerindians was hardly accidental—this was not simply a "virgin soil epidemic" (e.g., Crosby 1986). To be sure, the infectious diseases Europeans brought with them outran the pace of conquest. But the duration of the demographic collapse attests to capitalism's reorganization of nature: diseases such as tuberculosis and malaria plagued indigenous peoples due to malnutrition, lack of sanitation, overcrowded labor settlements, and lethal exploitation in mines and plantations (Packard 2011; Arnold 1996).

The capitalist reorganization of New World natures boomeranged death upon Eurasia. The Little Ice Age peaked in the seventeenth century (Parker 2013), due partially to the Amerindian demographic collapse. The Americas' population decline allowed for forest regeneration. Reforestation of the Americas combined with strong El Niños and low sunspot activity (the maunder minimum) to precipitate socio-ecological disasters across Eurasia. By 1610, a "CO_2 minima" had been reached; carbon dioxide levels were among the lowest ever recorded in human history (Lewis and Maslin 2015; Nevle and Bird 2008).

Exploiting the demographic catastrophe, capitalism created a novel "tropical" ecology in the slave plantation. Tropical zones—as much created as discovered—became a homogenized equatorial region whose native diversity was destroyed and replaced by a few staple crops such as sugar, tobacco, and coffee. This climatic-geographic differentiation allowed for the ecological othering of colonial subjects, justifying capitalist expansion by creating zones of law and exclusion (Benton 2010). This geographical othering was a self-fulfilling prophecy: the more the plantation system grew, the more the ecological transformations it wrought allowed for malaria and yellow fever to thrive to new epidemic proportions, the more Europeans viewed these places as unsuitable for "civilization," and inhospitable to settlement by "civilized" peoples. The myth that the demand for West African slaves was due to their immunity to the Caribbean disease environment is backward. *First*, indigenous populations collapsed, propelled by the imperial reorganization of natures. *Then*, African slaves were imported well before the flourishing of malaria and yellow fever, which had not existed in the New World prior to the European invasion (Packard 2011; Webb 2009).

By the eighteenth century, thousands of fossils were pouring into the imperial epicenters of knowledge production. Colonial expansion had facilitated an unprecedented cooperation between the natural sciences and the state. Amateur biologists and botanists took advantage of colonial projects to pursue basic research, and at the same time to gather information for the sake of resource exploitation (Cushman 2013; Ax et al. 2011; Beinart and Middleton 2004; Worster 1994; Grove 1995). Strange, unidentifiable fossils flowed in from the peripheries of the French and British empires, hinting at the prospect of species disappearance. These cryptic specimens, such as the woolly mammoth, haunted the salons of the Enlightenment for nearly a century. The mammoth, whose bones were discovered across North America, presented a sort of anatomical Sphinx's riddle.

In 1796, Georges Cuvier proposed a radical solution to this riddle. He argued that the mammoth and the modern Indian elephant were not the same species. While his conclusion was based on anatomical comparison, the planetary reach of colonial "exploration" provided evidence to support his hypothesis. It seemed impossible, Cuvier argued, "that men who have collected and described the smallest insects in the least accessible climates would not have yet seen such substantial animals" if they were still existent (quoted in Rudwick 2005, 359). Cuvier believed he had discovered "the existence of a world previous to ours, destroyed by some kind of catastrophe.... What revolution was able to wipe it out to the point of leaving no trace of it except some half-decomposed bones?" (quoted in Rudwick 2005, 363). In 1804, Thomas Jefferson, haunted by the implications of Cuvier's hypothesis, sent Meriwether Lewis and William Clark to search—among other objectives—for mammoths that "should" have been roaming the American West during their expedition (Rudwick 2005, 414).

Of course Lewis and Clark did not find mammoths west of the Mississippi River. Cuvier had found a rupture in the chain of being, and advanced a revolutionary concept: extinction. Cuvier had proposed a theory of "catastrophism": disruptions in ecological homeostasis, driven by exogenous natural catastrophes such as floods and earthquakes, could cause the extinction of previously robust, well-adapted species.

The original theorists of geological deep time, James Hutton and Charles Lyell, as well as the early evolutionists Geoffroy St. Hilaire and Jean-Baptiste Lamarck refused to believe that mass extinction was possible. Catastrophism, in their view, was a relic of the Judeo-Christian mythology. A crucial vulnerability in Cuvier's theory was his denial of evolution. The discovery of deep time rendered Cuvier's time frame much too shallow for geologists, who had come to believe that only gradual, cumulative change across deep time affected species.

Lyell's uniformitarianism—which implied that biological change worked as a constant, rather than punctuated, rhythm—seemed to have triumphed with the publication of *On the Origin of Species* (1859). Darwin's conception of evolution consisted of tiny, accumulative changes occurring at a fairly constant speed through deep time. This appeared to strike a decisive blow against Cuvier's catastrophism. Nevertheless, uniformitarianism remained ill-equipped to explain major gaps in the fossil record; the strange, radiative qualities of species clustered in some strata and absent from others suggested variable speeds of evolutionary change. That pure uniformitarianism triumphed—for the moment—owed much to the *mentalité* of nineteenth-century Anglo-American laissez-faire empiricism. Its ontology assumed that species were autonomous units, in charge of their individual destinies, and whose extinctions were endogenously caused by their lack of adaptive robustness. Species were a sort of biological Horatio Alger. Marx quipped that Darwin had rediscovered nineteenth-century England in the world of the "beasts and plants" (quoted in Foster 2000, 198). Catastrophism was buried, but in a shallow grave, waiting for some tectonic spasm to awaken it.

Uniformitarianism may have pushed catastrophism to the margins of scientific thought, but reminders of past catastrophes were increasingly dredged up, now in the heartlands of capitalism. Quarrying, mining, and railroad construction came upon the bizarre relics of animals, plants, and other hominids that spoke of ancient and unknown disasters. Industrial capitalism increasingly exhumed extinct life: coal and oil. Capitalism had been reared by the "free gifts" of energy in charcoal, peat, water, solar, and wind, but the Cheap Nature of living energy was increasingly inadequate by the mid-nineteenth century. The transition from a biomass to hydrocarbon regime marked the moment when capital, having exhausted contemporary nature, tapped into deep time: the decayed, dead world now harnessed for sake of capital's world-ecology.

From 1492, early capitalism was premised on rapid forest clearance—for fuel especially (Williams 2003). Across Europe and the Americas, the forests retreated, or their ecologies were fundamentally altered. While today it is fashionable to see fossil fuels as fundamental to capitalist development, American capitalism made the switch to coal fairly late in the game. The United States found no need to use anthracite coke until the mid-nineteenth century—and coal did not become the leading energy source until after the Civil War (Pursell 2007, 61). Even with vast forest resources, it became clear by the 1860s that some form of "rational" forest management was necessary.

In 1867, George Perkins Marsh published *Man and Nature*. Marsh conceived "Man" as both parasite and prime mover. Having witnessed New England's deforestation, he believed humans lived in a perpetual imbalance with nature. Man, Marsh argued, had to find ways to address that imbalance—we had to maintain an "intelligent will" that could see beyond contemporary pressures (1965, 41). Nature could not afford the interest rate of our destruction. If the Enlightenment's "economy of nature" meant a balanced budget, then Marsh thought humans were running a great deficit. Marsh articulated the two main strains of environmentalist thought and practice. On the one hand, Marsh advanced a technocratic ethic of conservation that could control nature. On the other hand, he advocated a preservationist ethic that saw "man" as "everywhere a disturbing agent . . . [who] unsparingly persecutes, even to extirpation" all life around him (Marsh 1965, 43). These two tributaries of the "gospel of conservation" followed parallel, and often antagonistic, paths until the turn of the century (Hays 1959).

This antagonism crystallized in the dispute between Gifford Pinchot and John Muir. Arguing over the construction of Hetch Hetchy dam in Yosemite (California) during the 1910s, the dispute prefigured a century of conflicts between conservationism and preservationism. San Francisco's demand for water would ultimately triumph over the natural sublime of the valley. Conservation was tied to state building. In the United States, it was a response to the environmental problems of western expansion driven by homesteading, mining, forestry, and agriculture (Hays 1959; Worster 1985). Preservation was tied to an aesthetic-transcendentalist lexicon of Eden, and the protection of Nature (with an uppercase N) threatened by civilization. For the preservationist Muir, Pinchot's conservationism represented a plan "for the destruction of the first Garden" (Muir 2008,

111). For Muir, a pristine "Eden" was at stake—and it was threatened with extinction. Purged from Muir's vision were the Native Americans who had been expelled from their lands to establish his cherished Yosemite. Nor did Muir confront capitalism's rapacious appetite for Cheap Nature that made it necessary to "preserve nature" in parks such as Yosemite. "Beauty hunger" seemed more important than actually existing hunger and disease. Viewed in a wider context, the very terms of this debate— between preservationists and conservationists—separated questions of resource depletion and toxification. The first became a problem of a pristine Nature, existing "out there," beyond Society; the second became a non-natural problem of urban environments, excluded from environmental politics altogether.

I Am Become Death, the Savior of Worlds

"We knew the world would not be the same. A few people laughed, a few people cried. Most people were silent. I remembered the line from the Hindu scripture, the Bhagavad-Gita; Vishnu is trying to persuade the Prince that he should do his duty, and to impress him, takes on his multi-armed form and says, 'Now I am become Death, the destroyer of worlds.' I suppose we all thought that, one way or another."
—Robert Oppenheimer, 1965, reflecting on the first atomic bomb test

The return of catastrophism did not come from the upheavals of the Great Depression but from the system of total war that matured across the two world wars. Military-industrial production began to entrench itself in civilian life. It was led by chemical firms finding justification for the continued production of poison gas by transposing its surplus for use in a "war on insects" (Russell 2001). Here an eradication mentality, structured by metaphors of parasites and pests, sustained a new phase of the Necrocene. In the military-industrial production regime, capitalism attempted to save itself from destruction through the absolute intensification of destruction. The apotheosis of this process would be Hiroshima and Nagasaki. Capitalism found in the Atom Bomb the dark watery reflection of its own image. It realized that its logic could only lead to one thing: total extinction. It realized it had become the Necrocene.

Catastrophism's reemergence owes much to the Bomb and its unanticipated side effect in global fallout. Climate science came of age in the

Cold War "techno-politics" of altitude (Edwards 2010, 215). A complex web of satellites, numerical weather models, and weather modification now drove a growing global network of data capture that aimed at planetary surveillance. This atmospheric techno-politics was a reaction to—and catalyst of—the rapid expansion in the spatial and temporal scales of ecological risk. Experts studying the Bomb's environmental effects came to see humanity as a planetary actor in a fragile, finely tuned system—one that postwar humanity threatened to annihilate (Hamblin 2013; Edwards 2012).

Prometheanism, the view that humans could and indeed should control nature, went hand-in-hand with a new catastrophism. At its center of was a new cult of expertise. American world power justified expert political authority through the necessity of managing the hazards set in motion by its permanent war economy. But these experts' authority derived from more than a promise to mitigate catastrophic risks; it also owed much to their proclamations that such risks were *unavoidable*—and outside of political deliberation.[6] This was the birth of the biosecurity state. Vannevar Bush's *Science: The Endless Frontier* (1945) justified this cult of the expert in his reappropriation of Turner's frontier thesis (1898). Bush proposed a new, macho, techno-utopian ideology. The scientist was became a gunslinger in a sidereal wild west, an imperialist fantasy that would overcome the contradictions of capitalist surplus extraction. The *Endless Frontier* as scientific exploration was really the *Endless Frontier* as commodity expansion: apocalyptic fears of extinction would be vanquished by utopian fantasies of techno-omniscience. The scientized discourse of environmental risk obfuscated the close relationship between economic and environmental inequality. This excused the system of production that threatened environmental catastrophe by framing humanity as an undifferentiated mass that had become a "planetary agent."

Weather control was this planetary agent's first major goal. This required solving the problem of modeling and anticipating turbulence. The prospect of enlisting the computational power of the new "Electric Brains"—computers—seemed to make this possible. John von Neumann, mathematician and inventor of ENIAC computer (as well as the Mutually Assured Destruction nuclear strategy), initiated the Numerical Weather Prediction Project at the Institute for Advanced Studies at Princeton in 1946 for this purpose. Von Neumann had corresponded with Norbert Wiener, a pioneer in the analysis of complex nonlinear systems, born of his work designing antiaircraft targeting during World War II. Wiener had popularized systems theory in his 1948 *Cybernetics: Or Control and Communication in the Animal and the Machine.* For Wiener, complex systems were primarily structures governed by the "command and control" of information flows. Chaotic flows of information become entrained in recursive loops of positive and negative feedback, producing an emergent order from "noise." In this scheme, information regulation was a universal framework for all natural and social processes.[7] His conclusions made him skeptical of meteorologists' ability to control the weather due to the "amplification of small differences" leading to unpredictable outcomes (Weart 2008, 58). Edward Lorenz, running weather models in the late 1950s, confirmed Wiener's assertion. He discovered that very similar initial numerical conditions would quickly diverge in their trajectories—this would later become Lorenz's famous "butterfly theory." The weather displayed a chaotic character sensitive to fine-grained differences.

Atmospheric nuclear testing made the need for weather models practical—and urgent. When testing began in earnest in the 1950s, so too did the greatest experiment upon the earth: global radioactive fallout. Strontium-90 did not exist before a hot July day in 1945. As warlike Athena sprung from Zeus's head, strontium-90 burst forth from "the gadget's" plume, flying upward into the stratosphere. From there it dispersed and rained down upon the planet, a toxic blanket of human design and a moment of no return. The earth, capital, and body were now joined through the deep time of radioactive mutation. The notion of the atmosphere and the oceans as a bottomless sink was now put to the test.

Project Sunshine, a secret study initiated by the Atomic Energy Commission in the early 1950s, sought to trace this new twist in capitalism's planetary metabolism. It was an unprecedented effort to understand the global biosphere by tracing the radionuclides throughout the biosphere's trophic levels. The project began in 1949 under the apocalyptic title Project Gabriel. A health physicist at Oak Ridge, Nicholas Smith, calculated the limit point of how many nuclear bombs could be detonated before all life on earth was killed off (Hacker 1994, 181–82). He determined strontium-90 was the worst of a variety of nasty fission products, owing to its ability to mimic calcium, which allowed it to settle in the bone. Once in the bones, strontium-90 needed to knock just one electron from a nearby calcium molecule to begin a metastasized chain reaction (RAND Co. 1953, 2).

And so once again, bones from across the global periphery flowed into the new imperial center of the United States. Only this time around, human bodies—not extinct animals—were the prized objects. At Columbia University's Lamont Observatory, the "theochemist" Laurence Kulp avidly embraced the project. Up to this point, the Observatory had been something of a research backwater. The Bomb gave it purpose—and fame. Kulp and his students examined milk, wine, soil, plants, and animals, even accounting for dietary differences across the globe (Higuchi 2010, 306–7).

Most prized, however, were children's bones. This was their Holy Grail. When it came to these bones, the Observatory's scientists were gripped with an almost monomaniacal obsession. Discussions of children's bones seemed to dominate Sunshine meetings.[8] At a 1954 Atomic Energy Commission Project Sunshine conference, Commissioner Willard Libby lamented the tricky grey area that was "the law of body snatching.... If anybody knows how to do a good job of body snatching, they will really be serving their country."[9] The AEC hired body snatchers, coerced governments, bribed morticians, and instructed some of the best graduate students in geochemistry to steal samples from the Arctic to Australia to South Africa. Up to one thousand specimens were shipped to the United States from Australia alone, including 284 baby hearts—most without permission of the parents, who they believed should "remain in blissful ignorance" (Roff 2002, 304–5).

Meanwhile the catalyst for a new environmental politics of planetary catastrophe emerged from a different source: a university study of human biomineral specimens. Washington University's Baby Tooth Survey, led by the dentist Louise Reiss, was a citizen effort that collected over three hundred thousands children's "milk teeth" between 1958 and 1962. (Some eighty-five thousand of these teeth still linger in shoeboxes in an ammunition bunker at the university [St. Louis Post-Dispatch, 2013].) It was the "citizen science" answer to Project Sunshine. The survey's stated purpose was to provide the public with "objective" scientific knowledge about how radioactive fallout affected human bodies. In this they pioneered scientific data as tool of political protest (Egan, 2007; K. Moore, 2008; Higuchi, 2010). Most of Sunshine's data was already public by the time the project began. It was really the use of juvenile samples that made the Baby Tooth Survey a success. "Milk teeth" put a human face on the abstract, highly technical problem of "permissible dose." This human face was of a suburban white child—the unequal distribution of risks meant that environmental danger only became politically charged when influential groups felt threatened. The fear of bequeathing to our children a ruined planet was now a far more harrowing prospect than the deforestation denounced by Pinchot and his fellow conservationists in the early twentieth-century. Childhood innocence, the *raison d'être* of the era's suburban consumerism, now seemed besieged by unnatural, mutant, alien forces. Here the ancient struggle of monster and child was recapitulated as *Godzilla* v. *Leave it to Beaver*.

When Rachel Carson published *Silent Spring* (1962), the catatrophist synthesis of preservationism and conservationism became the dominant model of how we imagined planetary futures. Carson told the story of fallout through DDT (dichlorodiphenyltrichloroethane)—a seemingly mundane product widely used as an agricultural pesticide. Carson opens *Silent Spring* with Biblical language: "a strange blight crept over everything," bringing with it "mysterious maladies" (1962, 2). A "shadow of death" was cast over all life (ibid.). Something has invaded the Garden; the serpent has arrived. God brings down His wrath upon the inhabitants of the American pastoral, though they know not what they did. Like the first born of Egypt, even children are not spared. They are living, it seems, in a land so toxic they are stricken "suddenly while at play and die within a few hours." A chain reaction of disappearances leaves even that most resilient animal, "man," without succor. Its seems as if an atomic bomb had fallen—the vegetation looked "as if swept by fire, a white granular powder fell "like snow," a metaphor that evoked the horror of "atom dust." Carson extended the relationship between the human body and the radioactive isotope to all industrial chemicals. In so doing, she captured a deepening popular anxiety over the end of humanity through deformity and mutation: an "end" that was fundamentally tied to the practice of modern life, from geopolitics to the backyard. In the inadvertent consequences of our everyday life, a "grim specter has crept upon us almost unnoticed, and this imagined tragedy may easily become the stark reality we all shall know" (Carson 1962, 1–3). In a single sentence, Carson globalized this tragedy as a creeping catastrophe of deep time, not in the flashy mega-explosions of the Bomb, but in the slow violence of its unknown, invisible by-products. "I am Become Death" and "Save the Earth" had become two sides of the same coin.

Carson was not the only scholar who had become aware of deep-time catastrophe. In the 1950s, there were growing popular fears—in Japan, Britain, and America—that nuclear explosions would trigger large-scale climatic changes and extreme weather events (Edwards, 2010; Hamblin,

2013). Most atmospheric experts initially dismissed public concerns. By the early 1960s, once-skeptical scientists began to speculate about the possibilities of melting the polar ice caps with hydrogen bombs to create a "temperate" Arctic. Other scientists feared such an intervention would instead trigger an Ice Age (Wexler 1958). The mystery of the ice ages had been the holy grail of climatological research for nearly a hundred years. In the 1950s, earth scientists generally accepted that there had been four ice ages and interglacial epochs in regular intervals. But evidence remained scant. In the 1930s, the Serbian astronomer Milutan Milankovitch had proposed that orbital cycles based on the long-term elliptical eccentricities of the earth's rotation around the sun were involved. If this was the case, far more than four ice ages had occurred, given that the longest orbital cycle was only one hundred thousand years.

Geophysicists doubted Milankovitch's hypothesis. To them, it was exceedingly unlikely that slight alterations in solar radiation could cause such huge climatic changes. But the Lamont Observatory's scientists began to think otherwise. They dredged up deep sea core samples suggesting that Milankovitch might be correct. These suggestions implicated something profound: planetary climate could shift rapidly, and do so from even minor perturbations. The geochemist Wallace Broecker, a Lamont Project Sunshine veteran, proposed in 1963 that rapid climatic changes were possible. Milankovitch's theory, Broecker argued, must now be considered as "more than an interesting curiosity" (Weart 2008, 48). The head of the Lamont Observatory, Maurice Ewing, had already coauthored an article in 1956 proposing the possibility that albedo feedback loops might cause ice ages with rapid onset. Cesare Emiliani, studying the chemical markers of ancient foraminifera (tiny snails buried deep in the ocean's crust), proposed many more than four ice ages—and that their occurrence was neither so regular, nor so gradual, as scientists believed (Weart 2008, 45–47). Ice core sampling in the Arctic further confirmed the prospect of climatic instability. Now nuclear and climatic catastrophe merged into one larger complex in the expert mind. Robert Ayres, whose subsequent studies of industrial metabolism influenced sustainable development discourse, wrote a definitive three-volume study for RAND on the environmental effects of nuclear weapons. In it he applied these new theories of ice age instability to argue that nuclear weapons could alter the atmosphere through throwing up huge amounts dust aerosols (Ayres 1965)—what would later be known as a "nuclear winter."

The Cold War "command and control" mentality had pushed scientists to look for a single, overdetermining factor governing the biosphere (Weart, 2008). By the 1960s, that mentality was breaking down. Multidetermination was now favored. It became increasingly clear that the climate operated through sensitive feedback loops at variable speeds. General Circulation Models began to add more and more variables, from ocean currents to volcanic eruptions. By the 1980s, Broecker would even discover that the deep ocean "conveyor" (the thermohaline current), if shut down, could cause rapid and catastrophic climatic changes. It seemed every biospheric process was on a hair trigger, even the ocean.

In the 1950s, scientists assumed that the oceans possessed a nearly infinite capacity to absorb human waste, from radioactive waste to carbon dioxide. The oceanographer Roger Revelle, who had led the first biological study of fallout at Bikini Atoll in 1946, began to undermine even this assumption. In an article coauthored with Hans Suess in 1957, the two men discovered—contrary to their assumptions—that the oceans could not act as an infinite sink for CO_2. "Human beings," they declared, "were carrying out a large-scale geophysical experiment of a kind that could not have happened in the past—and could not be repeated (Revelle and Suess 1957, 19). But CO_2 as "inadvertent weather modification" was still one of several culprits, and not—*yet*—considered the main threat to climate stability. In the 1960s a plethora of anthropogenic atmospheric particulates preoccupied scientists. Walter Orr Roberts realized in 1963 that jet contrails increased cumulus clouds and hence absorbed incoming radiation (Fleagle 1969; Weart 2008), cooling the earth. In the early 1970s NASA scientists Mario Molina and Sherwood Rowland hypothesized that CFCs (from aerosols and refrigerants) were breaking down the ozone layer and could, potentially, warm the earth. Simultaneously, the atmospheric chemist Paul Crutzen found yet another ozone depleting process. This derived from skyrocketing use of artificial fertilizers, which increased nitric oxide in the atmosphere (Weart 2008, 122–23).

Atmospheric scientists remained unsure if the cooling or warming effects of human actions would triumph. One thing, however, was certain: the global atmosphere had been modified by industrial production. The National Science Foundation's 1965 report on the topic echoed George Perkins Marsh a century before, declaring that "man is becoming so numerous and his influences on his environment so profound that he cannot consider himself free to heedlessly or improvidently exploit the air, water, land, and growing things of this earth" (Special Commission on Weather Modification 1965, 1). As scientific studies accumulated, the convergence of chaos theory and catastrophism allowed for a universally shared lingua franca that cut across environmental activism, natural science research, national security strategy, and global development programs.

This discourse was not, of course, centered on the problem of capitalist production. Rather "mankind" as a species was the (catastrophic) agent of change. But even if the discourse of "man" obscured capitalism's primary culpability, the reality of its planetary effects had been clarified empirically—by the very experts who helped to solidify American world power in the 1950s. By the 1970s, it was apparent to many in the natural sciences that the temporal scale of negative-value accumulation had extended far beyond the reach of capital's managerial capacities.

The final variable at work in catastrophism was "population." The engine of environmental degradation seemed to lie with there simply being too many humans. The more people born, the more energy consumed, the more waste produced, the more the earth suffers. Here, it seemed, was a positive feedback loop with only negative consequences. Pollution, perhaps, would not be a problem if there just weren't so many people! Sound management of resources and populations was all that was needed. Global population control could ensure the containment of environmental upheaval. The techno-optimistic cult of expertise seen in many modernization and development programs hid an underlying fear of disaster. The idea of "containing" communism was not simply waged through military and economic means. The maxim *Keep 'Em Fed and They Won't Go Red* was as important as the domino theory to American Cold War strategy.

Hence environmental containment was a primary battleground of the Cold War (White, 2010; Cullather, 2010; Biggs, 2010; Kinkela, 2011). Whereas colonial administrators in 1930s worried about *under*-population stifling economic growth, a different obsession characterized the postwar era: the fear of *over*population (Hodge, 2007; Connelly, 2010; Bashford, 2014). The "population bomb"—the title of Paul Ehrlich's smash bestseller (1968)—transposed the lexicon of nuclear catastrophism into a new ecological threat: overpopulation. Now the very reproduction of "humanity" was a threat to human existence. The discourse of overpopulation resurrected a misanthropic neo-Malthusianism that perceived the greatest threat to the biosecurity of the globe as the growing "hordes" of the Global South (Amrith, 2006). But global capital could perhaps survive the upheavals it had produced via a new concept of ecological securitization. Launched in 1971, UNESCO's Man and the Biosphere Program embodied a new phase in the effort to use global biosecurity to save capitalism from itself. The initiative set aside "biosphere reserves" across the globe, desperately seeking to square the accumulation circle through "sustainable development."

The early 1970s marked a new phase of environmental awareness—punctuated in popular consciousness by the first Earth Day in 1970. In this context, *The Limits to Growth* critiqued catastrophism—and reinforced it (Meadows et al. 1972). Donella Meadows and her colleagues used computer simulations to argue that the exponential growth of the global population would outstrip finite resources. Here was Malthus brought into the digital age. *The Limits to Growth*, while criticizing industrial production in the abstract, placed the blame on population rather than production. This seemingly intractable feedback loop of population growth and resource depletion made some scientists to begin to search for the escape hatch to *Spaceship Earth*—before "man" hit the self-destruct button.

In the lean years of the mid-1970s energy crisis and budget cuts, Bush's *Endless Frontier* now became the more modest *High Frontier* (O'Neill 1976). Gerard O'Neill confronted the dilemma of limits to growth and provided a utopian solution. "We can colonize space, and do so without robbing or harming anyone and without polluting anything," he prophesied (O'Neill 1974, 32). Space colonization would be the capitalist's and the environmentalist's dream: habitats would be self-sustaining and cost-neutral, using solar energy, cultivating their own crops, mining minerals on the moon or asteroids. Even endangered species "may find havens for growth in space colonies, where insecticides are unnecessary . . . and industry has unlimited energy for recycling" (O'Neill 1974, 34). O'Neill claimed that the galaxy's effectively inexhaustible resources would sustain population booms and remove limits on economic growth: "if we are so prodigal as to run through the material of the asteroid belt the next 500 years, we can gain another 500 years by using up the moons of the outer planters" (O'Neill, 1974, 39).

Again we see the contradiction of sustainability. O'Neill begins with a description straight out of *The Limits to Growth* but ends by advocating a continuation of capitalism through an endless frontier movement, swallowing up the rest of the solar system's—even the Milky Way's—resources. The L5 Society, a group of space colonization advocates inspired by O'Neill, symbolized the culmination of planetary catastrophism's contradiction of capitalist expansion and environmental protection (Michaud 1986). Their slogan, "Love the Earth: Leave it," might be considered the white flag of Cold War environmentalism: no solution could be found but more of the same in the interstellar beyond.

The environmental imaginary's movement from earth to space also facilitated its inverse: those who studied space began to look back upon the earth. Astrophysicists leapt into planetary climatology. The entry of the astronomers shifted the focus of research in climatic catastrophes back out toward the stars. The astrobiologist Carl Sagan solved the mystery of why Venus, a planet so similar to ours and marginally closer to the sun, could be so much hotter than the earth. It was the work of an amplifying feedback loop: the "Venus Effect" of greenhouse warming. In Venus we saw the hellish reflection of our future. It is no coincidence that NASA's Godard Institute of Space Studies, under the leadership of Jim Hansen, became the central node for climate research in the 1980s. Hansen's testimony before the U.S. Congress in 1988 brought to the public's attention the dire prospect of a rapidly warming atmosphere. He felt confident in his predictions after his team's general circulation models had shown how sulfate aerosols could trigger sufficient albedo feedback to cool the globe. The model, by inverse, also implied how *warming* could occur through the same amplifying feedback process (Weart 2008, 116–18).

Preoccupation with asteroids mirrored a renewed fear of nuclear climate modification, now described as "nuclear winter." Rapid climatic alterations meant that life could be thrown into adaptation crises that led to extinction events, exactly what Cuvier proposed over a century before. Population biologists realized as much. Gould and Eldredge proposed the evolutionary theory of "punctuated equilibrium" (1972), giving a plausible explanation for gaps in the fossil record that had puzzled nineteenth-century naturalists. They posited that periods of rapid species diversification, such as the Cambrian explosion, were followed by long periods of stasis (equilibrium). Eventually another exogenous geological event, such as an asteroid or increased volcanism, disrupted environments too quickly for most species to adapt. From these catastrophes, new species would evolve. The "Alvarez hypothesis" in 1980 would be final icing on the catastrophist cake (Alvarez 1980). Luis and Walter Alvarez argued that the bizarre global strata of the rare element iridium in the geological record suggested an asteroid impact. The extinction of the dinosaurs was most likely caused by such an impact, which sent enough dust aerosols into the atmosphere to cause a cooling feedback loop. Cuvier was vindicated. But where he had seen catastrophe as a product of divine intervention, scientists now saw it in terms of extraterrestrial accidents. Life became *speeds* on a razor's edge of oblivion.

The new catastrophism also made clear that planetary life had experienced multiple mass extinctions. An extinction event is defined as a rapid disappearance of at least three-quarters of all living species, something that occurred five times before the human era (Barnosky et al. 2011, 51). The discovery of mass extinction was certainly disturbing. But in the 1980s, scientists still assumed that such catastrophes occurred only through errant extraterrestrial impacts or nearby supernova bursts, "a somewhat comforting finding" (Ward 2009, 83). It even appeared there was perhaps there was some kind of "natural" periodicity to these events (Raup and Sepowski Jr. 1984). By the 1990s, those comforting findings gave way to something much less comfortable: the idea that life itself could be the catalyst of its own destruction (Ward 2009, 84). The evidence suggested "humanity" as the driver of a new mass extinction event (Leakey and Lewin 1995).

Today, after five centuries of global capitalist expansion, accumulation by extinction has produced a Sixth Extinction (Kolbert 2014). The Sixth Extinction is the material result of the Necrocene's convergence—conceptually, between chaotic systems theory and deep-time biogeological planetary catastrophism; practically, through the actually existing processes of extinction and necrosis under capital. We can analyze the rise of negative-value through the historical geographies of extinction, and the production of knowledge regarding its process. Accumulation by extinction has become dominant. Capital hopes it will invent new corpses upon which to feast.

The Future Is Past Forever

The Anthropocene argument explains capital's evils by pointing to human nature. It then calls the suffering born from this evil useful because humanity has brought it upon ourselves, *and only through collapse* can a great rebirth justify this hour of darkness. The Anthropocene argument seems to lead us, again and again, to the idea that only technological cocooning can protect us against life's inherent self-destructive tendencies. "Only engineering will save us now, for 'nature' is simply the facts on the page, staring us in the face" (Ward 2009, 156). This argument seems the very justification for catastrophic capitalism's continuation. If the capitalism's game is Russian roulette, would we not assume that every player is suicidal? The suggestion that we must "save life from itself" through technological manipulation could not be more useful to its ends. Capital now seeks to postpone its demise through planetary geoengineering, intensifying the contradictions of negative-value through "environmental" protection. After thirty years of trying remove sulfur dioxide from the atmosphere, it is now seriously proposed that we inject it back into the stratosphere to save us (National Research Council 2015).

The overwrought sense of "humanity" on the brink of near-term extinction is a pernicious perspective that short-circuits the ability to act (Lilley et al. 2012). Today has born witness to the transformation of "Love the Earth: Leave it" to "Love the Earth: Kill Yourself." The death wish of the deep ecologists and the death drive of capital lies in the same misanthropic fantasy of a world emptied of ourselves—the former in a masochistic longing to erase our sins, the latter in the hope to become pure abstract value unmoored from material entropy and death. Deep ecology and geoengineering schemes are two sides of the same coin. Environmental catastrophism is a politics based upon a thousand Cassandras ringing the death knell of "civilization," a belief that leads either to a fatalist neoprimitivism or a fascistic Darwinian-Malthusian fight for survival.

If we live in the Anthropocene, it is because the Capitalocene wants us to think this way. The "environment" must be discarded as a fiction of capital, and with it "environmentalism." "Green Arithmetic"—adding up Nature and Society (Moore 2015a)—has for too long obfuscated capital's interpenetration of bodies, ecologies, and geological strata. The real subsumption of the earth under capital is impossible: capital will never escape the material world in which it acts. The logic of accumulation is not capable of outrunning extinction because accumulation and extinction are the same process. They cannot be decoupled. But the human being *can* be decoupled from Capital. Capital is extinction. We are not.

Notes

1   A new rock has been proposed: plastiglomerate, made from "the intermingling of melted plastic, beach sediment, basaltic lava fragments, and organic debris" (Corcoran et al. 2014, 4).

2   "The Four Cheaps are central to the resolution of recurrent overaccumulation crises in historical capitalism. Consequently, the cyclical end of the 'Four Cheaps,' in successive accumulation cycles, corresponds to a growing mass of surplus capital with nowhere to go. The exhaustion of commodity frontiers, and the slowed growth of unpaid work, is consequently linked strongly to the peculiar forms of financialization which have emerged since the 1970s" (Moore 2015a, 227).

3   "Photosynthesis triggered one of the world's worst climate disasters, the Paleoproterozoic snowball Earth. Intensive investigation of the time period of the Paleoproterozoic glaciations may reveal whether a novel biological trait is capable of radically altering the world and nearly bringing an end to life on Earth" (Kopp et al. 2005).

4   Lewis and Maslin conclude that "5 centuries of human scientific investigation" had eradicated a belief in humanity's uniqueness in the web of life (2015, 177). Science had transmuted humanity from the top of the chain of being to mere primate to invasive parasite overrunning a fragile biosphere. They called upon their readers to look at the Anthropocene not simply as a stratigraphic classification but as the means for humanity to reassert itself as the central protagonist in the great struggle of life. They seem to have taken a page from Nietzsche, who had observed this decentering brought by science long before. Only, what he said with irony, is repeated now with sincerity. For Nietzsche saw in science a "hard-won *self-contempt* of man as his ultimate and most serious claim to self-respect" (Nietzsche 2000, 592). So too could we say of the Anthropocene: the more we vanquish our uniqueness the more we hold ourselves up as unique. The Anthropocene wants to put us back at the top of the chain of being while banishing us further into what Nietzsche had called "a penetrating sense of our own nothingness" (2000, 591).

5   Disaster taxa typically populate areas after an environmental catastrophe wipes out native species. Mammals, for instance, would not have radiated across the globe in the wake of the K-T extinction event if not for their willingness to be scavengers.

6   The pianist Tom Lehrer summed up this idea in his satirical homage to the V-2 rocket inventor Werner von Braun when he quipped, "Once the rocket goes up, who cares where it comes down? That's not my department, says Werner von Braun" (quoted in Vaver 2006, 175).

7   The Macy Conferences of 1948–1950 included Wiener, Gregory Bateson, Claude Shannon, Talcott Parsons, John von Neumann, and Margaret Mead. These actors led the development of a new "cybernetic" episteme. Talcott Parsons's "grand theory" of social action saw emergent structures of "pattern variables" and "pattern maintenance" as structural evolutionary universals of socialization and the formation of social norms. The engineer Claude Shannon proposed a solution to the problem of "information entropy" at

the 1948 conference. Information entropy was sort of like the game of tele-phone—a signal's relevant information deteriorates as a function of time due to "noise." Shannon argued that all information is essentially uniform, the content or meaning of the signal itself irrelevant, all analog signals could be compressed to binary code. Life and labor became essentially packets of binary "information."

8   Kulp also seemed to have particular zeal for "sawing up bodies and ashing them"—so many, in fact, that the man "who ran the machine shop bought Larry his own bandsaw because he didn't want him cutting up bodies on his bandsaw in the shop" (Imbrie 1997).

9   AEC Division of Biology and Medicine, January 18, 1955 ("Biophysics Conference") (ACHRE No. NARA-061395-B). In response to Kulp's sugges-tion that they try the city of Houston because "they don't have all these rules there . . . they have a lot of poverty cases and so on," Libby displayed a rather disquieting joy, exclaiming, "That is wonderful!" (ibid.).

FIVE

The Capitalocene, or, Geoengineering against Capitalism's Planetary Boundaries

Elmar Altvater[1]

In the last few decades, climate scientists have discovered the "planetary boundaries" of economic growth. They warn of a possible collapse of earth systems after trespassing certain tipping points (Rockström et al. 2009). "Man"—the *Anthropos*—followed the biblical message, to subdue the earth under his rule so effectively that "we have started a new kind of evolution: technology." Through this development, says the former chief engineer of Google, Ray Kurzweil, the human progress that started with biological evolution could continue "until the whole universe is in our hands" (2005). Kurzweil's statement on humanity's *reliance* on increasingly autonomous technologies is not a promise (or a threat) directed to the next generations; it is already a reality. His statement on "human progress" is much more questionable.

Mankind has created the world economy and thus realized the "propagandistic" tendency of the global expansion of capitalism, which Marx mentions in the *Grundrisse* (1973). However, today's transformations are about far more than capitalism as a global social formation; they are perhaps equally about capitalism as a geological formation. Today's great questions are about how capitalism works through, and actively creates, planetary nature.

Marx used an unequivocally geological term to comprehend the long stages of history (Braudel's *longue durée*): that of the "formation." Marx called capitalism a mode of production and also a "social *formation*." He adopted the term as an analogy to "earth formation" used by the geological science of his time. In *The German Ideology* (1971), Marx and Engels remark that "mankind must live" in order to make their human and social history. And Marx added a footnote: "Hegel. Geologische, hydrographis-che etc. Verhältnisse" (geological, hydrographical relations)—a reminder to study not only the social conditions of human life, but also the physical ones. Human history thus is, as Friedrich Engels in *Dialectics of Nature* emphasized, a "dialectical totality" (*dialektischer Gesamtzusammenhang*) of natural and social processes (1987).

The social moment of this dialectical totality is "abstract" value, the natural moment, the domain of "concrete" use values (Marx 1977). This is crucial to his analysis of capitalism's contradictions, which center on the double character of the commodity—of commodity producing labor in the production process as well as in the reproduction process of capitalism as a whole. Marx conceived it mostly as a national economic system, but he was obviously aware that a comprehensive analysis of the "conditions of life" included the social relations beyond production as well as biological and geological formations: the earth-systems. In Boulding's words (1966), the "energy system" comprises not only fossil fuels but climate, raw materials, and the system of information. To these systems we must add what Boulding forgot: the world economy. The decisive systems of "our" spaceship Earth are connected; they have been—and will continue to be—reshaped.

Flows of information are therefore tightly connected to nature. Here we might reflect upon the connections between the planetary surveillance and imperial surveillance. We are witnessing the globalized data theft by the U.S. National Security Agency (NSA) and other intelligence "services," in order to appropriate information necessary for control of the other earth systems. The twenty-first century is also the era of the robot world war. Killer drones, from Afghanistan to Somalia, Iraq, Syria, Yemen, and Palestine, are deployed to kill "terrorists"—defined as those who threaten the normal working of world systems which (we are told) are indispensa-ble for "free peoples" in a "free world." The struggles over energy and the climate have repercussions for all other earth systems and for human rights in general. The dominant narrative on capitalism's globalization, a quarter century after the end of "actually existing socialism," seems almost kitschy against the background of these planetary developments. Its repercussions are felt across all spheres of life: in politics and cultures, in the economy and in daily life.

A New Geological—*and Geopolitical*—Era?
At the same time, a new geological and geopolitical era has begun.

The impending transformation of our earth-systems could be interpreted as a great triumph over the "four offenses of mankind" committed in modern history (Klingholz 2014, 108). For Klingholz, Nicolas Copernicus is responsible for the first offense. In the sixteenth century, Copernicus proved that, contrary to popular belief, the earth is not the center of the Universe—it is not even the center of the solar system. The second offense came from Charles Darwin in the nineteenth century. Darwin's offense was the claim that Man is not the crown of creation, but only one possible result of natural selection: evolution. In the twentieth century, Sigmund Freud committed a third offense, with the discovery that we do not act always consciously and rationally but also unconsciously and irrationally. This is an obvious negation of the belief that European rationality is the best guideline for intentional action in the world.

Finally, a twenty-first-century offense: the discovery that humanity does not preserve or sustain nature but destroys the conditions for human-friendly life in pursuit of economic growth. Daly calls this the "failed growth economy" (2010). Of course, it would be reasonable to include other "offenses" on our list. But one last offense is crucial. This is Marx's analysis of capitalism as a crisis-ridden mode of production (a failed growth economy), driven by class struggle. Capitalism, therefore, cannot be the ultimate answer to the challenges of the present as history.

For Kurzweil, however, all these offenses can be treated with advanced technology. Therefore the "singularity is near," and social transformation is unnecessary. From this perspective, geoengineering offers perfectly reasonable solutions to planetary crisis (see also McBrien, "Accumulating Extinction," in this volume). Crutzen also argues for geoengineering as the most effective way to stop global warming: "Scientists and engineers . . . [must] guide society towards environmentally sustainable management during the era of the Anthropocene. This will require appropriate human behavior at all scales, and may well involve internationally accepted, large-scale geoengineering projects, for instance to 'optimize' climate" (2002, 23). In Crutzen's vision, engineering, not social transformation, is the best way to meet the challenges of climate change. Technology will pardon modernity's "four offenses"—inherited from the Enlightenment but still at work in the twenty-first century. Crutzen's vision commits the error that Albert Einstein asked us to avoid: to think that humanity can resolve problems by applying the same methods that caused them.

The vision of a technological solution to modernity's problems is optimistic and inconsistent at the same time. Kurzweil praises the incessant acceleration of technical progress as a "singularity," even as he admits that we do not know what may occur beyond the "event horizon" of our "rational" perception. So we have to take the warnings seriously that humanity has already transgressed at least two "planetary boundaries"—with more transgressions to come (Rockström et al. 2009). The peak exploitation of many resources (peak oil, peak everything) has already been reached, or exceeded (Bardi 2013; Heinberg 2007). But today's conjuncture is about more than resource scarcity: the planet's carrying capacity and resilience in the face of runaway climate change is now under siege. Rising atmospheric concentrations of CO_2 and other greenhouse gases, the accumulation of nuclear wastes in our soils and water, the acidification and pollution of the oceans—all have made the Anthropocene argument unavoidable. Its core argument—that humanity has changed the biosphere in fundamental ways—has become very plausible. Climate change, the loss of biodiversity, the contamination of habitats, the inhospitality of cities, global economic and financial instability, global poverty—these processes, entwined with permanent acceleration, implicate a systemic crash that may have already begun (Virilio 2007). Perhaps the point of no return has been reached, even if we cannot know it with any precision.

Now the literati swarm the planetary ruins in the wake of the crash, some write of friendly and bright utopias while others imagine dark dystopias. Filmmakers shoot Oscar-winning dystopian, transhumanist films, such as *Avatar*. So humanity transforms more than the nature of planet Earth in a "real dystopia." In such narratives, humanity remakes itself, as avatars, transhuman cyborgs, hybrids of organic and technical elements (Hörz and Hörz 2013). Communication between people turns into "interface management," as mobile phones, laptops, and tablets become indispensable control points in worldwide information flows. Here the surveillance society enters in full force: it becomes possible to tap these interfaces and to collect the exchanged data between the technically connected masses. This is the opportunity that the NSA and other "security services" have seized upon. But we can only fully understand the dimensions of the planetary data theft when we bring it into the context of the new geoeconomic and geological era, and the deepening capitalist project of planetary surveillance. This project comprises the widest range of activities: attempts to create a unified system of control for planetary energy provision, climate management, global finance, world trade, and of course the global information system.

It's the Capitalocene, Stupid!

In this cyborg world, the old discourse on "globalization" is increasingly displaced—and replaced—by a discourse on the Anthropocene. This is neither utopia nor dystopia, a friendly or less friendly view of an unknown future. The Anthropocene has arisen in the past, at the end of the warm period of the Holocene. The past twelve thousand years—the Holocene—were exceptionally favorable for the emergence and development of human civilizations (Davis 2010). There have been, naturally, significant climate fluctuations—warm periods and even ice ages—during this long era. But all was not natural climate fluctuations. Since the dawn of civilization, humans have made the Earth their home by transforming the planet into a human-friendly world. The Earth's soils have been cultivated and depleted, its crust ransacked for raw materials, its rivers moved, its atmosphere changed. Unlike earlier periods of climate change, twenty-first-century climate change is due to human influence on earth systems, on the energy system, the economic system, and systems of resources and information. That is why the Anthropocene is a plausible name for the new planetary era.

It is impossible to give an exact date for onset of the Anthropocene. Most likely, this occurred between the beginning of European modernity in Braudel's "long sixteenth century" (2009), and the industrial-fossil revolution of the second half of the eighteenth century. In these centuries, labor productivity advanced as never before (Maddison 2001). All processes in production, reproduction, communication, circulation, and consumption accelerated. Time and space were compressed: in shorter periods more things were produced, and transported more rapidly, over longer distances. Things—and also information—moved faster, exchanged faster. Commodities traveled farther and faster—and so did people. The onset of fossil fuel–driven industry and transportation amplified and accelerated those earlier trends. Modern machinery, more and more concentrated in big factories, allowed for new technical divisions of labor. Adam Smith describes these as the decisive force that increased labor productivity and thus the wealth of nations ([1776] 1937). New cities—and especially industrial cities—took shape as land and agriculture become less important relative to industrial production. Life and working conditions radically changed. Therefore it is completely justified to call it a revolution. Marx and Engels already interpreted the industrial revolution as a rupture in human history (see Altvater 2015). Industrialization "brought into existence those forms of labor and styles of living distinguishing the modern world from the past" (Kemp 1978, 9). During the later nineteenth century, oil succeeded coal as capitalism's most important energy source, and in the twentieth century natural gas was added—not to mention unconventional fossil fuels today. They still satisfy up to four-fifths of world energy demand (IEA, 2013).

Before the nineteenth century, water, wind, and forest energy had been used extensively to increase the surplus product, with the result of large-scale civilizational progress—and large-scale ecological destruction (Varchmin and Radkau 1981, 42–77). For this reason, Moore questions the unique importance of the industrial and fossil revolution in the second half of the eighteenth century (Moore, "The Rise of Cheap Nature" in this volume). For Moore, the socio-ecological transformations of the Industrial Revolution originated in the long sixteenth century. The rise of capitalism, in this interpretation, was enabled by a "Cheap Nature" strategy, centered on the Four Cheaps: labor-power, food, energy, and natural resources (Moore 2015a). These Four Cheaps were indeed an important factor in the formation of early modern capitalism—what Marx calls the era of the original, or "primitive," accumulation of capital.

The Industrial Revolution therefore marks the end of "protoindustrial" capitalism, and at the same time the rise of *modern* capitalism. It might also be interpreted as the transition from the "formal" to the "real" subsumption of labor (and of nature) by capital (Marx 1977). While formal subsumption only allows the production of absolute surplus value (by extending the working day, for example), real subsumption activates the potential for relative surplus value production, and dramatically rising labor productivity. The first method already is part of the early modern transition to capitalism, to the systematic exploitation of labor by capital and the emergence of a world-system of trade and investment. But accumulation and growth based on powerful fossil fuels and driven by modern machinery only became reality in the course of the Industrial Revolution. Therefore we have to distinguish two points from which capitalist development begins. The first is not a point but a period of time, the era of the "great discoveries" after 1492, coming to an end with the Westphalia Treaty and the emergence of a modern system of states (1648). This is the interpretation of Braudel (1983), who is therefore critical of Polanyi's dating of the "great transformation": the rise of a "disembedded" capitalist market economy in the late eighteenth and early nineteenth centuries (1944). As it turns out, *both* authors are right. The transition to the social formation of capitalism and the impact on earth formations took place across these four centuries.

Since then, capitalist social formations have spread across the globe. At some times capitalism's planetary expansion has been violent and brutal, at others, a relatively peaceful and mercantile process. In this context, the dissemination of science and of arts took place, with the assistance of missionaries, and also with the wars of colonial conquest. In this—Polanyi's great transformation—societies were revolutionized: politically, economically, culturally, mentally. Landscapes were plowed, ecosystems altered, and social and political revolutions took place. In the process, capitalism became the horizon of evolution, the pattern of reference for all social formations that emerged in the centuries after the first capitalist experiments.

The driver of these changes was not "humanity" in the abstract; it was the people living and working and above all *owning* in the capitalist mode of production who have caused the thoroughgoing changes to *all* earth systems and formations. To be sure, precapitalist social formations brought about major changes in culture and politics, in the economy and in techno-structures; but earth systems have been overstretched only under capitalist conditions—in the process transforming humans themselves into a biotic-technical Avatar hybrid. Modern capitalism thus is more than a social formation. Capitalism changed human existence; it has interpenetrated both earth systems and the mental worlds of each (social) individual. This has significant consequences for our politics. Because there are no longer "just" social antagonisms: each such antagonism embodies the socio-ecological implications of the altered earth systems that also trigger class conflicts and keep society on the move.

What this means can be observed in the history of civilizations. It would not make sense to call the transition to sedentary agriculture—the Neolithic Revolution about eight thousand years ago—a transition to the "Agrarocene." The Neolithic Revolution fundamentally changed social relations and the energy system. But the geology of planet Earth was not affected by agriculture's systematic use of solar energy. Instead, the geology of the earth remained largely untouched and unchanged.

Thousands of years later, the Industrial Revolution was very different. The earth was scoured and transformed in search of precious metals, fossil fuels, and other raw materials. Without matter and energy from Earth's crust, industrialization would not have been possible. In contrast to the Neolithic Revolution, industrial capitalism not only transformed *social* relations, but the societal relation to nature—and in its course, the relations of physical and living nature as well. The "productive forces" were augmented rapidly and radically, motivated by the compulsions of relative surplus-value production. In the process, earth systems were changed, increasingly so over time. Fossil fuels provided the physical power for capitalism's acceleration through time, and its expansion across space—that is, for advancing labor productivity, decisive to capitalist accumulation. The capitalists who strove to maximize profitability discovered the positive effects of advancing labor productivity. This propelled the generalization of big machinery and of big energy to power the machines. The dawning era of fossil energy powering the modern capitalist industrial system should therefore be referred to as the Capitalocene. This is why Marx and Engels interpret the industrial transformation as a *revolution* in human history.

The Capitalocene is about ideology as well as energy, class, and machinery. In the Capitalocene, "nature" has been transformed into a capital asset. Nature has been reduced to something that can be valued and traded and used up just as any other asset: industrial capital, human capital, knowledge capital, financial claims, and so forth. This is the ideological way of incorporating nature into capitalist rationality and its monetary calculus. This is, of course, the dominant way of thinking in mainstream economics.

Capitalism's success made it possible to incorporate nature into this peculiar economic rationality. For the first time in planetary history, humanity—acting through capitalist imperatives—is organizing nearly all its productive and consumptive activities by tapping (and depleting) the planet's energetic and mineral reserves. This planetary dominance—like the Industrial Revolution—is also a revolution. By using fossil fuels capitalist humanity has substituted an open solar energy system for a closed and even isolated fossil energy system. This exactly makes the difference between the Neolithic and the Industrial Revolutions. The former involved no rupture in the use of solar energy. People after the Neolithic Revolution used it more efficiently than before. They cultivated plants in order to transform the sun's energy into food; they exploited the power of animals for labor; they captured the kinetic energy of wind and water for transport and material processing.

The Neolithic Revolution opened the path for a great progress of mankind, for the production of surplus, also for an increase of labor productivity. Therefore Moore is right to emphasize the preindustrial dynamics of capitalism and its Cheap Nature strategy (2015a). One turning point—across Braudel's "long" sixteenth century—led to another, more profound rupture. Taking shape first in eighteenth-century Britain, the marriage of abundant fossil fuels and modern machinery quickly transformed Europe and North America, and then the rest of the world. Far from a narrowly technical development, this industrial transformation was a child of European rationalism, of profit-seeking greed and of the dynamics of money and the market. *Industrial* capitalism, underwritten by cheap fossil fuels, became the dominant model of modern economic development. No less important, it also created a *new global socio-ecological reality*. The planet was transformed into a closed system on the input side as well as on the output side of the earth systems. From the Industrial Revolution, a new era begins: the earth under the rule of capital and capital under the rule of the most powerful imperialists. *It's the Capitalocene, stupid!*

In Capitalism, Externalization Is Rational
When hunters and gatherers became sedentary farmers, their conditions of work and life changed from the ground up. The Neolithic Revolution, without any doubt, *was* a revolution—just not in the same sense of storming the Bastille in 1789 Paris, or the Winter Palace in 1917 St. Petersburg. It was, rather, a *longue durée* process, one occurring over centuries. Towns sprang up. Cultures flourished. All this took place within the interglacial period of the Holocene, so richly favorable to human development.

Times changed with the birth of instrumental rationality and the rise of capitalism in the long sixteenth century. That rationality underpinned subsequent scientific discourses, among them classical political economy and later, neoclassical economics. Moral deliberations which were still intrinsically linked to political economy in Adam Smith's writings subsequently became irrelevant compared to the rules of rational decision-making. But the moral economy never disappeared from history, as E.P. Thompson showed (1971). Nevertheless, the alleged rationality of the profit-maximizing individual became everything. That rationality—*capitalist* rationality—is reckless when it comes to the requirements of the whole system. It is a rationality of the parts and not the whole.

For classical political economy, the coordination of individual decisions is left to the market's "invisible hand." Its advocates argued that market rationality supersedes the logic of individual rationality because the invisible hand guarantees the best for each and for the whole. But observing only the means to an end covers only a small part of a totality. It is an observation from the point of view of the fragment rather than the totality. It becomes impossible to take the "web of life" (Moore 2015a) or the "totality of the system" (Friedrich Engels's *Gesamtzusammenhang*) into consideration. The web of life's vast interdependencies are disregarded, and therefore the rationality of capitalist modernity can only be partial. In this scheme of things, interdependencies cannot be planned, they cannot be controlled. Thus, the modern form of rationality is the decisive principle of the European world domination that influences—and at times determines—popular thoughts and action.

European (*capitalist*) rationality cannot be holistic. Surprises are inevitable. Economic plans fail, expected profits must be written off, losses must be absorbed. If these failures and losses begin to spread, a crisis breaks out. This is a specifically economic disruption of normality and routine and enforces an adjustment to the changed conditions. This can be very destructive and creative at the same time. Capital must be written off. The survival of workers—and even capitalists—can be jeopardized. Economically depreciated capital can be physically destroyed. Scandalous irrationalities appear, as an increasing number of homeless people appear in America, in Spanish and German cities—alongside a rising number of vacant homes. But the phoenix can rise from the ashes. This is the reason for Schumpeter's optimism with regard to "creative destruction" (1950).

Today capital may be confronting new limits to its creativity. Modernity, with its Occidental rationality of world domination, is running into barriers beyond the "event horizon." As if by magic, what was once rational is becoming irrational. But this looping is irrelevant, because the destructive forces of the crisis belong to capitalist normality. Capitalism's rationalization of the world is based on externalization, on tapping resources and on loading the spheres of the planet with solid, fluid, and gas waste.[2] For capital, societies and earth systems exist only insofar as they are incorporated into the world of rationality, of monetary calculus, of capitalist valorization. Capital sees only what it can price. On the input side, the appropriation of resources takes place solely to valorize capital. "Nature" under the rule of capital therefore leads an unduly narrow existence: as "natural capital" (e.g., Wackernagel et al. 1999). The pursuit of cheap inputs is fundamental to the pursuit of capitalism's decisive principle: seek out the highest possible return on the capital employed, find the largest possible levers to increase profitability and shareholder value. On the output side, everything that cannot be valorized has to be dumped into planetary landfills—"landfills" that include, of course, the atmosphere. Capital seeks to rationalize the "external world" in the same way that it rationalizes inputs: this is Cheap Nature as Cheap Garbage. But there's a problem: that external world does not work in quite the same way. The physical working of the energy system, for instance—from extraction to greenhouse gas emissions—follows a logic quite different from that of capital. Value circulation and the transformation of use values are two sides of the double character of the capitalist reproduction process. But they are different. The one is immaterial, the other is material and substantial. The one follows the logic of circularity (capital must return to capital), the other has cumulative effects—for instance, the CO_2 in the atmosphere has increased rapidly since the nineteenth century, from 280 to 400 parts per million. In mining, raw materials extraction has a "negative cumulation effect": first comes the peak of extraction, but eventually only a "black hole" remains.

So it is not only the external world that is limiting capital, but also capital's own mode of rationality. This cost-benefit rationality is revealed in the microeconomic calculations of individual companies. The indicators for capital's rational comparison of costs and benefits are as diverse as modernity, and they are adapted to the business needs of individual companies. They are also historically specific. In a Fordist company in the 1960s, they were different from the indicators used by an investment or hedge fund in today's finance-driven capitalism.

Nevertheless, the core of this rationality has remained constant. In these calculations, neither the spatial nor temporal dimensions of "external" impacts—on society and on nature—can be considered. Such impacts are not considered in capitalist measures of rationality: the profit rate or the interest rate. At the same time, this logic of microeconomic calculation generates contradictions in the social and macroeconomic environment. This occurs because some of the "external" effects—at the level of the firm—are internalized at the level of society. They can become extremely negative for other capitalists and for society, which can generate pressures for (at least some) firms to "internalize" externalities, to pay attention to the "social costs of private enterprise" (Kapp 1950). It then becomes necessary that "prices tell the truth" of these externalities. Only when price tell the truth can there be a return of capitalist rationality. In more elaborate approaches, algorithms are developed for private sector negotiations between polluters and victims of environmental damage (Coase 1960); or official taxes levied to compensate for environmental damage (a Pigouvian tax) (Pigou 1932). Also, certificates are used to acquire the right of emissions into the environment, e.g., into the atmosphere with CO_2 emissions (Dales 1968). If damage done to nature is expressed in monetary terms, they are accessible to the rational calculus of benefits and costs. The world of economists is now back in order.

The world of the ecologist, however, is still out of joint. Whenever "externalized" costs are internalized, even to a small degree, economists celebrate the triumph of economic rationality. But, we might ask, is not externalization highly purposive-rational? Is not externalization an element of modernity? The project of the "rational mastery of the world" (Weber 1964, 248), could not exist without an "external" world, into which the undesirable effects of rational action can be transferred. Bacon would not have been able to develop his theories of the domination of nature without dissecting external nature. The separation of nature and society that characterizes modern thought since Descartes has no basis in reality— only a basis in the European rationality of world domination.

Therefore, the external world—what Marx calls external nature—is a creation of capitalist modernity. For European modernity, nature is encaged in value, torn from its natural context and integrated into an economic circuit of value circulation. The complexity of nature is reduced to a simple, fetishized category: natural capital. This gives economists the chance to calculate nature like any other asset. The waste is dumped into planetary systems without consideration for the totality of living organisms and organic/inorganic relationships. This is a clear sign of the existence of two contradictions in modern capitalism, which James O'Connor (1998) mentioned: a contradiction between capital and labor and a contradiction between capital and nature and thus between capital as a social and political power and the environmental movements. The systemic complexity of the societal relation of different classes to a singular nature can be noticed—as today—only when "tipping points" are reached. The quality of the system then changes, and a shocked public becomes receptive to discourses such as the Anthropocene. Ecosystems can collapse, as well as civilizations (Diamond 2004; Tainter 1998). But—as yet—only a few people think that capitalism may be also be reaching its tipping point, signaling its historical demise (Mahnkopf 2013).

The earth is changed, a new era has begun. On this, Friedrich Engels was quite realistic and not optimistic at all:

> Let us not, however, flatter ourselves overmuch on account of our human victories over nature. For each such victory takes its revenge on us. . . . Thus at every step we are reminded that we by no means rule over nature like a conqueror over a foreign people, like someone standing outside nature—but that we, with flesh, blood and brain, belong to nature, and exist in its midst, and that all our mastery of its consists in the fact that we have the advantage over all other beings to be able to learn its laws and apply them correctly. (1987, 461)

In the Capitalocene, we have lost the optimism of Engels's last sentence—because we obviously have not properly applied the laws of nature. The earth's "external" worlds to capital have been progressively incorporated into the circuit of capital, so that nature is reshaped as a provider of resources and a dumping site for emissions. As an arena of externalization—of the consequences of "rational" capitalist economies—the external world is no longer available. Luxemburg's *landnahme*—the annexation of *new* territories—is no longer possible. The economic irrationality of our internalization of external effects is obvious. The assumption that it is ecologically rational is wrong. It is, moreover, quite certain that the destruction of planetary life that results from externalization is not Schumpeterian. It is not *creative* destruction—only, simply, *destruction*.

Planetary Engineering

The expectation somehow persists that the economically rational—and ecologically irrational—actors should be able to cope with the "great transformation" of a global civilization which "is increasingly aware of its importance as a formative force" (Schwägerl 2010, 33). At this point, the distinction between the Anthropocene and the Capitalocene becomes politically significant. In the Anthropocene "the people" (humanity) are the *dramatis personae* who can make their social, economic, political and geological history. But they only can influence their geological history on an insignificant scale—although it is growing in the course of economic and social development. In the Capitalocene, the major formative forces are the laws of motion of capital: of the capitalist *social formation*, of the financialized capitalism today. These also influence the geological history of the planet, the *geological formation*, as part of capital's drive to extend and deepen its reach, to externalize social and environmental costs. From this follows a mighty effort to regulate, control, and neutralize these externalized costs—costs which now encroach upon capital's costs of doing business.

Now the geoengineers enter the stage of capitalist modernity. Geoengineering faces a double task. On the one hand, they must create necessary resources on the input side of the planetary social and geological systems at a time when they can no longer be easily extracted from external nature. On the other hand, they must organize new methods of dumping all emissions into the earth's systems. It is a seemingly impossible task. Their task is much greater than building a car or a dam or a hotel; the geoengineers are tasked with controlling whole earth systems in order to combat—or at least to reduce—the negative consequences of capitalist externalization. However, the required internalization of externalized emissions is the internalization of external effects into production costs at the level of the corporation. Then indeed—*in principle*—the prices could "tell the truth," as in the neoclassical textbooks. But we would not be wiser still. Why? Because many interdependencies in society and nature *cannot be expressed in terms of prices*. Any effective rationalization would have to be holistic; it would have to be qualitative and consider much more than price alone. But that is impossible because it contradicts capitalist rationality, which is committed to fixing the parts and not the whole. In such a scenario, capitalist modernization through externalization would—*inevitably*—come to an end. The Four Cheaps would disappear behind the "event horizon." Would it be possible for geoengineers to bring the necessary moderation of modernization *and* of capitalist dynamics in coincidence? They cannot, for the engineers are not qualified to work holistically. They fight the effects of externalization (e.g., greenhouse gas emissions) by externalizing the external effect once again (e.g., by obscuring the sun to reduce solar heat radiation). This would amount to an absurd secondary externalization of primary external effects.

Geoengineering cannot respond to the limitations of earth systems in the Capitalocene. More effective could be many "small" responses to the planetary challenges—experiments to test a variety of alternative projects and explore potential solutions. If they are small enough, it does not come to path dependence—something as dangerous to humanity as drug addiction is to the individual. One can take a different direction when the path turns out to be too bumpy, or misleading. Small projects are also not "too big to fail"; they do not attract many others in a self-produced mess. There are many roads to Rome. Because there are many who share a common goal, it is possible to decide deliberately and democratically about alternatives, based on the emancipatory guidelines, that respect the "planetary boundaries" now being crossed in the Capitalocene.

Notes

1   Thanks to David Barkin for helpful comments on this essay.
2   This already was a theme in Rosa Luxemburg's writings before the First World War. She called capitalism's externalization strategies a *Landnahme* (annexation of territories).

PART III
Cultures, States, and Environment-Making

SIX

Anthropocene, Capitalocene, and the Problem of Culture

Daniel Hartley[1]

The object of world-ecology is contained in the word "culture." Originally denoting "the tending of something, basically crops or animals" (Williams 1983, 87), during the sixteenth century culture came to mean a process of human development. Thus, Francis Bacon could write of the "culture and manurance of minds" in "a suggestive hesitancy between dung and mental distinction" (Eagleton 2000, 1). A cognate of "civilization," culture came ultimately to mean three things: (1) a "process of intellectual, spiritual and aesthetic development"; (2) "a particular way of life"; and (3) "the works and practices of intellectual and especially artistic activity" (Williams 1983, 90). Given that world-ecology aims to overcome a philosophy—and narrative—of human history premised upon the "Cartesian divide" between man and nature (Moore 2014b, 3), *culture* is clearly a very important—yet deeply problematic—term. As Eagleton writes, "it is less a matter of deconstructing the opposition between culture and nature than of recognizing that the term 'culture' is already such a deconstruction" (2000, 2). The problem is to think "culture" in its historically recent sense of a way of life or set of artistic activities—or even, as we shall see below, as "hegemony" or "ideology"—whilst never losing sight of its etymological roots in the soil. Like world-ecology itself, "culture" denotes a historical, philosophical and conceptual problematic.

In what follows, my intention is to explore this problematic of "culture" in conversation with world-ecology as a philosophy and historical method that seeks to move beyond dualisms, especially the Nature/Society binary. I do so in three principal steps. I begin by considering the increasingly popular discourse of the Anthropocene. This discourse claims that "humanity' has become a geological force in its own right (Crutzen 2002; Steffen et al. 2011; Zalasiewicz et al. 2011). Yet the Anthropocene's implicit philosophy of history is deeply problematic, leading to practical proposals that are apolitical and narrowly technological, and a grasp of modernity that is entirely ignorant of the complex historical processes at the heart of the capitalist world-ecology and its cultures. Turning to Moore's far more convincing term, "Capitalocene" (the Age of Capital), I briefly set out what I take to be the major claims of the world-ecology perspective before returning to the problem of culture. I conclude with some tentative suggestions as to how the study of culture may inform the evolving world-ecology conversation—and our understanding of the Capitalocene.

The Anthropocene Discourse: Five Problems

As a way of talking about geological changes, the Anthropocene discourse is relatively harmless. Danger arises, however, when geologists enter the political arena, calling for collective ecological intervention on the basis of the Anthropocene. For there exists something like a "spontaneous ideology" of Anthropocene scientists; they have produced an implicit philosophy of history. It is an abstract, naturalistic materialism, one that "excludes the historical process," and whose weaknesses "are immediately evident from the abstract and ideological conceptions expressed by its spokesmen whenever they venture beyond the bounds of their own specialty" (Marx 1977, 494). It is just such "venturing beyond," and the incoherent discourse which inspires it, that warrants a radical critique. The Anthropocene's abstract materialism gives rise to five problems that deserve special attention.

1. Ahistorical, Abstract Humanity

At the heart of the Anthropocene lies the *Anthropos*: the human. But what or who is this *Anthropos*? No clear definition is ever given. Yet the literature on the Anthropocene regularly refers to such phenomena as "the human enterprise" (Steffen et al. 2011a, 849). Such a conception—of humanity in general—presupposes "an internal, 'dumb' generality which *naturally* unites the many individuals" (Marx 1975, 423). A historical conception of humanity, in contrast, would see humans as internally differentiated and constantly developing through contradictions of power and re/production. To speak of the "human enterprise" is to make of humanity an abstract corporation in which "we're all in this together" (the David

Cameron maxim of 2009), thus belying the reality of class struggle, exploitation, and oppression.

2. *Technological Determinism*

The dating of the Anthropocene to some time around 1800 points to its technological bias—the steam engine changed the world. But did it? Technological determinism is always tempting, and much easier to communicate than the messy processes of class struggle. As Moore observes, the historical roots of the phenomena covered by the term "Anthropocene" lie, not in the invention of the steam engine, but in "the rise of capitalist civilization after 1450, with its audacious strategies of global conquest, endless commodification, and relentless rationalization" (Moore 2014a, 5). This marked "a turning point in the history of humanity's relation with the rest of nature, greater than any watershed since the rise of agriculture and the first cities" (ibid. 17). Inherent to the Anthropocene discourse is a conception of historical causality which is purely mechanical: a one-on-one billiard ball model of technological invention and historical effect. But that is simply inadequate to actual *social* and *relational* modes of historical causation. The fact that technology itself is bound up with social relations, and has often been used as a weapon in class war, plays no role in Anthropocene discourse whatsoever. Marx's (1977, 563) dictum that "it would be possible to write a whole history of the inventions made since 1830 for the sole purpose of providing capital with weapons against working-class revolt" is unthinkable within such a purview. To put it bluntly, then, for the Anthropocene technology is not *political*.

3. *Annihilation of the Time of Praxis*

Even from a literary perspective the Anthropocene is problematic. Take this representative passage, for instance: "Pre-industrial humans, still a long way from developing the contemporary civilization that we know today, nevertheless showed some early signs of accessing the very energy-intensive fossil fuels on which contemporary civilization is built" (Steffen et al. 2011a, 846). Sartre once remarked that the biographies of "great men" only ever see the child as the retrospectively projected necessity of what came after, thereby voiding the past present of its true contradictory presence, i.e., as a time of multiple possibilities leading to a range of potential futures (Sartre 1964). So too the Anthropocene can only ever think the past in its proleptic trajectory toward our present. Its specific narrative mode translates the time of initiative and praxis into the time of pure physical necessity. For precisely this reason, it can only think *our own present* as part of the empty, homogeneous time of linear succession, which increasingly contracts as catastrophe approaches.

4. A Whig View of History

This view of historical time goes hand in hand with a Whig view of history as one endless story of human progress and enlightenment. Two passages clearly exemplify this tendency:

> 1) "Migration to cities usually brings with it rising expectations and eventually rising incomes, which in turn brings an increase in consumption"; and
> 2) "The onset of the Great Acceleration may well have been *delayed* by a half-century or so, *interrupted* by two world wars and the Great Depression." (Steffen et al. 2011, 850; emphases added)

The first sentence seems almost willfully blind to the history of mass urban poverty, gentrification and accumulation by dispossession. The second seems to claim that the bloodiest century in human history— including Hiroshima, Nagasaki, the Dresden bombing, the Gulags, and the Holocaust—is a mere blip on the rising line of progress.

5. Apolitical Technical and Managerial Solutions

Finally, the Anthropocene discourse is extraordinarily technocratic. The majority of the solutions proposed by scientists are technical (e.g., mass climate and geoengineering projects) and managerial in nature—often couched in the language of "governance systems"—rather than political. The scientists arrive at such apolitical solutions precisely because they never pose the Anthropocene as a political problem in the first place. Kim Stanley Robinson's claim that "Justice has become a survival technology" is practically unthinkable within the presuppositions of the scientific representations of the Anthropocene (Robinson 2010, 213). Just as Anthropocene scientists cannot see *technology* as a *political* force, so they cannot see *politics* as a *material* force. Indeed, they have a problematic conception of materiality as such.

From this sketch, we can see quite clearly how the Anthropocene's diagnosis of planetary crisis powerfully shapes the range and quality of the possible solutions. An alternative sketch, drawing on Marxism and the world-ecology argument, suggests a very different range and quality of possibilities. Particularly useful is Moore's suggestion that we replace Anthropocene with Capitalocene, the "Age of Capital." Where many would see capitalism as an economic and social system, Moore's argument for world-ecology calls for thinking capitalism as producer *and* product of the web of life. Capitalism's economic and social relations are thus "bundled"—in Moore's language—with (and within) nature as a whole. Such a formulation points toward a synthesis of humanist and post-human thought. For one of the many paradoxes of the current conjuncture is that at the very moment in which scientists are using the term Anthropocene—forcing us to focus on our natural existence as a human species and collective human agent—the speculative realists and object-oriented ontologists are trying to problematize and move beyond the "human" as such (Harman 2011). The two appear to be flip sides of one another and, arguably, equally politically toothless.

Capitalocene as World-Ecology

World-ecology is a "framework of historical interpretation that dialectically unifies capital, power and nature" (Moore 2014a, 2). This is an argument for a conception of capitalism that extends beyond the purely economic, and sees capitalism as a civilization "co-produced by humans and the rest of nature" (ibid., 1). As such, world-ecology seeks to transcend accounts of human history—capitalism included—premised on a "Cartesian divide" between Humanity and Nature (2014b, 3).

For Moore, the world-ecology framework allows for a reconceptualization of Marx's theory of value: "While Marxist political economy has taken value to be an *economic* phenomenon with systemic implications, I argue that value-relations are a *systemic* phenomenon with a pivotal economic moment" (ibid.). For classical Marxism, "value" has been understood as "abstract social labor." Its dynamics center on socially necessary labor time, or the average labor time in the average commodity. (With the caveat, as we shall see, that only *some* work is counted as labor time.) This occurs within the "zone of exploitation" (Moore 2015a, 73)—Marx's "hidden abode" of commodity production, ruled by the capital-labor relation. What Moore does is simultaneously to affirm Marx's insight on this question, whilst highlighting how the zone of exploitation depends on a tight relation with *another* zone: the "zone of appropriation." This refers to all those realms of human and extra-human "unpaid work/energy," including not only so-called "women's work" but also the work of forests, soils, and rivers. In this perspective, capitalism cannot be reduced to the realm of paid work alone. Without the constant (and rising) appropriation of unpaid work—performed by human and extra-human natures—capitalism could not expand and develop:

> If we take the nexus paid/unpaid work as our premise—implicitly suggested by ecological and feminist scholars—the implications are significant. Capitalism and value relations cannot be reduced to a relation between the owners of capital and the possessors of labor-power.... The historical condition of socially necessary labor-time is socially necessary unpaid work. This observation opens a vista on capitalism as a contradictory unity of production and reproduction that crosses the Cartesian boundary [Nature/Society]. The crucial divide is between the zone of paid work (the exploitation of commodified labor-power) and the zone of unpaid work (the reproduction of life). (2014b, 9)

In other words, for Moore there are *two* fundamental contradictions—unified through an expanded conception of value—which structure capitalism as a civilization. One is between capital and labor, another between the zone of exploitation (commodity production) and the zone of appropriation (unpaid work/energy). Because this appropriation of unpaid work/energy cannot be conceptualized purely in terms of the capital/labor relation, Moore proposes a new concept: "abstract social nature" (2015, chapter 8). Abstract social nature comprises "the family of processes through which capitalists and state-machineries map, identify, quantify, measure, and code human and extra-human natures in service to capital accumulation" (2014b, 12). These activities and methods seek out and make legible to capital realms of unpaid work/energy—what Mies calls the work of "women, nature and colonies" (1986, 77). One might think, for instance, of those nineteenth-century American land surveyors who measured, mapped, rationalized and parceled out the land in order to sell it to investors (Johnson 2013, 34*ff*; see also Parenti's essay "Environment-Making in the Capitalocene," in this volume).

World-Ecology and Culture

Moore distinguishes abstract social nature from Stephen Shapiro's conception of the "cultural fix." For Shapiro, the cultural fix comprises those "social and cultural matters involving the reproduction of class identities and relations over time-lengths greater than a single turnover cycle" of capital. These identities and relations "*are intrinsic, not superficial, to the [accumulation] of capital*" (Shapiro 2013 quoted in Moore 2015a, 198). The cultural fix thus seems to refer to all those hegemonic and ideological processes that legitimate the long-term reproduction of the social relations of production. "If cultural fixes naturalize capitalism's punctuated transitions in the relations of power, capital, and nature," writes Moore, "abstract social natures make those transitions possible" (Moore 2015a, 16).

The distinction between abstract social nature and the cultural fix works only so long as it is provisional. Moore's account of the history of capitalism turns on the idea that capitalism reinvents itself—and the web of life—in successive eras. There are *transitions* from one phase of capitalism to the next, and consolidations of these accumulation regimes during which specific orders of culture, food, social reproduction, etc., stabilize. By equating those cyclical periods of transition with abstract social nature, and stabilization with the cultural fix, Moore risks overlooking just how important each moment is to the other. *Both* processes—abstract social nature and cultural fix—are constituted through the other, albeit in shifting relations of dominance. Culture is a constitutive moment of abstract social nature and vice versa. This dialectical relation of abstract social nature and culture is a constitutive moment of value in a Marxist sense.

Let me give me two brief illustrations, so as better to draw out the implications of this mutual constitution of culture and abstract social nature. The examples show the mutual imbrication of abstract social nature and the cultural fix within any period of historical capitalism. But they do not account for the shifting configurations between abstract social nature and culture in any historically *singular* period of transition or consolidation. A far lengthier engagement awaits.

In *River of Dark Dreams*, Walter Johnson describes the way in which slaves' bodies were standardized for the market: "The reports [filed by slaving firms] formalized a system of grading slaves—'Extra Men, No. 1 Men, Second Rate or Ordinary Men, Extra Girls, No. 1 Girls, Second Rate or Ordinary Girls,' and so on—which allowed them to abstract the physical differences between all kinds of human bodies into a single scale of comparison based on the price they thought a given person would bring in the market" (2013, 41). Here, we see abstract social nature in practice. Slave bodies are being standardized and made measurable for the market.

Could we not also say, however, that such standardization was possible only through a racist culture capable of legitimizing this practice and—here's the rub—producing the callousness of the human gaze? Here we see a cultural fix that was instrumental in effecting this standardization and in consolidating its social and material payoff. Indeed, Johnson himself writes with remarkable insight into the co-implication of abstract social nature and cultural fix:

> The agricultural order of the landscape, the standing order of slavery, the natural order of the races, and the divine order of earthly dominion were not separable for a man like Harper [a slaveholder]; they were fractal aspects of one another. His eschatology was rooted in his ecology. . . . Slaveholders were fully cognizant of slaves' humanity—indeed, they were completely dependent on it. But they continually attempted to conscript—signify, channel, limit, and control—the forms that humanity could take in slavery. The racial ideology of Harper and Cartwright [another slaveholder] was the intellectual conjugation of the daily practice of the plantations they were defending: human beings, animals and plants forcibly reduced to limited aspects of themselves, and then deployed in concert to further slaveholding dominion. (Johnson 2013, 206–8)

The second example is Federici's *Caliban and the Witch* (2004), which explicates the systematic violence perpetrated against women in the transition to capitalism. She highlights the highly gendered—and unequal—character of enclosure and the spread of wage-work in early modern Europe. With the enclosure of the commons, women lost a vital source of sociality and relative power. This was compounded by two further phenomena. One was the Price Revolution, in which the costs of food increased so steeply that many were condemned to chronic hunger. The other was the European demographic crisis of the seventeenth century. Federici sees this crisis as the root cause of a new "biopower" regime, in which "the question of the relation between labor, population, and the accumulation of wealth came to the foreground of political debate and strategy" (2004, 86). This was the crucible in which the witch-hunt emerged: "the enslavement of women to procreation" that "literally demonized any form of birth-control and non-procreative sexuality, while charging women with sacrificing children to the devil" (ibid. 89, 88). The witch-hunt involved a series of socio-cultural measures: the limiting of women's legal rights;

the surveillance and curtailing of women's spatial freedom; the criminalization of prostitution; the introduction of publicly humiliating punishments; the construction of new cultural canons to maximize perceived differences between the sexes and about women's innate inferiority; and an entire literary and theatrical discourse dedicated to the vilification of the "scold," the "witch," the "whore," and the "shrew," with Shakespeare's *Taming of the Shrew* being "the manifesto of the age" (ibid., 101). If women's unpaid work has been historically vital to capitalism, then we must conclude from Federici's history that culture is more than a force of ideological *legitimation*; it is itself a materially *constitutive* and *productive* moment in capitalist value relations. The ideological attacks on women were precisely about controlling them, confining them, and making their unpaid work appropriable by capital. Thus, whilst "abstract social nature" and the "cultural fix" can be *analytically* separated, in practice they always go together.

Let us now consider the ingenious notion of the cultural fix more closely. Shapiro (2014) connects the cultural fix to what he claims is a missing, but logically inferable, category in Marx's *Capital*: "fixed labor-power"—the dialectical complement of "fluid" or "circulating" labor-power and the counterpart to fixed capital. He further distinguishes between "absolute fixed labor-power" and "relative fixed labor-power." The former denotes "the materials that labor needs, but which capitalists do not provide, to ensure their human survival [. . .]: food, clothing, shelter, healthcare and educational training." The latter "include[s] everything that shapes class subjectivity, such as the social infrastructures responsible for durability of class solidarity and subordination. This is the realm of Gramscian hegemony" (Shapiro 2014, 1261–62). The ingeniousness of the term "fixed labor-power" is undeniable: it effectively combines social reproduction theory (Marxist-feminism) with theories of ideology and hegemony, and it transcends simplistic theories of culture as a non-constitutive "reflection" of the economic "base." Consequently, Shapiro claims to have discovered the "'object' for which the 'domain' of cultural materialism has been searching" (ibid., 1252).

As with any pioneering work, however, local blind spots are the condition of its insights. Shapiro focuses on the recurrent or cyclical features of capitalism—"periodicity" (2014, 1250)—as opposed to conjuncture-specific "periodizations." His categories are therefore transhistorical to the extent that they name structural features of *more than one* capital accumulation cycle. This abstraction is a necessary first step in the production of new theoretical knowledge. However, in naming "cultural fix" the operation of reproducing class identities over the *longue durée*, he has also rendered transhistorical the term "culture." As we have seen, the contemporary meaning of culture is deeply historical and has been reinvented as a "keyword" in successive eras of capitalism (Williams 1976). If one looks at "culture" across these successive eras—abstracting the cyclical reinvention of culture as a keyword—Shapiro's conception works ably to encompass social reproduction, hegemony, ideology, and so forth. If one looks at culture *within* these successive eras, however, this abstraction underestimates the extent to which these words are immanent, constitutive elements of the very problems they are used to discuss. (The same holds for "nature" and any number of other keywords.) The question must then arise: Is the abstraction of "culture" in Shapiro's work the reflection of a real, historical abstraction—as the abstraction of 'labor' for Marx presupposed the "developed totality of real kinds of labor" (Marx 1973, 104)—or is it a purely conceptual abstraction?

The cost of abstracting the historical meaning of culture is the excision of shifting constellations of keywords. The title of Williams's *Culture and Society* (1958), for example, implies the gradually emergent opposition of culture (as a repository of ideal values) to society throughout the nineteenth and twentieth centuries. Likewise, the terms "political" and "hegemony" invite a historical analysis of the changing role of the state throughout capitalist modernity. Gramsci himself argued that in bourgeois society the "political" is "a real abstraction or hypostatization that subordinates and organizes civil society," this latter providing the "subaltern 'raw material'" (Thomas 2009, 31). "The political" in bourgeois society quite simply *is* the form of bourgeois hegemony: "As a distinctively modern political practice aiming to compose atomized, juridically free individuals into larger collective social bodies, bourgeois hegemony has traversed the boundaries between civil society and political society, simultaneously a form of both 'civil' and 'political' organization and leadership" (ibid.) We must therefore take care to situate the historically specific struggles to shape and reshape culture within successive eras, as well as across the *longue durée* of capitalist history. Cultural history must incorporate the profound *interrelation* of historically and geographically specific struggles with their fundamental symbolic components and the long-run arc of "fixed labor-power" in capitalist history as a whole.

Historical capitalism produces a total social formation whose material constitution is such that the topographical relation of its elements—"culture," "nature," "politics," "society," and "the state"—is constantly shifting, and continually altering the internal compositions of that which the terms denote. The relations of nature to culture, of culture to politics, or of politics to the "economy" are remade through successive eras of capitalism. Each rearticulation transforms the very meaning of the terms themselves. This is certainly not to deny the presence of recurrent or cyclical features of capitalism, but we have yet to hit upon a sufficient terminology for thinking periodicity and periodization together. "Fixed labor-power" and the "cultural fix"—like abstract social nature—must be taken provisionally, as points of departure rather than "fixed" concepts. Otherwise, they risk sacrificing historical specificity. Our conceptual vocabulary—and historical method—for articulating the historical specificity within the *longue durée* of the Capitalocene is only now beginning to be elaborated.

Conclusion

How, then, should world-ecology proceed? Firstly, we should attempt to respect the complex historical trajectories and shifting relations of the words and phenomena that fall under the broad term "cultural fix": culture, society, ideology, hegemony, identity, generation, etc. That is, world-ecology should integrate and build on the historical semantics of Raymond Williams's *Keywords*, resisting the temptation to narrow itself only to those terms directly connected to the "Cartesian dualism" it wishes to sublate (Humanity/Nature, Culture/Economy, etc.) Such terms are themselves articulated with other keywords: politics, the state, work, etc. Secondly, extending the insights of Johnson and Federici, we should continue the world-ecological project of overcoming the Two Cultures by rethinking the precise relations between abstract social nature and ideology or hegemony—and by understanding how these specific relations change and evolve in successive cycles of capitalism, and over the *longue durée* of the Capitalocene.

Moreover, we must insist on the importance of culture in justifying the theoretical and political superiority of the term Capitalocene. Strictly speaking, the Anthropocene is cultureless: it is the result of "man" and technology, or "man" insofar as he develops and wields technology. Politics proper (as opposed to "governance") does not enter the Anthropocene discourse since social relations are presumed to possess no effective materiality. Yet the history of the word "culture" belies this disavowal, for it contains within itself the violent separation—and insepa-rability—of the spirit from the soil in historical capitalism. Conceived in Williams's terms as "a theory of relations between elements in a whole way of life," culture demonstrates the inadequacy of static notions like "man," "technology," and "environment," whose relation to each other is one of pure externality. "Culture" names the shifting constellations of mutually articulated elements in the social formation and, at the same time, is one of those elements itself. Each constellation constitutes a "way of life," the broadest definition of culture—and one very much akin to Moore's own term *oikeios*, "a co-production of specifically bundled human and extra-human natures" (Moore 2014a, 11). Thus, culture is a crucial element of the Capitalocene, both in Shapiro's broad cyclical sense (ideology, hegemony) and in my own conjunctural one. It is also that the Capitalocene is the only term capable of reasonably accounting for the historical trajectory of the keyword "culture" itself. For the great irony of the Anthropocene discourse is that it was developed to explain the merger of "man" and "nature," yet at the conceptual level has split them further apart than ever.

What *culture*, *world-ecology*, and the *Capitalocene* show is that the battle against the capitalist production of climate change must be waged at several levels simultaneously. Of course, we must attack self-evidently "ecological" phenomena such as new oil pipelines, deforestation, frack-ing, etc. But—and this is crucial—we must also attack those elements of capitalist civilization *which appear to have no immediate relation to ecology, but which are in fact internal conditions of its possibility*: violence against women both literal and symbolic, the structural obscurity of domestic labor, institutional racism, and so on. At its outer limit, ecological strug-gle is nothing but the struggle for universal emancipation: world-ecology unifies these struggles at the level of theory.

Notes
1   An earlier version of this article was published under the title "Against the Anthropocene" in the inaugural issue of *Salvage* magazine (2015). I thank the editors for their kind permission to reproduce parts of it here.

SEVEN

Environment-Making in the Capitalocene
Political Ecology of the State

Christian Parenti

Climate change brings extreme weather, drought, wild fires, flooding, in short, emergencies. Under conditions of modern capitalism, these emergencies, in turn, call forth the state. When the routine functioning of production and consumptive reproduction is paralyzed by some weather event, we see the real relationship between capital and the state. In these moments, capital's profound, even existential, dependence upon the core features of government comes into focus: legal authority, backed by legitimized organized violence; production for use, as in the public sector; and the need for mass, unified collective action and planning. Capital's world of self-interest and private accumulation depends upon non-capitalist values, non-capitalist institutions, and non-capitalist forms of production and reproduction to survive. All this becomes glaringly apparent in a moment of crisis.

In responding to the climate crisis, it appears that the state will have to take on a broadly defined environmental mission. At first glance this might seem like a new task. In fact, *the capitalist state has always been an inherently environmental entity*. Elements of this argument can be found elsewhere (Smith 1987; Cronon 1991; Emel et al. 2011).[1] Just as capital does not *have* a relationship to nature but rather *is* a relationship to nature, so too is that relationship always also a relationship with the state, and mediated through the state. To put it even more directly: the state does not have a relationship with nature, *it is a relationship with nature* because the web of life and its metabolism—including the economy—exist upon the surface of the earth, and because the state is fundamentally a territorial institution.

Thus, I am bringing the state into Moore's conception of capitalism as a world-ecology of capital, power, and nature (2015a). My core argument is this: the state is an inherently environmental entity, and as such, it is at the heart of the value form. The state is at the heart of the value form because the use values of nonhuman nature are, in turn, central sources of value. The modern state delivers these use values to capital. The state is therefore central to our understanding of the valorization process and to our discussion of the Capitalocene.

This argument becomes clear by explicitly connecting a few common ideas that are already implicitly linked. First, accept that the capitalist state by definition must work to reproduce the conditions of accumulation. Second, acknowledge the importance of nonhuman nature's "use values" in the production of exchange values. Third, consider the location of these preexisting natural use values. Where do we find "nature" and its utilities? In the biosphere, which is to say: upon the surface of the earth. Fourth, now consider again the state's obvious but undertheorized "territoriality." The modern state is fundamentally geographic; it *is* territory. Now tie all these together: the preexisting use values of nonhuman nature are essential to capitalist accumulation, and these are found upon the surface of the earth. What institutions ultimately control the surface of the earth? States.

It is the state that delivers nonhuman nature's use values to capital. More specifically, the modern state's territoriality delivers nonhuman nature to capital accumulation by way of its place-based property regimes, its production of infrastructure, and its scientific and intellectual practices that make nonhuman nature legible and thus accessible.

Value and "Nature"

Marx was clear—more than many Marxists—that nonhuman nature provides use values to capital, which through the labor process are converted into exchange values. This is a key point for understanding all of his thinking. In the *Critique of the Gotha Programme* Marx put it this way: "Labor is *not the source* of all wealth. *Nature* is just as much the source of use values (and it is surely of such that material wealth consists!) as labor, which itself is only the manifestation of a force of nature, human labor power" (1970, 1).

In this statement, Marx does two things: First, he puts human beings back inside nature. In particular, he draws our attention to the fact that *labor power* is a natural force that is delivered to production. The capitalist buys the worker's *labor time*. And in the production process the worker delivers a natural force to production, i.e., her *labor power*. Second, he notes that nonhuman nature provides use values to the accumulation process—that is the utility or usefulness of things, like the structural strength of wood, the nourishment of potatoes, the stored solar energy of coal. Through production, which is the application of labor power upon the external world, the use values of nonhuman nature are transformed into exchange value, i.e., money, i.e., capital, which is value in motion.[2]

For an explicit discussion of "external nature" and its contributions to capitalist production, consider Marx's discussion of the "natural forces" of production in the short chapter on "Differential Rent in General" in the third volume of *Capital*. Here he describes the advantages that accrue to a capitalist who owns a waterfall:

> To what circumstances does the manufacture in the present case [owning a waterfall] owe his surplus profit . . . ?
>
> In the first instance, to a natural force, the motive force of water-power which is provided by nature itself and is not itself the product of labor, unlike the coal that transforms water into steam, which has value and must be paid an equivalent, i.e. cost something. It is a natural agent of production, and no labor goes into creating it.
>
> But this is not all. The manufacturer who operates with the steam-engine also applies natural forces which cost him nothing but which make labor more productive, and . . . increase surplus value and hence profit." (Marx 1981, 782)

To put this point somewhat differently, nonhuman nature provides *rents* in the form of use values that exist outside of the labor process, but are captured through it as unearned income. This is clear when thinking about oil and its tremendous power. But are other biophysical use values so different? The nitrogen of guano, the malleability and strength of clay, whale blubber, water's ability to become steam—all could be read as offering rents, use values that are captured in production rather than produced by labor power.

Capital as a process—not to be confused with capitalism as a social system—always has an outside upon which it is dependent. It is as if we were viewing the logic of the enclosures at the molecular level. The seizure of external nature's utilities is actually at the heart of the valorization process. We see this logic of *micro-enclosure* within the labor process.

But the "outside" of capital includes not only places but social relations. Consider how non-capitalist social relations like kinship, linguistic solidarity, and other forms of precapitalist solidarity, are routinely utilized in capitalist production. The teamwork of migrant workers cutting lettuce in the Salinas Valley would be an example (Bardacke, 2012).

For Marx, labor power is similar to the motive force of a waterfall, or the infinite energy of the sun, in that it is a *preexisting force external to capital*. Marx describes labor power as "the aggregate of those mental and physical capabilities existing in the physical form, the living personality, of a human being, capabilities which he sets in motion whenever he produces a use value of any kind" (1977, 271). Capital harnesses (or captures by using) labor power in the labor process. Thus the "use of labor power is labor itself." In both the mobilization of labor power, and the delivery of nonhuman nature's preexisting utilities to production, the valorization process has something of the enclosure to it. We can see an enclosure of energies at the micro scale; the capture of preexisting utilities within the matrix of exchange value.

More broadly, the labor process leads on to questions of metabolism. For Marx:

> Labor is, first of all, the process between man and nature, a process by which man, through his own actions, mediates, regulates and controls the metabolism between himself and nature. He confronts the materials of nature as a force of nature. He sets in motion the natural forces, which belong to his own body, his arms, legs, head and hands, in order to appropriate materials of nature in a form adapted to his own needs. Through this movement he acts upon external nature and changes it, and in this way he simultaneously changes his own nature. He develops the potentialities slumbering within nature, and subjects the play of his forces to his own sovereign power" (1977, 283).

But all of this assumes a certain type of political geography: the territorial power of the state.

Placing the State

If these ubiquitous natural forces and instruments of production are essential to capital's valorization and accumulation, then where are they found? In the biosphere, which is to say: upon the surface of the earth. What ensures their delivery to production? The state, because in the modern world states are the ultimate arbiters of territory. The modern state makes and delivers "nature" through its place-based property regimes, production of infrastructure, and its geographically oriented forms of biopower. The state's manifold scientific, juridical, and economic practices facilitate conjuring, knowing, and managing the utilities of nonhuman nature.

After all, *where* are property rights enforced? In particular places, by particular states. What institution is almost always the final arbiter of where and how infrastructure is developed? The state. Use values are delivered to production by the legal-rational, territorially defined, framework of the law and attendant state practices. And, by the *massive* public investments that are essential to the development of actually existing capitalism.

In other words, behind Marx's waterfall-owning capitalist stands a bailiff—and a hangman ready to enforce property rights. The state is the ultimate "landlord"; it controls nonhuman nature's use values, and delivers these rents to capital.[3] And more often than not, behind the roads and canals stands the scientific knowledge, good credit, and direct investment of public agencies.

Before capital can harness energy, as labor power, or as the preexisting "rents" of nonhuman nature, the state must control terrain, portions of the surface of the earth where these utilities exist. The state must seize parts of the surface of the earth. The state must then measure it, understand it, represent it, contain it, and control it militarily, legally, and scientifically. In other words, for capital to use the biosphere, the state must control it.

We can call this subset of biopower, *geopower* (Tuathail 1997; Luke 1995). For Foucault, biopower is about eliciting and harnessing the power of populations, not repressing and destroying them. Biopower encompasses those "mechanisms through which the basic biological features of the human species became the object of a political strategy, of . . . how, starting from the eighteenth century, modern Western societies took on board the fundamental biological fact that human beings are a species" (Foucault 2007, 1). At one point, Foucault is prepared to go still further, introducing—but not elaborating—the relation of the state and nonhuman nature. Reflecting upon town planning, he writes that the state "deals with . . . the perpetual conjuncture, the perpetual interaction of a geographical, climatic, and physical milieu with the human species in so far as it has a body and a soul, a physical and a moral existence; and the sovereign will ... have to exercise power at that point of connection where nature, in the sense of physical elements, interferes with nature in the sense of the nature of the human species, at that point of articulation where the milieu becomes the determining factor of nature" (2007, 23).

If biopower is about harnessing, channeling, enhancing, and deploying the powers of bodies at the scale of territorially defined populations, then *geopower* is similarly the statecraft and technologies of power that make territory and the biosphere accessible, legible, knowable, and utilizable. This latter is Moore's "abstract social nature" (2015)—the results of geopower's remaking of territory. Here I lean into geopower's materialist possibilities. I am less concerned with the "writing" of the landscape and more concerned with geopower's actual technologies and practices of measurement, regulation, and resource management. This is the historical geography of roads, canals, railroads, telegraphs, property rights, and policed borders. Geopower technologies include exploring, surveying, militarily policing, cadastral mapmaking, and all the applied physical and geosciences, like botany and geology (Linklater 2002, 2007).[4]

It is in large part this geopower matrix of state-centric, earth-focused techno-rational practices that opened nonhuman nature to effective capitalist exploitation. Consider the U.S. Geological Survey, established in 1879 as a scientific arm of the federal government. Its charge was the "classification of the public lands, and examination of the geological structure, mineral resources, and products of the national domain" (1879, 394)—in other words, to identify the potential sources of nature's wealth for the whole of American continental space.

The State as Geography

How does the state deliver nonhuman nature and its utilities to production? The state does this abstractly with territorially based property laws. And it does it concretely—physically, geographically—in conquering territory and building infrastructure. Biophysical use values—the strength of wood, nourishment of potatoes—must travel through physical space, regardless of property law. Nonhuman nature's utilities are quite literally *channeled* into production through infrastructure, the built environment of communications and transportation networks: canals, railroads, highways, pipelines, ports, and airports. These geographically fixed public goods (even when they are privately operated, like oil pipelines) are highly dependent on state power and public financing.

These insights about the state and geography are deceptively obvious. The state *is* territory. Marxist traditions of state theorizing are well aware of this. Bob Jessop recently reminds us, "Statehood rests on the territorialization of political power: its three key features are state territory, a state apparatus, and a state population" (2013, 22). But the link between territory and value is not much developed. An environmentally minded Marxist political economy has not quite linked up with Marxist state theory (e.g., Miliband 1969, 1970; Poulantzas 1969; Aglietta 1979; Brenner et al. 2003). Needed is a theory that connects the role of nonhuman nature's use values to accumulation and the territoriality of the state. Neither do Hardt and Negri (2001), whose conception of sovereignty is all politics and no place. Here is an unrealistically dematerialized view of capital. Sounding all the familiar themes of mainstream globalization theory they write: "The informalization of production and the increasing importance of immaterial production have tended to free capital from the constraints of territory and bargaining. Capital can withdraw from negotiation with a given local population by moving its site to another point in the global network—or merely by using the potential to move as a weapon in negotiations" (Hardt and Negri 2001, 297). But all points in "the global network" are not created equal—not least because specific states create specific infrastructures and other capacities to channel the work of nature into the circuit of capital.

When the state and geography do meet in these discussions, the focus is on how "geographical scale" modifies and articulates the state's political functions. The biophysical significance of the state's geography rarely enters the discussion as *the place of nature's use values*. Environmentally minded theories of value, on the other hand, do much better at thinking geography as part of the actual means of production (Burkett 1999; Moore 2015a). But here the problem of state theory is inverted—value is highlighted, but the state drops away.

Classical Social Theory and the State

Let us now review some classic definitions of the state. For Engels the state arises through an "admission that . . . society has become entangled in an insoluble contradiction with itself, that it has split into irreconcilable antagonisms which it is powerless to dispel. But in order that these antagonisms, classes with conflicting economic interests, might not consume themselves and society in fruitless struggle, it became necessary to have a power seemingly standing above society that would alleviate the conflict and keep it within the bounds of 'order'; and this power, arisen out of society but placing itself above it, and alienating itself more and more from it, is the state" (1973, 204–334, 157). This is the state as the product and arbiter of class struggle. Lenin, reading Engels, summarizes: "The state is a product and manifestation of the *irreconcilability* of class contradictions. The state arises where, when and to the extent that class contradictions objectively *cannot* be reconciled" (1976, 5).

Flowing directly from this we have Weber's classic and more mainstream definition of the modern state, which he arrived at while trying to define "politics" amidst the violent class struggle of the German Revolution. He delivered his lecture "Politics as Vocation" in Munich on January 19, 1919. Less than three months later, Munich and all of Bavaria would see revolution and the short-lived creation of the Bavarian Soviet Republic. Then, just as Weber warned, "a polar night of icy darkness and hardness" arrived and the revolution was violently crushed. In this lecture, Weber was very much in conversation not just with Marx but with "actually existing" Leninism. At points, he even sounds like he is paraphrasing Lenin's *State and Revolution.*

"Ultimately, one can define the modern state sociologically," says Weber, "only in terms of the specific *means* peculiar to it . . . namely, the use of physical force." From there he concurs with Trotsky's assertion that "Every state is founded on force," noting that "force is a means specific to the state." Weber then arrives at the famous formulation: "We have to say that a state is a human community that (successfully) claims the *monopoly of the legitimate use of physical force* within a given territory. Note that 'territory' is one of the characteristics of the state" (1978, 54).

That last line is key. I would go further still. Territory is one of the central characteristics of the state and therefore so too is the state's role in managing the web of life and that portion of its metabolism that we know as modern production. Like Marx, Weber is only recently emerging as a fully ecological thinker (Foster and Holleman 2012).

What then are the economic and environmental implications of the "monopoly on the legitimate use of violence *within* a given territory"? John Simmons, a legal theorist at the University of Virginia, has begun to address this question. For Simmons, sovereignty implies: "(1) rights to jurisdictional authority (to make laws across the geographical domain), (2) a right to control, extract and tax resources within the territory, and (3) a right to control entry and exit of goods and people" (2001). This package of state powers can be read as the regulation of both human and nonhuman nature: bodies, labor power, and the use values of "natural" resources, all the crucial components of value. Again we see that it is precisely *the territoriality of the state* that gives it its *inherently environmental characteristics*. And this makes the state central to what Moore (2015a) calls capitalism's "world-ecological" project of accumulation. Similarly, it means the state is central to any realistic effort at climate mitigation and adaptation.

As we have seen, for Marx space and nature can become forces of production under capitalism:

> The more production comes to rest on exchange value, hence on exchange, the more important do the physical conditions of exchange—the means of communication and transport—become for the costs of circulation. Capital by its nature drives beyond every spatial barrier. Thus the creation of the physical conditions of exchange—of the means of communication and transport—the annihilation of space by time—becomes an extraordinary necessity for it. Only in so far as the direct product can be realized in distant markets in mass quantities . . . is the production of cheap means of communication and transport a condition for production based on capital, and promoted by it *for that reason.* (1973, 524)

Marx's discussion of water power versus steam power as a source of extra surplus suggests how "space acts as a force of production" (Swyngedouw 1992, 417–33). This alerts us to the importance of political (which is to say, the violent and administrative) control over place as the precondition for capital's appropriation of the "productive powers" and use values of nonhuman nature. Thus, returning to Marx's discussion of water and steam power, we find that:

> The increased productivity of the labor he applies arises neither from the capital and labor themselves. . . . What is used is rather a monopolizeable natural force which, like the waterfall, is available only to those who have at their disposal particular pieces of the earth's surface and their appurtenances. It is in no way just up to the capital to call into being this natural condition of greater labor productivity, in the way that any capital can transform water into steam. The condition is to be found in nature only at certain places, and where it is not found it cannot be produced by a particular

capital outlay.... Possession of this natural force forms a monopoly in the hands of its owner, the condition of higher productivity for the capital invested, which cannot be produced by capitals unproductive processes; *the natural force that can be monopolized in this way is always chained to the earth.* (1977, 784, emphasis added)

Just as the waterfall is "chained to the earth," so too are other natural use values (fish and game being partial, though not total, exceptions).[5] Trees, like waterfalls, confer utility and value, while growing they too are bound in place, though they can be cut down and carted away. Marx's waterfall is only a dramatic illustration of a more common set of relationships.

To those who control territory flow the utilities of specific spaces. But the small private monopolies over space and nature that are private property depend upon a larger system of political control over space. Thus capitalism is an inherently political-geographic project with the state as its central mechanism. At the heart of capital's process is nature, and that dynamic interplay between violence and space which is the state process. Capitalism emerged through state and imperial power—and continues to depend upon it (Moore 2002).[6] The state appropriates nature for capital *directly* by force; during conquest, enclosure, and the creation of functional property rights; and *indirectly* by its development of landscape and its infrastructure.

Primitive Accumulation and State in the Early Republic

To better understand the capitalist state's imbrication with land and non-human nature, let us look at the capitalist state's historical origins. The history of the early United States offers a clear example of state formation through environment-making. The American Revolution was a struggle over: (1) who controlled extra-human nature; (2) which institutions would control access to it; and (3) how would it be digested, metabolized and transformed. In October 1780—a year before the Articles of Confederation were ratified—the Continental Congress had already adopted a general policy for administering any lands transferred to the federal government. During the 1780s, the national government slowly but steadily collected western lands from the states (Linklater 2002, 2007). The Northwest Ordinance of 1784 was the first step. Virginia agreed to cede its huge and much-contested claims. This was followed by the more complete Northwest Ordinance of 1787, in which New York, Massachusetts, and Connecticut ceded their claims. That same year, the new constitution addressed the issue with a mere twenty-six words in Article IV, Section 3: "The Congress shall have Power to dispose of and make all needful Rules and Regulations respecting the Territory or other Property belonging to the United States." Georgia was the last to cede trans-Appalachian land in 1802.

The federal government's promise to pay off state debts incurred during the war facilitated this massive land transfer. Yet, in a stroke of brilliant geographic alchemy it was the land transfers themselves that created the *federal* territory against which the national government could borrow to pay down the states' debts. Here the vision of Alexander Hamilton, the country's first secretary of the treasury, moves to center stage. Hamilton's vision for strong federal government was not just a political arrangement; it became strong when it acquired territory, which in turn could fund the American state. In 1790, three new bond issues backed by the federal government replaced the miscellany of various state and federal bonds that had structured the new nation's debt. Early the following year, Congress chartered the Bank of the United States for twenty years.

Hamilton understood geopower. As the country's first treasury secretary, Hamilton faced the monumental task of creating a national economy out of thirteen largely independent and stagnant subunits. Fearing social collapse, civil war, and even reconquest by Britain, Hamilton presented a plan for economic survival in his "Report on Manufactures," presented to Congress in 1791. The report advocated a robustly interventionist role for federal government using tariffs on imported manufactured goods, but easy importation of necessary raw materials; international recruitment of skilled labor; government support for "new inventions and discoveries at home" and for the acquisition of foreign technology; government investment in infrastructure, or "internal improvements"; a partially government-owned national bank and national credit system with federal debt as its bedrock; and subsidies and support for innovation including legal protection for intellectual property rights for inventors.

Hamilton's report incorporated a practical grasp of geopower, and through it, environment-making. The report quotes Adam Smith with approval: "Good roads, canals, and navigable rivers, by diminishing the expence of carriage, put the remote parts of a country more nearly upon a level with those in the neighborhood of the town. They are upon that account the *greatest of all improvements*. . . . Though they introduce some rival commodities into the old market, they open many new markets to its produce" (Hamilton 1791 quoting Smith [1776] 1937; Parenti 2014a, 2014b, 2015). Here, Hamilton as an agent of state power was operationalizing capital's "extraordinary necessity" to "drive beyond every spatial barrier," its quest for "the annihilation of space by time" (Marx 1973). We see in Hamilton's thought that capital does not actually annihilate all by itself, but rather does so in symbiosis with the state. Hamilton's plans to use federal lands and build an integrated national market were instrumental to his larger project of a manufacturing-based form of economic development. Though deeply concerned with creating finance and manufacturing sectors, Hamilton never lost sight of what we could call (pace Marx) the "substratum" of preexisting use values, lying within nonhuman nature. "It is manifest that our immense tracts of land occupied and unoccupied are capable of giving employment to more capital than is actually bestowed upon them" (Hamilton 1791).

In the decades after Hamilton, the struggle between the forces of pro-industrial modernization and the forces of agrarian underdevelopment continued. By the 1820s, the Hamiltonian package of development policies became known as "the American System" and Henry Clay of Kentucky was its tribune. Clay added to the developmentalist policy menu the controlled release of federal lands in a fashion that set minimum prices. Ultimately, the American System was only partially realized. Its grander vision fell victim to steadfast opposition by Southern proponents of states' rights and laissez-faire. Largely defeated at the national level, much of the Hamiltonian vision was operationalized by the states. New York State's construction of the Erie Canal is perhaps the best example, but there were many such projects during the canal building mania of the 1820s and 1830s.

The story of the Erie Canal illustrates well the role of the state in developing and reproducing the metabolic arrangements that are capitalism. Put differently, the canal shows us how states make ecologies. It reveals the connection between nonhuman nature's use values, geo-power, and the expanded reproduction of capital. Famously, the canal connected Atlantic trade circuits, via New York City to the Great Lakes, the Mississippi River, and thus the whole interior West and South. New York City became the pivot point of a huge international network of financial and biological flows and as such became the capital of American finance, and thus later world finance. But the rise of New York City was merely the urban manifestation of a primarily rural process: the radical ecological transformation of a huge swath of interior territory; a transformation that involved the displacement of the Iroquois' "regime of nature" with a nascent capitalist one. Great swaths of previously Iroquois-controlled land were opened to white settlers and their environmental practices. In this sense the Erie Canal was a revolutionary moment, massive rupture, a great leap forward, in American capitalism's production of nature.

At the physical and financial heart of this de facto national project was a massive gift of public land, and with it public water. By one count no less than 4.5 million acres of federal land were given to canal companies (Rae 1944, 167). This land provided the territory and water for canals, as well as land to be developed next to them. The land grants also functioned as collateral against which to finance the canals. There was something else about the canals that made them state-centric—the unwieldy properties of water.

Dewitt Clinton's "Hydraulic State"

Few forces call forth the state so consistently as water. The peculiar link between water management and state power was not lost on canal-loving eighteenth-century European observers. Water management demands collective action. And only when the general cause of canals was taken up by the public sector—the state—did the dream of an American network of canals come to fruition.

As early as 1777 Gouverneur Morris "predicted the eventual union of the waters of the Great Lakes with those of the Hudson" (Bulletin 1932, 6). He said this even as most of what is now upstate New York was still controlled by the Iroquois who sided with the British during the American Revolution. After the Revolution, about two-thirds of the Iroquois decamped to land grants in British Canada. Conflicting land claims between New York and Massachusetts were resolved in the mid-1780s, and huge tracts of land were given to land speculators, who in turn tried to encourage settlement. But they had limited success. In 1792, the New York State Legislature chartered (the mostly privately funded) Western Inland Company and passed an "Act for establishing and opening lock navigation within the state (ibid.). Like many other private experiments with canal building the Western Inland Company failed spectacularly, one of its principles was even jailed. Jefferson denied New York State's requests for federal money, calling "talk of making a canal of 350 miles through the wilderness . . . little short of madness" (Hosack 1829, 347).

European accounts of Chinese canals played an important role in exciting the imagination of American canal proponents (Hanyan 1961).

Much of what canal proponents learned from reading about China's thousand-mile-long Grand Canal, linking Beijing in the north to the southeastern coast at Hangzhou, was technical. But just as important were the political insights about the essential role of government in producing and maintaining this amazing waterway. British diplomat Sir George Staunton, who wrote one of the most widely read investigations of China's Grand Canal, took pains to note the role of state planning and investment. "This canal," wrote Staunton in the 1790s,

> is not nor indeed is any in China, a private concern, carried on at the expense and for the profit of individuals but is under the regulation and immediate inspection of the government, whose policy it is to maintain an easy communication between the several parts of the empire, as tending to promote the commerce and agriculture of the country, thereby increasing the revenues of the state and the comforts of the people. (Hanyan 1961, 562)

In 1817, New York State finally allocated money to start building its canal. As president, Jefferson rebuffed New York's would-be canal builders when they came looking for federal money, but his treasury secretary, Albert Gallatin, did commit plenty of adjacent federal land to the canal, informing Congress as he did that a successful canal would greatly enhance the value of those lands (Koeppel 2009, 93). In all, the canal would cost $6 million; its primary contractor was a not-for-profit public entity, the Canal Commission, which in turn doled out work to local for-profit contractors—a methodology that set the template for public contracting thereafter.

These state-centric political lessons from China were as important as—or more important than—any technological vision:

> During the next decade many states made efforts in this direction, building canals in profusion. These projects were carried out under government control, following the pattern set by New York State's well-known Canal Commission and Canal Fund. Drawing more heavily from legislative allotments, rather than private shareholders and controlled more by state commissions than corporate directors, these new waterways indicated that the day of the [private] canal company was passing. If not providing new methods of building, then, the oriental example played a part in this change. . . . To a

New York provided only with the inadequate works of the Western Company, China gave the vision of a government-built Grand Canal. (Hanyan 1961, 566)

Completed in 1825, the economic, and therefore ecological, effect of the Erie Canal was massive. The cost of moving a ton of freight dropped 95 percent. This is the state making a regime of nature unintentionally—but very directly and forcefully, sharply accelerating agrarian change. New England farming began its long contraction with the canal's completion (Hedrick 1933, 243–44). It was "the first step in the transportation revolution that would turn an aggregate of local economies [and ecologies] into a nationwide market economy" (Howe 2007, 118). Before long, the Erie Canal was carrying twice as much cargo as flowed down the Mississippi to New Orleans. This state-led transportation revolution was also an environmental revolution. The famous canal-triggered growth of New York City (an environmental event in itself) was only one side of a broader spatial, environment-making transformation—the other was the radical capitalist transformation of Midwestern agriculture, especially after 1840. Away went one "regime of nature," in came another.

The pre-Canal landscape of the Iroquois was no pristine nature. It had hinged on massive anthropogenic burning. Regularly setting fire to the landscape created what we now call "edge habitat" which is preferred by deer and other game. Burning also facilitated food gathering, berries for example still need burning; and of course burning returned nutrients to the soil thus aiding cultivation of corn, squash, and beans. Adriaen van der Donck, a Dutch chronicler of life in New Amsterdam writing in the 1640s and 1650s, described the role of fire: "The Indians are in the habit—and we Christians have also adopted it—once a year in the fall to burn the woods, plains, and those marshlands that are not too wet as soon as the leaves have dropped and the herbage has withered. Portions that were missed, as may happen, get their turn later in the months of March and April. This is known among our people as well as the Indians there as bush burning" (2008, 21).

After the American Revolution, a majority of the Iroquois withdrew to land grants in Canada. Some white settlers moved in and cleared land for subsistence farming. But it was the government-built canal that really opened the interior west to white settlement and capitalist agriculture, shaped its economy and ecology, its social nature, and tied these regional metabolisms to broader markets. Gone was selective burning. In came forest clearing and the monocropping of wheat and other grains. Isolated subsistence farmers now became wheat exporters, and in the process developed new types of "nature." Monocropping would soon invite fungal disease and pests like the midge and Hessian fly. In the face of these eco-logical transformations, Hudson Valley farmers had to put "all available land under cultivation, some of it inferior land that had been previously depleted" (Wermuth 1998, 188).

Ultimately, Hudson Valley agriculture converted from wheat to dairy production—under pressure from disease and cheaper grain flowing from the Midwest, and responding to New York City's growing demand. At the same time, Hudson Valley farmers intensified household-based manufacturing of barrels and coarse cloth, drawing in and transforming resources from further afield. All these were ecological transformations driven, directly and indirectly, by the government-built canal. Canals more generally, as a development of the means of production, facilitated the extension and intensification of agriculture, which is to say, greatly facilitated the capitalist production of nature. Much of the Erie Canal's freight, therefore, can be seen as not merely carried by the new waterway, but as conjured and created by geopower:

> Wheat flour from the Midwest was stored in New York alongside the cotton that the city obtained from the South through its domination of the coastal trade; both could then be exported across the Atlantic. New York merchants began to buy wheat and cotton from their pro-ducers before shipping them to the New York warehouses. Soon the merchants learned to buy the crops before they were even grown; that is they could advance the grower money on the security of his harvest. Thus the city's power in commercial markets fostered its development as a financial center. (Howe 2007, 119–20)

As such, New York was merely one spatial expression of an emerging "regime of nature" that had as a central mechanism the geopower of the state, which built the canal and helped create the agricultural economy of the Midwest.

Conclusion

The unacknowledged centrality of the state to the functioning of capital-ism is especially relevant today, with a devastating climate crisis already upon us in the form of desertification, powerful storms, ocean acidification, melting glaciers, incrementally rising sea levels, and mass migrations. The crisis requires immediate action on a truly massive scale.

I have laid out an analysis of the state rooted in a political ecological reading of value. As a central catalyst of social nature, the capitalist state does not *have* a relationship to "nature"—it *is* a relationship with nature. The state is not merely "part" of the Capitalocene but central to it. Why? Because the *geopower* of the capitalist state makes it possible for capital to treat the surface of the earth as a warehouse of Cheap Nature.

As we have seen, the history of capitalist development is almost always the history of state-guided development. To reform capitalism—and to move beyond it—the Left needs to place the state front and center in its strategic considerations. Appeals to corporate social responsibility, attempts to shame capital into reform, strategies that declare politics "broken" and seek to circumvent the state, or escapist hyperlocalism—all hallmarks of American environmentalism—are fundamentally unrealistic.

This argument has political implications. First, the state cannot be avoided, as scholars like Holloway suggest (2002). For Left politics to become effective, especially in the face of the climate crisis, they must come up with strategies that engage and attempt to transform the state. The idea of escaping the state is to misrecognize the centrality and immutably fundamental nature of the state to the value form and thus to capitalist society (Mazzucato 2013).

The chairman of the Export-Import Bank of the United States (the export credit agency of the federal government) tried to explain the centrality of the state to reporters after a business trip to the Czech Republic: "It's time to drop the fantasy that a purely free market exists in the world of global trade.... In the real world our private enterprises are pitted against an array of competitors that are often government-owned, government-protected, government-subsidized, government-sponsored or all of the above" (*Economist* 2013).

In other words, the legal frameworks of property are territorially fixed and states remain the crucial political units of global capitalism. Managing, mediating, producing, and delivering nonhuman nature to accumulation is a core function of the modern, territorially defined, capitalist state. When we speak of capital having a metabolism, we must think of the state as an indispensable mediating membrane in that process. In that regard, the climate crisis does not require a new role for the state, but merely a different and better version of the environment-making that it already does. For that to happen, critical scholars need a renewed theoretical engagement with the state. I have suggested that we begin by considering the state as the central environmental actor within the larger world historical drama of capitalism. The state remains at the center of modern political struggle. More specifically, the state's seemingly new role as an economically crucial, environmental agent, which can appear to be merely a political by-product of climate change and the broader ecological crisis, is actually not new at all. Climate change brings disasters and emergencies that call forth the state. How the state responds is a different question: sometimes it fails, but always it is called.

Notes

1   Very few scholars have approached the state in this fashion. For all its flaws, Wittfogel's theory of the hydraulic state is one example (1957). The elements of such a theory of the state as environment-making entity are readily available in Cronon's masterful *Nature's Metropolis* (1991) — without however making the connections explicit.

2   At another level this indicates that capital, or the production and accumulation of value, always needs an outside to take from and deposit back into. Its takes up utilities and deposits back externalities.

3   When I made this point in my 2013 Antipode Lecture, Matt Huber brought to my attention that he had made a similar point in an earlier article (see Emel et al. 2011).

4   It is no coincidence that surveying was one of the first skills learned by prominent young men like George Washington. From these adventures in geo-measurement they got rich by first plotting and mapping then buying up choice pieces of Western lands. The knowledge of surveying in mapmaking was crucial to all colonial land companies. Frequently all they needed to assert their claim was the map, no "improvement" of the land like selling trees was necessary. As a young George Washington explained: "The greatest Estates we have in this Colony" were made "by taking up and purchasing at very low rates the rich back Lands which were thought nothing of in those days, but are now the most valuable lands we possess" (quoted in Cleland 1955, 237).

5   I say partial exceptions because even schools of fish that migrate hundreds or thousands of miles nonetheless have ecological ranges and thus specific territories, portions of which can fall under state control.

6   "Medieval Europe was driven by profound socio-ecological contradictions. Feudalism's environmental degradation pivoted on the lord-peasant relationship, which limited the possibilities for reinvestment in the land. Consequently, feudalism exhausted the soil and the labor power from which it derived revenues, rendering the population vulnerable to disease. The Black Death

decisively altered labor-land ratios in favor of Western Europe's peasantry. This new balance of class forces eliminated the possibility of feudal restoration and led the states, landlords, and merchants to favor geographical expansion—an external rather than internal spatial fix to feudal crisis. This external fix, beginning in the Atlantic world, had capitalist commodity production and exchange in scribed within it. Capitalism differed radically from feudalism in that where earlier ecological crises had been local, capitalism globalized them" (Moore 2002).

References

Aglietta, Michel. 1979. *A Theory of Capitalist Regulation*. London: Verso.

Agricola, Georgius. (1556) 1950. *De Re Metallica*. Translated by Herbert and Lou Hoover. New York: Dover.

Akrich, M., and M. Berg, eds. 2004. *Bodies on Trial*. Special issue of *Body and Society* 10 (2–3): 111–34.

Allen, Robert C. 2011. *Global Economic History*. Oxford: Oxford Univ. Press.

Altvater, Elmar. 2006. "The Social and Natural Environment of Fossil Capitalism." In *Socialist Register 2007: Coming to Terms with Nature*, edited by Leo Panitch and Colin Leys. London: Merlin Press.

———. 2015. *Engels neu entdecken. Das hellblaue Bändchen zur Einführung in die "Dialektik der Natur" und die Kritik von Akkumulation und Wachstum*. Hamburg: VSA.

Alvarez, Luis W., et al. 1980. "Extraterrestrial Cause for the Cretaceous-Tertiary Extinction." *Science*, no. 208: 1095–108.

Amin, Samir. 2009. "Capitalism and the Ecological Footprint." *Monthly Review* 61 (6): 19–30.

Angus, Ian. 2015. "When Did the Anthropocene Begin . . . and Why Does It Matter?" *Monthly Review* 67 (4): 1–11.

Arendt, Hannah. 1964. *Eichmann in Jerusalem*. New York: Penguin.

———. 1977. *Between Past and Future*. New York: Penguin.

Arens, Nan Crystal, and Ian D. West. 2008. "Press-Pulse: A General Theory of Mass Extinction?" *Paleobiology* 34 (4): 456–71.

Arnold, David. 1996. *The Problem of Nature*. Oxford: Blackwell Press.

Arrighi, Giovanni. 1994. *The Long Twentieth Century*. London: Verso.

Ax, Christina Folke, Niels Brimnes, Niklas Thode Jensen, and Karen Oslund, eds. 2011. *Cultivating the Colonies*. Athens: Ohio Univ. Press.

Ayres, Robert U. 1965. *Environmental Effects of Nuclear Weapons*. H1-518-RR: Contract No. OCD-OS-62-218, Department of Defense, Office of Civil Defense, OCD Task Number 3511A. Harmon-on-Hudson, NY: Hudson Institute.

Bairoch, Paul. 1973. "Agriculture and the Industrial Revolution, 1700–1914." In *The Fontana Economic History of Europe*, edited by Carlo M. Cipolla, 452–506. London: Fontana.

Bakewell, P.J. 1987. "Mining." In *Colonial Spanish America*, edited by Leslie Bethell, 203–49. Cambridge: Cambridge Univ. Press.

Balter, Michael. 2013. "Archaeologists Say the 'Anthropocene' Is Here—But It Began Long Ago." *Science*, no. 340: 261–62.

Barad, Karen. 2007. *Meeting the Universe Halfway*. Durham: Duke Univ. Press.

Barash, David. 2012. "Only Connect." *Aeon*. Accessed May 10, 2015. http://aeon.co/magazine/world-views/david-barash-buddhist-ecology/.

Barca, Stefania. 2010. "Energy, Property, and the Industrial Revolution Narrative." *Ecological Economics* 70 (7): 1309–15.

Bardacke, Frank. 2012. *Trampling Out the Vintage*. London: Verso.

Bardi, Ugo. 2013. *Der geplünderte Planet*. Munich: Oekom-Verlag.

Barnes, Trevor J., and Matthew Farish. 2006. "Between Regions: Science, Militarism, and American Geography from World War to Cold War." *Annals of the Association of American Geographers* 96 (4): 807–26.

Barnosky, Anthony D., et al. 2011. "Has the Earth's Sixth Mass Extinction Already Arrived?" *Nature*, no. 471: 51–57.

Barnosky, Anthony D., Elizabeth A. Hadly, Jordi Bascompte, Eric L. Berlow, James H. Brown, Mikael Fortelius, Wayne M. Getz, et al. 2012. "Approaching a State Shift in Earth's Biosphere." *Nature*, no. 486: 52–58.

Barry, John. 2007. *Environment and Social Theory*. 2nd ed. New York: Routledge.

Bashford, Alison. 2004. *Imperial Hygiene*. New York: Palgrave.

van Bavel, Bas. 2001. "Land, Lease and Agriculture: The Transition of the Rural Economy in the Dutch River Area from the Fourteenth to the Sixteenth Century." *Past & Present*, no. 172: 3–43.

———. 2010. "The Medieval Origins of Capitalism in the Netherlands." *BMGN-Low Countries Historical Review* 125 (2–3): 45–79.

Beard, Charles. 1901. *The Industrial Revolution*. London: George Allen & Unwin.

Beck, Ulrich. 1992. *Risk Society*. New York: Sage.

Beinart, William, and Karen Middleton. 2004. "Plant Transfers in Historical Perspective." *Environment and History*, no. 10: 3–29.

Benjamin, Walter. 2006. "On the Concept of History," in *Selected Writings*, vol. 4. Cambridge, MA: Harvard Univ. Press.

Benton, Lauren. 2010. *A Search for Sovereignty*. Cambridge Univ. Press.

Berry, Thomas. 1999. *The Great Work: Our Way into the Future*. New York: Bell Tower.

———. 2008. "The Ecozoic Era." In *Environment: An Interdisciplinary Anthology*, edited by Glenn Adelson, James Engell, Brent Ranalli, and K.P. Van Anglen, 356–61. New Haven: Yale Univ. Press.

Bieleman, Jan. 2010. *Five Centuries of Farming: A Short History of Dutch Agriculture, 1500–2000*. Wageningen: Wageningen Academic Publishers.

Biggs, David. 2010. *Quagmire: Nation-Building and Nature in the Mekong Delta*. Seattle: Univ. of Washington Press.

Biggs, Michael. 1999. "Putting the State on the Map." *Comparative Studies in Society and History* 41 (2): 374–405.

Blackburn, Robin. 1998. *The Making of New World Slavery*. London: Verso.

Blanchard, Ian. 1995. *International Lead Production and Trade in the 'Age of the Saigerprozess': 1460–1560*. Wiesbaden: Franz Steiner Verlag.

Blickle, Peter. 1981. *The Revolution of 1525*. Baltimore: Johns Hopkins Univ. Press.

Blum, Jerome. 1957. "Rise of Serfdom in Eastern Europe." *American Historical Review* 62 (4): 807–36.

van Bochove, Christiaan Jan. 2008. *The Economic Consequences of the Dutch: Economic Integration around the North Sea, 1500–1800*. Amsterdam: Amsterdam Univ. Press.

Bolthouse, Jay. 2014. "Rethinking Capital's Relations to Nature: From the Production of Nature Thesis to World-Ecological Synthesis." *Japanese Journal of Human Geography* 66 (6): 580–94.

Bond, Patrick. 2012. *Politics of Climate Justice*. Durban, South Africa: Univ. of Kwazulu-Natal Press.

Boomgaard, Peter. 1992a. "Forest Management and Exploitation in Colonial Java, 1677–1897." *Forest & Conservation History* 36 (1): 4–14.

———. 1992b. "The Tropical Rain Forests of Suriname." *NWIG: New West Indian Guide / Nieuwe West-Indische Gids* 66 (3/4): 207–35.

Boserup, Ester. 1965. *The Conditions of Agricultural Growth*. London: Allen & Unwin.

Boulding, Kenneth. 1966. "The Economics of the Coming Spaceship Earth." In *Environmental Quality in a Growing Economy*, edited by Henry Jarrett, 3–14. Baltimore: Johns Hopkins Univ. Press.

Boxer, Charles R. 1965. *The Dutch Seaborne Empire, 1600–1800*. London: Hutchinson.

———. 1969. *The Portuguese Seaborne Empire 1415–1825*. New York: Alfred A. Knopf.

Braudel, Fernand. 1953. "Qu'est-ce que le XVIe siècle?" *Annales E.S.C.* 8 (1): 69–73.

———. 1961. "European Expansion and Capitalism, 1450–1650." In *Chapters in Western Civilization*, edited by Contemporary Civilization Staff of Columbia College, 245–88. New York: Columbia Univ. Press.

———. 1983. *The Perspective of the World*. Translated by Siân Reynolds. New York: Harper & Rowe.

———. 2009. "History and the Social Sciences: The *Longue Durée*." *Review* 32 (3): 171–203.

Brenner, Neil, Bob Jessop, Martin Jones, and Gordon Macleon, eds. 2003. *State/Space: A Reader*. Oxford: Blackwell.

Brenner, Robert. 1976. "Agrarian Class Structure and Economic Development in Pre-Industrial Europe." *Past & Present*, no. 70: 30–75.

———. 2001. "The Low Countries in the Transition to Capitalism." *Journal of Agrarian Change* 1 (2): 169–241.

Brinley, Thomas. 1993. *The Industrial Revolution and the Atlantic Economy*. New York: Routledge.

Broadberry, Stephen, Bruce Campbell, Alexander Klein, Mark Overton, Bas van Leeuwen. 2011. "British Economic Growth, 1270–1870." unpublished paper, Department of Economic History, London School of Economics. Accessed August 8, 2014. http://www.unileipzig.de/~eniugh/congress/fileadmin/eniugh2011/dokumente/ComparingLivingStandards_BroadberryCampbellKleinOvertonvan Leeuwen_2011_04_16.pdf.

Burke, Edmund. (1795) 1958. *A Philosophical Inquiry into the Origin of our Ideas of the Sublime and Beautiful*. Indiana: Univ. of Notre Dame Press.

Burkett, Paul. 1999. *Marx and Nature*. New York: St. Martin's.

Busby, Kimberly Sue. 2007. "The Temple Terracottas of Etruscan Orvieto." PhD diss., Univ. of Illinois.

Büscher, Bram, and Robert Fletcher. 2015. "Accumulation by Conservation." *New Political Economy* 20 (2): 273–329.

Bush, Vannevar. 1945. *Science: The Endless Frontier*. Washington, DC: U.S. Government Printing Office.

Cafaro, Philip, and Eileen Crist, eds. 2012. *Life on the Brink*. Athens: Univ. of Georgia Press.

Calarco, Matthew. 2012. "Identity, Difference, Indistinction." *The New Centennial Review*, no. 11: 41–60.

Camba, Alvin A. 2015. "From Colonialism to Neoliberalism: Critical Reflections on Philippine Mining in the 'Long Twentieth Century.'" *Extractive Industries and Society* 2 (2): 287–301.

Campbell, Chris, and Michael Niblett, eds. 2016. *The Caribbean: Aesthetics, World-Ecology, Politics*. Liverpool: Liverpool Univ. Press.

Caro, Tim, Jack Darwin, Tavis Forrester, Cynthia Ledoux-Bloom, and Caitlin Wells. 2011. "Conservation in the Anthropocene." *Conservation Biology* 26 (1): 185–88.

Carr, E.H. 1962. *What Is History?* New York: Penguin.

Carson, Rachel. 1962. *Silent Spring*. New York: Signet.

Certini, Giacomo, and Riccardo Scalenghe. 2011. "Anthropogenic Soils Are the Golden Spikes for the Anthropocene." *The Holocene* 21 (8): 1269–74.

Chakrabarty, Dipesh. 2009. "The Climate of History: Four Theses." *Critical Inquiry*, no. 35: 197–222.

Charna, Suzy McKee. 1974. *Walk to the End of the World*. New York: Ballantine.

Cicero. 1933. *Cicero in Twenty-Eight Volumes*. Translated by H. Rackham. Cambridge, MA: Harvard Univ. Press.

Cipolla, Carlo M. 1976. *Before the Industrial Revolution: European Society 1000–1700*. New York: W.W. Norton.

Cleland, Hugh. 1955. *George Washington in the Ohio Valley*. Pittsburgh: Univ. of Pittsburgh Press.

Clifford, James. 1997. *Routes: Travel and Translation in the Late Twentieth Century*. Cambridge, MA: Harvard Univ. Press.

———. 2013. *Returns: Becoming Indigenous in the Twenty-First Century*. Cambridge, MA: Harvard Univ. Press.

Coase, Ronald H. 1960. "The Problem of Social Cost." *Journal of Law and Economics*, no. 3: 1–44.

Corcoran, Patricia, Charles J. Moore, and Kelly Jazvac. 2014. "An Anthropogenic Marker Horizon in the Future Rock Record." *GSA Today* 24 (6): 4–8.

Costanza, Robert, Lisa J. Graumlich, and Will Steffen, eds. 2007. *Sustainability or Collapse?* Cambridge, MA: MIT Press.

Cox, Christopher R. 2015. "Faulty Presuppositions and False Dichotomies: The Problematic Nature of 'the Anthropocene." *Telos*, no. 172: 59–81.

Crist, Eileen. 2012. "Abundant Earth and the Human Population Question." In *Life on the Brink*, edited by Philip Cafaro and Eileen Crist, 141–51. Athens, GA: Univ. of Georgia Press.

———. 2013. "Ecocide and the Extinction of Animal Minds," in Marc Bekoff, ed., *Ignoring Nature No More*. Chicago: Univ. of Chicago Press, 45–61.

———. 2014. "Ptolemaic Environmentalism." In *Keeping the Wild*, edited by George Wuerthner and Eileen Crist, 16–30. Washington, DC: Island Press.

Cronon, William. 1991. *Nature's Metropolis*. New York: W.W. Norton.

———. 1995. "The Trouble with Wilderness; or, Getting Back to the Wrong Nature." In *Uncommon Ground*, edited by William Cronon, 69–90. New York: W.W. Norton.

Crosby, Alfred W., Jr. 1972. *The Columbian Exchange*. Westport, CT: Greenwood Press.

———. 1986. *Ecological Imperialism*. Cambridge: Cambridge Univ. Press.

———. 1997. *The Measure of Reality*. Cambridge: Cambridge Univ. Press.

Crutzen, Paul J. 2002. "Geology of Mankind: The Anthropocene." *Nature*, no. 415: 23.

———. 2006. "Albedo Enhancement of Stratospheric Sulfur Injections." *Climate Change*, no. 77: 211–19.

Crutzen, Paul J., and Eugene F. Stoermer. 2000. "The Anthropocene," *IGBP* [International Geosphere-Biosphere Programme] *Newsletter*, no. 41: 17–18.

Crutzen, Paul J., and Will Steffen. 2003. "How Long Have We Been in the Anthropocene Era?" *Climatic Change* 61 (3): 251–57.

Cullather, Nick. 2010. *The Hungry World: America's Cold War Battle Against Poverty in Asia*. Cambridge, MA: Harvard Univ. Press.

Cushman, Gregory. 2013. *Guano and the Opening of the Pacific World*. Cambridge: Cambridge Univ. Press.

Dales, John H. 1968. *Pollution, Property and Prices*. Toronto: Univ. of Toronto Press.

Daly, Herman E. 2010. "From a Failed-Growth Economy to a Steady-State Economy." *Solutions* 1 (2): 37–43.

Darby, H.C. 1956. "The Clearing of Woodland in Europe." In *Man's Role in Changing the Face of the Earth*, edited by William L. Thomas Jr., 183–216. Chicago: Univ. of Illinois Press.

Davis, Heather, and Etienne Turpin. 2013. "Matters of Cosmopolitics." in Etienne Turpin, ed., In *Architecture in the Anthropocene*, edited by Etienne Turpin, 171–82. London: Open Humanities Press.

Davis, Mike. 2010. "Who Will Build the Ark?" *New Left Review*, no. 61: 29–46.

Davis, Ralph. 1962. "English Foreign Trade, 1700–1774." *Economic History Review* 15 (2): 285–303.

———. 1973. *The Rise of the Atlantic Economies*. Ithaca: Cornell Univ. Press.

Dean, Warren. 1995. *With Broad Ax and Firebrand: The Destruction of the Brazilian Atlantic Forest*. Berkeley: Univ. of California Press.

Deckard, Sharae. 2015. "Mapping the World-Ecology." Academia.edu. http://www.academia.edu/2083255/Mapping_the_World-Ecology_Conjectures_on_World-Ecological_Literature

Deléage, Jean-Paul. 1989. "Eco-Marxist Critique of Political Economy." *Capitalism Nature Socialism* 1 (3): 15–31.

Dempster, Beth M. 1998. *A Self-Organizing Systems Perspective on Planning for Sustainability*. MSc thesis. Department of Environmental Studies, Univ. of Waterloo.

Descartes, René. 2006. *A Discourse on the Method of Correctly Conducting One's Reason and Seeking Truth in the Sciences*. Ian Maclean, ed. Oxford: Oxford Univ. Press.

Descripción de la Villa y Minas de Potosí—Ano de 1603. 1603 (1885). In *Relaciones Geograficas de Indias*, vol. 2, edited by Ministerio de Fomento, 113–36. Madrid: Ministerio de Fomento.

Despret, Vinciane. 2004. "The Body We Care For: Figures of Anthropo-zoo-genesis." *Body & Society* 10 (2–3): 111–34.

Detienne, Marcel, and Jean-Pierre Vernant. 1978. *Cunning Intelligence in Greek Culture and Society*. Translated by Janet Lloyd. Sussex: Harvester Press.

de Vries, Jan. 1974. *The Dutch Rural Economy in the Golden Age, 1500–1700*. New Haven, CT: Yale Univ. Press.

———. 1976. *The Economy of Europe in an Age of Crisis*. Cambridge: Cambridge Univ. Press.

———. 1984. *European Urbanization, 1500–1800*. London: Methuen & Co.

———. 1993. "The Labour Market." In *The Dutch Economy in the Golden Age*, edited by Karel Davids and Leo Noordegraaf, 55–78. Amsterdam: Nederlandsch Economisch-Historisch Archief.

———. 2001. "Economic Growth before and after the Industrial Revolution." In *Early Modern Capitalism*, edited by Maarten Prak, 175–91. New York: Routledge.

———. 2008. *The Industrious Revolution*. Cambridge: Cambridge Univ. Press.

de Vries, Jan, and Ad van der Woude. 1997. *The First Modern Economy*. Cambridge: Cambridge Univ. Press.

deVries, Karen. 2014. *Prodigal Knowledge: Queer Journeys in Religious and Secular Borderlands*. PhD dissertation. Department of History of Consciousness, Univ. of California, Santa Cruz.

Diamond, Jared. 2004. *Collapse: How Societies Choose to Fail or Succeed*. New York: Viking.

Dirzo, Rodolfo, Hillary S. Young, Mauro Galetti, Gerardo Ceballos, Nick J.B. Isaac, and Ben Collen. 2014. "Defaunation in the Anthropocene." *Science*, no. 345: 401–6.

Dixon, Marion. 2015. "Biosecurity and the Multiplication of Crises in the Egyptian Agri-food Industry." *Geoforum*, no. 61: 90–100.

Drengson, Alan. 2004. "The Wild Way." *The Trumpeter* 20 (1): 46–65.

DuPlessis, Robert S. 1997. *Transitions to Capitalism in Early Modern Europe*. Cambridge: Cambridge Univ. Press.

Dussel, Enrique. 1998. "Beyond Eurocentrism." In *The Cultures of Globalization*, edited by Frederic Jameson and Masao Miyoshi, 3–31. Durham: Duke Univ. Press.

Eagleton, Terry. 2000. *The Idea of Culture*. Oxford: Blackwell.

Economist. 2011a. "A Man-Made World." (May 26). http://www.economist.com/node/18741749.

———. 2011b. "Welcome to the Anthropocene." (May 26). http://www.economist.com/node/18744401.

————. 2013. "Protectionism: The Hidden Persuaders." (October 12). http://www. economist.com/news/special-report/21587381-protectionism-can-take-many-forms-not-all-them-obvious-hidden-persuaders.

Edwards, Paul. 2010. *A Vast Machine*. Cambridge, MA: MIT Press.

————. 2012. "Entangled Histories: Climate Science and Nuclear Weapons Research." *Bulletin of Atomic Scientists* 68 (4): 28–40.

Egan, Michael. 2007. *Barry Commoner: The Science of Survival*. Cambridge, MA: MIT Press.

Ehrlich, Paul R. 1968. *The Population Bomb*. New York: Ballantine.

Ehrlich, Paul R., and John P. Holdren. 1971. "Impact of Population Growth." *Science* 171 (3977): 1212–17.

Elden, Stuart. 2006. *Speaking against Number*. Edinburgh: Edinburgh Univ. Press.

Eldredge, Niles and Stephen J. Gould. 1972. "Punctuated Equilibria." In *Models in Paleobiology*, edited by T.J.M. Schopf, 82–115. San Francisco: Freeman Cooper.

El Khoury, Ann. 2015. *Globalization, Development, and Social Justice*. New York: Routledge.

Ellis, Erle C. 2009. "Stop Trying to Save the Planet." *Wired* (May 6). http://www.wired.com/wiredscience/2009/05/ftf-ellis-1/.

————. 2011. "Anthropogenic Transformation of the Terrestrial Biosphere." *Philosophical Transactions of the Royal Society A* 369 (1938): 2010–35.

————. 2012. "A Planet of No Return." *The Breakthrough Journal*, no. 2: 37–41.

Ellis, Erle C., Kees Klein Goldewijk, Stefan Siebert, Deborah Lightman, and Navin Ramankutty. 2010. "Anthropogenic Transformation of the Biomes, 1700 to 2000." *Global Ecology and Biogeography* 19 (5): 589–606.

Eltis, David. 2015. "A Brief Overview of the Trans-Atlantic Slave Trade." *Voyages: The Trans-Atlantic Slave Trade Database*. Accessed June 13, 2015. http://www.slavevoyages.org/tast/assessment/estimates.faces.

Emel, J., et al. 2011. "Extracting Sovereignty." *Political Geography* 30 (2), 70–79.

Engels, Friedrich. 1973. "The Origin of the Family, Private Property and the State." In *Karl Marx and Frederick Engels, Selected Works*, vol. 3., 204–334. Moscow: Progress Publishers.

————. 1987. "Dialectics of Nature." In *Karl Marx and Friedrich Engels, Collected Works*, vol. 25, 318–588. London: Lawrence and Wishart.

Enzensberger, H.M. 1974. "A Critique of Political Ecology." *New Left Review* I/84: 3–31.

Escobar, A. 1999. "After Nature" *Current Anthropology* 40 (1): 1–30.

Febvre, Lucien, and Henri Martin. 1976. *The Coming of the Book*. Translated by David Gerard. London: Verso.

Federici, Silvia. 2009. *Caliban and the Witch*. Brooklyn: Autonomedia.

Fisher, Elizabeth. 1975. *Women's Creation*. New York: McGraw-Hill.

Fischer-Kowalski, Marina, and Helmut Haberl. 1997. "Tons, Joules, and Money." *Society & Natural Resources* 10 (1): 61–85

————. 1998. "Sustainable Development: Socio-Economic Metabolism and the Colonization of Nature." *International Social Science Journal*, no. 158: 573–87.

Fischer-Kowalski, Marina, Fridolin Krausmann, and Irene Pallua. 2014. "A Sociometabolic Reading of the Anthropocene." *The Anthropocene Review* 1 (1): 8–33.

Fleagle, Robert, ed. 1969. *Weather Modification*. Seattle: Univ. of Washington Press.

Flynn, Dennis O., and Arturo Giráldez. 2012. *China and the Birth of Globalisation in the 16th Century*. Burlington, VT: Ashgate Variorium.

Foreman, Dave. 2007. "The Arrogance of Resourcism." *Around the Campfire* 5 (1). http://www.rewilding.org/pdf/campfiremarch107.pdf.

———. 2011. *Man Swarm and the Killing of Wildlife*. Durango, CO: Raven's Eye Press.

Fossier, Robert. 1968. *La Terre et les Hommes en Picardie jusqu'à la Fin du XIIIe Siècle*, 2 vols. Louvain and Paris: B. Nauwelaerts.

Foster, John Bellamy. 1994. *The Vulnerable Planet*. New York: Monthly Review Press.

———. 2000. *Marx's Ecology*. New York: Monthly Review Press.

Foster, John Bellamy, and Hannah Holleman. 2012. "Weber and the Environment." *American Journal of Sociology* 117 (6): 1625–73.

Foster, John Bellamy, Brett Clark, and Richard York. 2010. *The Ecological Rift*. New York: Monthly Review Press.

Foucault, Michel. 2003. *Society Must Be Defended*. New York: Picador.

———. 2007. *Security, Territory, Population*. New York: Picador.

Fouquet, Roger. 2008. *Heat, Power and Light*. Northampton, MA: Edward Elgar.

Fraser, Caroline. 2009. *Rewilding the World*. New York: Picador.

Funes Monzote, Reinaldo. 2008. *From Rainforest to Cane Fielde in Cuba*. Translated by Alex Martin. Chapel Hill: Univ. of North Carolina Press.

Galeano, Eduardo. 1973. *Open Veins of Latin America*. New York: Monthly Review Press.

Gilbert, Scott F., Jan Sapp, and Alfred I. Tauber. 2012. "A Symbiotic View of Life." *Quarterly Review of Biology* 87 (4): 325–41.

Gill, Bikrum. 2015. "Can the River Speak? Epistemological Confrontation in the Rise and Fall of the Land Grab in Gambela, Ethiopia." *Environment and Planning* A. http://epn.sagepub.com/content/early/2015/10/13/0308518X15610243.abstract.

Gilson, Dave. 2011. "Octopi Wall Street!" *Mother Jones* (October 6). http://www.motherjones.com/mixed-media/2011/10/occupy-wall-street-octopus-vampire-squid.

Gimbutas, Marija. 1999. *The Living Goddesses*. Miriam Robbins Dexter, ed. Berkeley: Univ. of California Press.

Glacken, Clarence J. 1967. *Traces on the Rhodian Shore*. Berkeley: Univ. of California Press.

Godinho, Vitorino Magalhaes. 2005. "Portugal and the Making of the Atlantic World." *Review* 28 (4): 313–17.

Gowdy, John and Lisi Krall. 2013. "The Ultrasocial Origin of the Anthropocene." *Ecological Economics*, no. 95: 137–47.

Grigg, David B. 1980. *Population Growth and Agrarian Change*. Cambridge: Cambridge Univ. Press.

Groenewoudt, B.J. 2012. "Versatile Land, High versus Low: Diverging Developments in the Eastern Netherlands." *Proceedings of the Latvian Academy of Sciences*, section A, no. 66–63: 54–69.

Grove, Richard H. 1995. *Green Imperialism*. Cambridge: Cambridge Univ. Press.

Hacker, Barton. 1994. *Elements of Controversy: The Atomic Energy Commission and Radiation Safety in Nuclear Weapons Testing*. Berkeley: Univ. of California Press.

Hacking, Ian. 2000. *The Social Construction of What?* Cambridge, MA: Harvard Univ. Press.

Hamblin, Jacob Darwin. 2013. *Arming Mother Nature.* Oxford: Oxford Univ. Press.

Hamilton Alexander. 1791. "Alexander Hamilton's Final Version of the Report on the Subject of Manufactures, [5 December 1791]." Founders Online, National Archives. http://founders.archives.gov/documents/Hamilton/01-10-02-0001-0007. Source: *The Papers of Alexander Hamilton*, vol. 10, *December 1791–January 1792*, ed. Harold C. Syrett. New York: Columbia University Press, 1966, 230–340.

Hansen, James. 2009. *Storms of My Grandchildren.* New York: Bloomsbury.

Hanyan, Craig R. 1961. "China and the Erie Canal." *Business History Review* 35 (4): 558–66.

Haraway, Donna. 1988. "Situated Knowledges," *Feminist Studies* 14 (3): 575–99.

———. 1989. *Primate Visions.* New York: Routledge.

———. 2004. *Crystals, Fabrics, and Fields: Metaphors that Shape Embryos.* Berkeley, CA: North Atlantic Books.

———. 2008. *When Species Meet.* Minnesota: Univ. of Minnesota Press.

———. 2010. "Jeux de ficelles avec les espèces compagnes: rester dans le trouble." In *Les Animaux*, edited by Vinciane Despret and Rafaël Larrière, 17–47. Paris: Hermann.

———. 2011. *SF: Speculative Fabulation and String Figures/SF: Spekulative Fabulation und String-Figuren.* Ostfildern, Germany: Hatje Cantz Verlag.

———. 2013a. "Cosmopolitical Critters, SF, and Multispecies Muddles." Paper presented at Gestes Spéculatifs au Centre Culturel de Cerisy, Cerisy, France, June 28–July 5.

———. 2013b. "Sowing Worlds: A Seed Bag for Terraforming with Earth Others." In *Beyond the Cyborg*, edited by Margaret Grebowicz and Helen Merrick, 137–46. New York: Columbia Univ. Press.

———. 2014a. "Staying with the Trouble: Sympoiesis, String Figures, Multispecies Muddles." Lecture, Univ. of Alberta, March 23. http://new.livestream.com/aict/DonnaHaraway.

———. 2015. "Anthropocene, Capitalocene, Plantationocene, Chthulucene," *Environmental Humanities.* 6 (1): 159–65.

———. 2016. *Staying with the Trouble: Making Kin in the Chthulucene.* Durham: Duke Univ. Press.

Haraway, Donna, and Martha Kenney. 2015. "Anthropocene, Capitalocene, Chthulucene: Donna Haraway in Conversation with Martha Kenney." In *Art in the Anthropocene*, edited by Heather Davis and Etienne Turpin, 255–70. London: Open Humanities Press.

Harding, Susan. 2014. "Secular Trouble: Anthropology, Public Schools, and De/regulating Religion in Late 20th Century America." Lecture, Center for Cultural Studies, Univ. of California, Santa Cruz, April 23.

Hardt, Michael, and Antonio Negri. 2001. *Empire.* Cambridge, MA: Harvard Univ. Press.

Harman, Graham. 2011. *Quentin Meillassoux: Philosophy in the Making.* Edinburgh: Edinburgh Univ. Press.

Hartouni, Valerie. 2012. *Visualizing Atrocity.* New York: New York Univ. Press.

Harvey, David. 1974. "Population, Resources, and the Ideology of Science." *Economic Geography* 50 (3): 256–77.

Hays, Samuel P. 1959 *Conservation and the Gospel of Efficiency*. Cambridge, MA: Harvard Univ. Press.

Hayward, Eva. 2010a. "FingeryEyes: Impressions of Cup Corals." *Cultural Anthropology* 24 (4): 577–99.

———. 2010b. "SpiderCitySex." *Women & Performance* 20 (3): 225–51.

———. 2012a. "Sensational Jellyfish." *Differences* 23 (1): 161–96.

———. 2012b. "The Crochet Coral Reef Project Heightens Our Sense of Responsibility to the Oceans" *Independent Weekly*. http://www.indyweek.com/indyweek/the-crochet-coral-reef-project-heightens-our-sense-of-responsibility-to-the-oceans/Content?oid=3115925.

Heidegger, Martin. 1977. "The Question Concerning Technology." in *The Question Concerning Technology and Other Essays*, 3–35. New York: Harper.

Heinberg, Richard. 2007. *Peak Everything*. Gabriola Island, BC: New Society Publishers.

Hiebert, Lauren, Kara Treibergs, and Marley Jarvis. 2011. "Octopi Wall Street." http://deepseanews.com/2011/11/octopi-wall-street/.

Higuchi, Toshiro. 2010. "Atmospheric Nuclear Weapons Testing and the Debate on Risk Knowledge in Cold War America, 1945–1963." in J.R. McNeill, ed., In *Environmental Histories of the Cold War*, edited by J. R. McNeill, 301–22. Cambridge: Cambridge Univ. Press.

Hildebrand, Karl-Gustaf. 1992. *Swedish Iron in the Seventeenth and Eighteenth Centuries*. Translated by Paul Britten Austin. Stockholm: Jernkontorets bergshistoriska skriftserie.

Ho, Engseng. 2004. "Empire through Diasporic Eyes: A View from the Other Boat." *Society for Comparative Studies of Society and History* 46 (2): 210–46.

———. 2006. *The Graves of Tarem: Genealogy and Mobility across the Indian Ocean*. Berkeley: Univ. of California Press.

Hodge, Joseph Morgan. 2007. *Triumph of the Expert: Agrarian Doctrines of Development and the Legacies of British Colonialism*. Athens: Ohio Univ. Press.

Holloway, John. 2002. *Changing the World without Taking Power*. London: Pluto.

Horkheimer, Max and Theodor Adorno. 1972. *Dialectic of Enlightenment*. Continuum.

Hormiga, Gustavo. 1994. *A Revision and Cladistic Analysis of the Spider Family Pimoidae (Araneoidea: Araneae)*. Washington, DC: Smithsonian Institution Press.

Hornborg, Alf. 2015. "The Political Ecology of the Technocene." In *The Anthropocene and the Global Environmental Crisis*, edited by Clive Hamilton and François Gemenne, 57–69. New York: Routledge.

Hörz, Helga, and Herbert Hörz. 2013. *Transhumanismus: Ist der zukünftige Mensch ein Avatar?* Unpublished manuscript.

Hosack, David. 1829. *Memoir of Dewitt Clinton*. New York: J. Seymour.

Howe D.W. 2007. *What Hath God Wrought: The Transformation of America, 1815–1848*. Oxford: Oxford Univ. Press

Hribal, Jason C. 2003. "Animals Are Part of the Working Class." *Labor History* 44 (4): 435–53.

Huber, Matthew T. 2009. "Energizing Historical Materialism." *Geoforum*, no. 40: 105–15.

Huei, Sim Yong. 2008. "War and Diplomacy in the Estado da India, 1707–50." *Portuguese Studies Review* 16 (2): 49–80.

Hustak, Carla and Natasha Myers. 2012. "Involutionary Momentum: Affective Ecologies and the Sciences of Plant/Insect Encounters." *differences* 23 (3): 74–118.

Imbrie, John. 1997. Interview by Ronald Doel. College Park, MD: Niels Bohr Library & Archives, American Institute of Physics (May 21). http://www.aip.org/history-programs/niels-bohr-library/oral-histories/6924.

Ingold, Tim. 2007. *Lines, a Brief History*. New York: Routledge.

IEA (International Energy Agency). 2013. *World Energy Outlook 2013*. Paris: IEA.

Invisible Committee, The. 2009. *The Coming Insurrection*. Los Angeles: Semiotext(e).

Jacobsen, Thorkild. 1976. *The Treasures of Darkness*. New Haven: Yale Univ. Press.

Jakes, Aaron. Forthcoming. "Booms, Bugs, and Busts: Ecologies of Interest on Egypt's Commodity Frontier, 1882–1914." *Antipode*.

Jensen, Derrick. 2002. *Listening to the Land*. White River Junction, VT: Chelsea Green.

———. 2013. "Age of the Sociopath." *Earth Island Journal* 28 (1). http://www.earthisland.org/journal/index.php/eij/article/age_of_the_sociopath/.

Jessop, Bob. 2013. "The World Market, Variegated Capitalism, and the Crisis of European Integration." In *Globalization and European Integration*, edited by Petros Nousios, Henk Overbeek, and Andreas Tsolakis, 91–111. London: Routledge.

Johnson, Walter. 2013. *River of Dark Dreams*. Cambridge, MA: Harvard Univ. Press.

Jonas, Hans. 1974. *Philosophical Essays*. Englewood Cliffs, NJ: Prentice Hall.

———. 2010. "Toward a Philosophy of Technology." In *Technology and Values*, edited by Craig Hanks, 11–25. Oxford: Wiley-Blackwell.

Jones, Eric L. 1987. *The European Miracle*. Cambridge: Cambridge Univ. Press.

Jones, Nicola. 2011. "Human Influence Comes of Age." *Nature*, no. 473: 133.

Kaijser, A. 2002. "System Building from Below: Institutional Change in Dutch Water Control Systems." *Technology and Culture* 43 (3): 521–48.

Kane, Robert. 1845. *The Industrial Resources of Ireland*, 2nd ed. Dublin: Hodges and Smith.

Kapp, K. William. 1950, *The Social Costs of Private Enterprise*. New York: Schocken.

Kareiva, Peter, and Michelle Marvier. 2012. "What Is Conservation Science?" *BioScience* 62 (11): 962–69.

Kareiva, Peter, Michelle Marvier, and Robert Lalasz. 2011. "Conservation in the Anthropocene." *Breakthrough Journal*, no. 2: 26–36.

Katz, Cindi. 1995. "Major/Minor: Theory, Nature, and Politics." *Annals of the Association of American Geographers* 85 (1): 164–68.

Kellenbenz, Hermann. 1974. "Technology in the Age of the Scientific Revolution 1500–1700." In *The Fontana Economic History of Europe, II*, edited by Carlo M. Cipolla, 177–272. London: Fontana.

———. 1976. *The Rise of the European Economy*. London: Weidenfeld and Nicolson.

Kemp, Tom. 1978. *Historical Patterns of Industrialization*. New York: Longmans.

Kenney, Martha. 2013. *Fables of Attention*. PhD dissertation. Department of History of Consciousness, Univ. of California, Santa Cruz.

Kidner, David. 2014. "The Conceptual Assassination of Wilderness." In *Keeping the Wild*, edited by George Wuerthner, 10–15. Washington, DC: Island Press.

Kinahan, G.H. 1886–87. "Irish Metal Mining" *The Scientific Proceedings of the Royal Dublin Society*, no. 5: 200–317.

King, Katie. 2011. *Networked Reenactments*. Durham: Duke Univ. Press.

———. 2012. "A Naturalcultural Collection of Affections: Transdisciplinary Stories of Transmedia Ecologies Learning." *S&F Online* 10 (3). http://http://sfonline.barnard.edu/feminist-media-theory/a-naturalcultural-collection-of-affections-transdisciplinary-stories-of-transmedia-ecologies-learning/.

King, Peter. 2005. "The Production and Consumption of Bar Iron in Early Modern England and Wales." *Economic History Review* 58 (1): 1–33.

Kingsnorth, Paul. 2013. "Dark Ecology." *Orion* (January/February). https://orionmagazine.org/article/dark-ecology/.

Kinkela, David. 2011. *DDT and the American Century*. Chapel Hill: Univ. of North Carolina Press.

Klare, Michael. 2013. "The Third Carbon Age." http://www.huffingtonpost.com/michael-t-klare/renewable-energy_b_3725777.html.

———. 2014. "What's Big Energy Smoking?" http://www.commondreams.org/view/2014/05/27-5.

Klein, Naomi. 2013. "How Science Is Telling Us All to Revolt." *New Statesman* (October 29). http://www.newstatesman.com/2013/10/science-says-revolt.

———. 2014. *This Changes Everything*. New York: Simon and Schuster.

Klingholz, Reiner. 2014. *Sklaven des Wachstums: Die Geschichte einer Befreiung*. Frankfurt: Campus-Verlag.

Knutson, April. 2011. *Les faiseuses d'histoires: Que font les femmes à la pensée?* Paris: Découverte.

Koeppel, Gerard T. 2009. *Bond of Union: Building the Erie Canal and the American Empire*. New York: Da Capo Press.

Kohn, Eduardo. 2013. *How Forests Think*. Berkeley: Univ. of California Press.

Kolbert, Elizabeth. 2011. "Enter the Anthropocene—Age of Man." *National Geographic*. hhttp://ngm.nationalgeographic.com/2011/03/age-of-man/kolbert-text/1.

———. 2014. *The Sixth Extinction*. New York: Henry Holt & Co.

Kopp, Robert E., Joseph L. Kirschvink, Isaac A. Hilburn, and Cody Z. Nash. 2005. "The Paleoproterozoic Snowball Earth." *Proceedings of the National Academy of Sciences* 102 (32): 11131–36.

Kotchen, Matthew, and Oran Young. 2007. "Meeting the Challenges of the Anthropocene: Towards a Science of Coupled Human-Biophysical Systems." *Global Environmental Change*, no. 17: 149–51.

Kröger, Markus. 2015. "Spatial Causalities in Resource Rushes," *Journal of Agrarian Change*. http://onlinelibrary.wiley.com/doi/10.1111/joac.12113/abstract.

Kunnas, Jan. 2007. "Potash, Saltpeter and Tar." *Scandinavian Journal of History* 32 (3): 281–311

Kurzweil, Ray. 2005. *The Singularity Is Near: When Humans Transcend Biology*. New York: Penguin.

Ladurie, Emmanuel Le Roy. 1981. *The Mind and the Method of the Historian*. Translated by Sian Reynolds and Ben Reynolds. Chicago: Univ. of Chicago Press.

Landes, David S. 1998. *The Wealth and Poverty of Nations*. New York: W.W. Norton.

Lane, Frederic Chapin. 1933. "Venetian Shipping During the Commercial Revolution." *American Historical Review* 38 (2): 219–39

Latour, Bruno. 1993. *We Have Never Been Modern*. Cambridge, MA: Harvard Univ. Press.

———. 2004. "Why Has Critique Run Out of Steam?" *Critical Inquiry* 30 (2): 225–48

———. 2011. "Love Your Monsters." In *Love Your Monsters*, edited by M. Shellenberger and Ted Nordhaus, 16–23. San Francisco: The Breakthrough Institute.

———. 2013a. "Facing Gaia: Six Lectures on the Political Theology of Nature." The Gifford Lectures on Natural Religion, Edinburgh, February 18–28. http://macaulay.cuny.edu/eportfolios/wakefield15/files/2015/01/LATOUR-GIFFORD-SIX-LECTURES_1.pdf.

———. 2013b. "War and Peace in an Age of Ecological Conflicts." Lecture, Peter Wall Institute, University of British Columbia, September 23. http://www.bruno-latour.fr/node/527.

Leakey, Richard, and Robert Lewin. 1995. *The Sixth Extinction*. New York: Doubleday.

Lefebvre, Henri. 1991. *The Production of Space*. Translated by Donald Nicholson-Smith. Oxford: Blackwell.

Le Guin, Ursula K. 1976. *The Word for World Is Forest*. New York: Berkeley Medallion.

———. 1985. *Always Coming Home*. Berkeley: Univ. of California Press.

———. 1988. *Buffalo Gals and Other Animal Presences*. New York: New American Library.

———. 1989. *Dancing at the Edge of the World*. New York: Harper & Row.

Leiss, William. 1972. *The Domination of Nature*. Boston: Beacon Press.

Leitner, Jonathan. 2005. "Commodity Frontier as Contested Periphery: The Fur Trade in Iroquoia, New York and Canada, 1664–1754." In *Nature, Raw Materials, and Political Economy*, edited by Paul S. Ciccantell and David A. Smith, 231–52. New York: Emerald Group.

Lenin, V.I. 1976. *The State and Revolution*. Peking: Foreign Languages Press.

Lenton, Tim. 2008. "Engines of Life." *Nature* 452 (7188): 691–92.

Lenzen, M., D. Moran, K. Kanemoto, B. Foran, and A. Geshke. 2012. "International Trade Drives Biodiversity Threats in Developing Nations." *Nature*, no. 486: 109–22.

Levine, David. 2001. *At the Dawn of Modernity*. Berkeley: Univ. of California Press.

Lewis, Simon L., and Mark A. Maslin. 2015. "Defining the Anthropocene" *Nature*, no. 519: 171–80.

Lilley, Sasha, David McNally, Eddie Yuen, and James Davis. 2012. *Catastrophism: The Apocalyptic Politics of Collapse and Rebirth*. Oakland: PM Press.

Lindgaard, Jade. 2015. "Clive Hamilton: «L'anthropocène est l'événement le plus fondamental de l'histoire humaine»." *Mediapart* (November 5). https://www.mediapart.fr/journal/culture-idees/051115/clive-hamilton-l-anthropocene-est-l-evenement-le-plus-fondamental-de-l-histoire-humaine.

Linklater, A. 2002. *Measuring America: How United States Was Shaped by the Greatest Land Sale in History*. New York: Plum Books.

———. 2007. *The Fabric of America: How Our Borders and Boundaries Shaped the Country and Forged Our National Identity*. New York: Walker & Company.

Lohmann, Larry. 2016. "What Is the 'Green' in Green Growth." In *Green Growth: Ideology, Political Economy and the Alternatives*, edited by Gareth Dale, Manu V. Mathai, and Jose Puppim de Oliveira. London: Zed.

Lordon, Frédéric. 2014. *Willing Slaves of Capital*. Translated by Gabriel Ash. London: Verso.

Lovecraft, H.P. 2009. *The Call of Cthulhu and Other Dark Tales*. New York: Barnes and Noble.

Lovelock, James E. 1967. "Gaia as Seen through the Atmosphere." *Atmospheric Environment* 6 (8): 579–80.

Lovelock, James E., and Lynn Margulis. 1974. "Atmospheric Homeostasis by and for the Biosphere." *Tellus* 26 (1–2): 2–10

Luke, Timothy W. 1995. "On Environmentality." *Cultural Critique*, no. 31: 57–81.

Luxemburg, Rosa. 2003. *The Accumulation of Capital*. Translated by Agnes Schwarzschild. New York: Routledge.

Lynas, Mark. 2011. *The God Species*. London: Fourth Estate.

Mace, Georgina M., Belinda Reyers, Rob Alkemadec, Reinette Biggse, F. Stuart Chapin III, Sarah E. Cornelle, Sandra Díaz, et al. 2014. "Approaches to Defining a Planetary Boundary for Biodiversity." *Global Environmental Change*, no. 28: 289–97.

Maddison, Angus. 2001. *The World Economy: A Millennial Perspective*. Paris: OECD

———. 2005. *Growth and Interaction in the World Economy*. Washington, DC: AEI Press.

Mahnkopf, Birgit. 2013. "Peak Everything—Peak Capitalism? Folgen der sozial-ökologischen Krise für die Dynamik des historischen Kapitalismus." *Working Paper* 02/2013. Post-Growth Research-Group, Univ. of Jena. http://www.kolleg-postwachstum.de/sozwgmedia/dokumente/WorkingPaper/wp2_2013.pdf.

Malanima, Paolo. 2001. "The Energy Basis for Early Modern Growth, 1650–1820." In *Early Modern Capitalism*, edited by Maarten Prak, 49–66. London: Routledge.

———. 2006. "Energy Crisis and Growth, 1650–1850." *Journal of Global History* 1 (1): 101–21

Malm, Andreas. 2013. "The Origins of Fossil Capital" *Historical Materialism* 21 (1): 15–68.

Małowist, Marian. 2009. *Western Europe, Eastern Europe and World Development, 13th–18th Centuries*. Leiden: Brill.

Manes, Christopher. 1992. "Nature and Silence." *Environmental Ethics*, no. 14: 339–50.

Manning, Richard. 2005. *Against the Grain: How Agriculture Hijacked Civilization*. New York: North Point Press.

Marley, Benjamin J. 2015. "The Coal Crisis in Appalachia." *Journal of Agrarian Change*. http://onlinelibrary.wiley.com/doi/10.1111/joac.12104/abstract.

Marris, Emma, Peter Kareiva, Joseph Mascaro, and Erle C. Ellis. 2011. "Hope in the Age of Man." *New York Times* (December 7). http://www.nytimes.com/2011/12/08/opinion/the-age-of-man-is-not-a-disaster.html?_r=0.

Marsh, George Perkins. 1965. *Man and Nature*. Seattle: Univ. of Washington Press.

Marx, Karl. 1967. *Capital*. 3 vols. Frederick Engels, ed. New York: International Publishers.

———. 1970. *Critique of the Gotha Programme*. Moscow: Progress Publishers.

———. 1972. *On the Jewish Question*. In *The Marx-Engels Reader*, edited by Robert C. Tucker. New York: W.W. Norton.

———. 1973. *Grundrisse*. Translated by Martin Nicolaus. New York: Vintage.

———. 1975. *Early Writings*. Rodney Livingstone and Gregor Benton. London: Penguin.

———. 1977. *Capital*, vol. 1. Translated by Ben Fowkes. New York: Vintage.

———. 1978. *Capital*, vol. 2. Translated by David Fernbach. New York: Pelican.

———. 1979. *The Letters of Karl Marx*. Translated by S.K. Padover. Englewood Cliffs, NJ: Prentice-Hall.

———. 1981. *Capital*, vol. 3. Translated by David Fernbach. New York: Pelican.

Marx, Karl, and Frederick Engels. 1971. *The German Ideology*. New York: International Publishers.

Marx, Leo. 1996. "The Domination of Nature and the Redefinition of Progress." In *Progress*, edited by Leo Marx and Bruce Mazlish, 201–18. Ann Arbor: Univ. of Michigan Press.

Massey, Douglas S., and Joaquin Arango. 1999. *Worlds in Motion*. Oxford: Oxford Univ. Press.

Mathias, Peter. 1969. *The First Industrial Nation*. London: Methuen & Co.

McAfee, Kathleen. 1999. "Selling Nature to Save It?" *Society and Space* 17 (2): 133–54.

———. 2003. "Neoliberalism on the Molecular Scale." *Geoforum* 34 (2): 203–19.

McCracken, Eileen. 1971. *The Irish Woods since Tudor Times*. Newton Abbot, Ireland: David & Charles.

McFall-Ngai, Margaret, Michael G. Hadfield, Thomas C.G. Bosch, Hannah V. Carey, Tomislav Domazet-Lošo, Angela E. Douglas, Nicole Dubilier, et al. 2013. "Animals in a Bacterial World." *Proceedings of the National Academy of Sciences* 110 (9): 3229–36.

McFall-Ngai, Margaret. 2014. "Divining the Essence of Symbiosis." *PLoS/Biology* 12 (2): 1–6.

McMichael, Phillip. 2013. *Food Regimes and Agrarian Questions*. Halifax, NS: Fernwood.

McNeill, J.R. 2008. "Global Environmental History in the Age of Fossil Fuels (1800–2007)." In *The Environmental Histories of Europe and Japan*, edited by K. Mizoguchi, 1–11. Kobe: Nagoya Univ. Press.

McSpadden, Russ. 2013. "Help Fund the Ecosexual Revolution and End Mountain-top Removal Mining in Appalachia." *Earth First! Journal* (May 16), http://earthfirstjournal.org/newswire/2013/05/16/help-fund-the-ecosexual-revolution-and-end-mountain-top-removal-mining-in-appalachia/.

Meadows, Donella H., et al. 1972. *The Limits to Growth*. New York: Signet.

"Medousa and Gorgones." http://www.theoi.com/Pontios/Gorgones.html.

Merchant, Carolyn. 1980. *The Death of Nature*. New York: Harper & Row.

———. 1989. *Ecological Revolutions*. Chapel Hill: Univ. of North Carolina Press.

Meszaros, Istvan. 1970. *Marx's Theory of Alienation*. London: Merlin Press.

Michaud, Michael. 1986. *Reaching the High Frontier: The American Pro-Space Movement, 1972–1984*. Westport, CT: Praeger.

Mielants, Eric H. 2007. *The Origins of Capitalism and the "Rise of the West."* Philadelphia: Temple Univ. Press.

Mies, Maria. 1986. *Patriarchy and Accumulation on a World Scale*. London: Zed.

Miliband, Ralph. 1969. *The State in Capitalist Society*. New York: Basic.

———. 1970. "The Capitalist State: Reply to Nicos Poulantzas." *New Left Review* 59 (1): 53–60.

Miller, J.C. 1988. *Way of Death: Merchant Capitalism and the Angolan Slave Trade 1730–1830*. Madison: Univ. of Wisconsin Press.

Mintz, Sidney W. 1978. "Was the Plantation Slave a Proletarian?" *Review* 2 (1): 81–98.

———. 1985. *Sweetness and Power*. New York: Penguin.

Mitchell, Timothy. 2002. *Rule of Experts*. Berkeley: Univ. of California Press.

———. 2011. *Carbon Democracy*. London: Verso.

Mokyr, Joel. 1990. *The Lever of Riches*. Oxford: Oxford Univ. Press.

Moore, Jason W. 2002. "The Crisis of Feudalism: An Environmental History." *Organization & Environment* 15 (3): 301–22.

———. 2003a. "Nature and the Transition from Feudalism to Capitalism." *Review* 26 (2): 97–172.

———. 2003b. "*The Modern World-System* as Environmental History? Ecology and the Rise of Capitalism." *Theory & Society* 32 (3): 307–77.

———. 2007. *Ecology and the Rise of Capitalism*. PhD dissertation. Department of Geography, Univ. of California, Berkeley.

———. 2009. "Madeira, Sugar, and the Conquest of Nature in the 'First' Sixteenth Century, Part I." *Review* 32 (4): 345–90.

———. 2010a. "'Amsterdam Is Standing on Norway' Part I: The Alchemy of Capital, Empire, and Nature in the Diaspora of Silver, 1545–1648." *Journal of Agrarian Change* 10 (1): 35–71.

———. 2010b. "'Amsterdam is Standing on Norway' Part II: The Global North Atlantic in the Ecological Revolution of the Long Seventeenth Century." *Journal of Agrarian Change* 10 (2): 188–227.

———. 2010c. "Madeira, Sugar, and the Conquest of Nature in the 'First' Sixteenth Century, Part II." *Review* 33 (1): 1–24.

———. 2010d. "'This Lofty Mountain of Silver Could Conquer the Whole World': Potosí and the Political Ecology of Underdevelopment, 1545–1800." *Journal of Philosophical Economics* 4 (1): 58–103.

———. 2010e. "The End of the Road? Agricultural Revolutions in the Capitalist World-Ecology, 1450–2010." *Journal of Agrarian Change* 10 (3): 389–413.

———. 2011. "Capital, Nature, and the Sugar Commodity Frontier in the Making of the Global Atlantic." Public lecture, Department of English and Comparative Literature, Warwick Univ., May 9.

———. 2012. "Cheap Food & Bad Money: Food, Frontiers, and Financialization in the Rise and Demise of Neoliberalism." *Review* 33 (2–3): 125–61.

———. 2014a. "The Capitalocene Part I: On the Nature & Origins of Our Ecological Crisis." http://www.jasonwmoore.com/uploads/The_Capitalocene_Part_I_June_2014.pdf.

———. 2014b. "The Capitalocene Part II: Abstract Social Nature and the Limits to Capital." http://www.jasonwmoore.com/uploads/The_Capitalocene_Part_II_June_2014.pdf.

———. 2015a. *Capitalism in the Web of Life*. London: Verso.

———. 2015b. "Cheap Food and Bad Climate." *Critical Historical Studies* 2 (1): 1–43.

Moore, Kathleen Dean. 2013. "Anthropocene Is the Wrong Word." *Earth Island Journal* 28 (1): 19–20. http://www.earthisland.org/journal/index.php/eij/article/anthropocene_is_the_wrong_word/.

Moore, Kelly. 2008. *Disrupting Science: Social Movements, American Science, and the Politics of the Military, 1945–1975*. Princeton: Princeton Univ. Press.

Morton, F.W.O. 1978. "The Royal Timber in Late Colonial Bahia." *Hispanic American Historical Review* 58 (1): 41–61.

Morton, Timothy. 2013. *Hyperobjects*. Minneapolis: Univ. of Minnesota Press.

Muir, John. 2003. *The Yosemite*. New York: Modern Library.

Mumford, Lewis. 1934. *Technics and Civilization*. London: Routledge and Kegan Paul.

Munro, John. 2002. "Industrial Energy From Water-Mills in the European Economy, Fifth to Eighteenth Centuries." In *Economia e Energia Secc. XIII–XVIII*, edited by Simonetta Cavaciocchi, 223–69. Paris: Le Monnier.

Naess, Arne. 1973. "Tee Shallow and the Deep, Long-Range Ecology Movement." *Inquiry* 16 (1): 95–100.

National Research Council. 2015. *Climate Engineering, Reflecting Sunlight to Cool the Earth*. Washington, DC: National Academies Press.

Needham, Joseph. 2013. *The Grand Titration: Science and Society in East and West*. London: Routledge.

Nef, John U. 1932. *The Rise of the British Coal Industry*. London: Routledge.

———. 1964. *The Conquest of the Material World*. New York: Meridian.

Nevle, Richard J., and Dennis K. Bird. 2008. "Effects of Syn-pandemic Fire Reduction and Reforestation in the Tropical Americas on Atmospheric CO_2 during European Conquest." *Palaeogeography, Palaeoclimatology, Palaeoecology* 264 (1–2): 25–38.

New Scientist. 2008. "The Facts about Overconsumption." *New Scientist* (October 15). http://www.newscientist.com/article/dn14950-special-report-the-facts-about overconsumption#.VWKSGvlVhBd.

New York Times. 2011. Editorial. "The Anthropocene." *New York Times* (February 27).

Niblett, Michael. 2013. "The 'Impossible Quest for Wholeness.'" *Journal of Postcolonial Writing* 49 (2): 148–60.

Nietzsche, Friedrich. 2000. *Basic Writings of Nietzsche*. Translated by Walter Kauffman. New York: Modern Library Classics.

Noordegraaf, Leo. 1993. "Dutch Industry in the Golden Age." In *The Dutch Economy in the Golden Age*, edited by Karel Davids and Leo Noordegraaf, 131–57. Amsterdam: Nederlandsch Economisch-Historisch Archief,.

Norgaard, Richard B. 2013. "The Econocene and the Delta," *San Francisco Estuary and Watershed Science* 11 (3): 1–5.

North, Michael. 1996. *From the North Sea to the Baltic*. Aldershot, VT: Variorum.

O'Connor, James. 1998. *Natural Causes*. New York: Guilford.

Octopus cyanea. 2014. Image for "Tentacles: The Astounding Lives of Octopuses, Squids, and Cuttlefish," Monterey Bay Aquarium Exhibit.

Oloff, Kerstin. 2012. "'Greening' the Zombie." *Green Letters* 16 (1): 31–45.

O'Neill, Gerard K. 1974. "The Colonization of Space." *Physics Today*, no. 27: 32–40.

———. 1976. *The High Frontier*. New York: William Morrow & Co.

Ortiz, Roberto José. 2014. "Agro-Industrialization, Petrodollar Illusions, and the Transformation of Capitalist World Economy in the 1970s: The Latin American Experience." *Critical Sociology.* http://crs.sagepub.com/content/early/2015/08/0 7/0896920514540187.

Overton, Mark. 1996. *Agricultural Revolution in England.* Cambridge: Cambridge Univ. Press.

Owen, James. 2010. "New Earth Epoch Has Begun, Scientists Say." *National Geographic News* (April 6). http://news.nationalgeographic.com/ news/2010/04/100406-new-earth-epoch-geologic-age-anthropocene/.

Packard, Randall. 2011. *The Making of a Tropical Disease.* Baltimore: Johns Hopkins Univ. Press.

Parenti, Christian. 2011. *Tropic of Chaos.* New York: Nation Books.

———. 2014a. "The Environment Making State." *Antipode* 47 (4): 829–48.

———. 2014b. "Reading Hamilton from the Left," *Jacobin* (August 26). https://www. jacobinmag.com/2014/08/reading-hamilton-from-the-left/.

———. 2015. "Why the State Matters." *Jacobin* (October 30). https://www.jacobinmag. com/2015/10/developmentalism-neoliberalism-climate-change-hamilton/.

Parikka, Jussi. 2014. *The Anthrobscene.* Minneapolis: Univ. of Minnesota Press.

Parker, Geoffrey. 2013. *Global Crisis: War, Climate Change & Catastrophe in the Seventeenth Century.* New Haven: Yale Univ. Press.

Parry, J.H. 1966. *The Spanish Seaborne Empire.* Berkeley: Univ. of California Press.

Patel, Raj. 2009. *The Value of Nothing.* New York: Picador.

———. 2013. "Misanthropocene?" *Earth Island Journal* 28 (1). Accessed April 13, 2015. http://www.earthisland.org/journal/index.php/cij/article/misanthropocene/.

Patterson, Orlando. 1982. *Slavery and Social Death.* Cambridge, MA: Harvard Univ. Press.

Peluso, Nancy L. 1992. *Rich Forests, Poor People.* Berkeley: Univ. of California Press.

Perlin, John. 1989. *A Forest Journey.* Cambridge, MA: Harvard Univ. Press.

Pignarre, Philippe, and Isabelle Stengers. 2005. *La sorcellerie capitaliste.* Paris: Decouverte.

Pigou, Arthur C. 1932. *The Economics of Welfare.* London: MacMillan.

Plumwood, Val. 1993. *Feminism and the Mastery of Nature.* New York: Routledge.

Polanyi, Karl. 1944. *The Great Transformation.* New York: Rinehart.

Pomeranz, Kenneth. 2000. *The Great Divergence.* Princeton: Princeton Univ. Press

Ponting, Clive. 1991. *A Green History of the World.* New York: St. Martin's Press

Poulantzas, Nicos. 1969. "The Problem of the Capitalist State." *New Left Review* 58, I: 67–78.

———. 2014. *State, Power, Socialism.* Translated by Patrick Camiller. London: Verso.

Poulsen, Bo. 2008. "Talking Fish: Cooperation and Communication in the Dutch North Sea Herring Fisheries, c. 1600–1850." In *Beyond the Catch: Fisheries of the North Atlantic, the North Sea and the Baltic, 900–1850,* edited by L. Sicking and D. Abreu-Ferreira, 387–412. Leiden: E. J. Brill.

Prado Júnior, Caio. 1967. *The Colonial Background of Modern Brazil.* Berkeley: Univ. of California Press.

Prak, Maarten, ed. 2001. *Early Modern Capitalism.* New York: Routledge.

Prigogine, Ilya, and Isabelle Stengers. 1984. *Order out of Chaos.* New York: Bantam.

Puig de la Bellacasa, María. 2009. "Touching Technologies, Touching Visions." *Subjectivity* 28 (1): 297–315.

———. 2011. "Matters of Care in Technoscience," *Social Studies of Science* 41 (1), 85–106.

———. 2013. *Penser nous devons. Politiques féminists et construction des savoirs.* Paris: Harmattan.

———. 2014. "Encountering bioinfrastructure," *Social Epistemology* 28 (1), 26–40.

Pursell, Carroll. 2007. *The Machine in America.* Baltimore: Johns Hopkins Univ. Press.

RAND Corporation. 1953. *The Worldwide Effects of Atomic Weapons: Project Sunshine.* Santa Monica: RAND Corporation. https://www.rand.org/content/dam/rand/pubs/reports/2008/R251.pdf.

Raup, David M., and J. John Sepowski Jr. 1984. "Periodicity of Extinctions in the Geologic Past." *Proceedings of the National Academy of Sciences* (81): 801–5.

Raworth, Kate. 2014. "Must the Anthropocene be a Manthropocene?" *The Guardian* (October 20). Accessed April 18, 2015. http://www.theguardian.com/commentisfree/2014/oct/20/anthropocene-working-group-science-gender-bias.

Reed, Donna. 2004. *Signs Out of Time.* https://www.youtube.com/watch?v=whfGbPFAy4w.

Revelle, Roger, and Hans E. Suess. 1957. "Carbon Dioxide Exchange between Atmosphere and Ocean and the Question of an Increase of Atmospheric CO_2 during the Past Decades." *Tellus* (9): 18–27.

Richards, J.F. 2003. *The Unending Frontier.* Berkeley: Univ. of California Press.

Roberts, William I., III. 1972. "American Potash Manufacture before the American Revolution." *Proceedings of the American Philosophical Society* 116 (5): 383–95.

Robin, Libby, and Will Steffen. 2007. "History for the Anthropocene." *History Compass,* no. 5: 1694–719.

Robinson, Kim Stanley. 2010. "Science, Justice, Science Fiction: A Conversation with Kim Stanley Robinson." By Gerry Canavan, Lisa Klarr, and Ryan Vu. *Polygraph,* no. 22: 201–17.

Rockström, Johan, Will Steffen, Kevin Noone, Åsa Persson, F. Stuart Chapin III, Eric F. Lambin, Timothy M. Lenton, et al. 2009a. "A Safe Operating Space for Humanity," *Nature* 461 (24): 472–75.

Rockström, Johan, Will Steffen, Kevin Noone, Åsa Persson, F. Stuart Chapin III, Eric F. Lambin, Timothy M. Lenton, et al. 2009b. "Planetary Boundaries," *Ecology and Society* 14 (2): 32.

Roff, Sue Rabbit. 2002, "Project Sunshine and the Slippery Slope." *Medicine, Conflict, and Survival* 18 (3): 299–310.

Rose, Deborah Bird. 2004. *Reports from a Wild Country.* Sydney: Univ. of New South Wales Press.

Rose, Deborah Bird, and Thom Van Dooren, eds. 2011. *Unloved Others: Death of the Disregarded in the Time of Extinctions.* Special issue of *Australian Humanities Review,* 50.

Rosenberg, Eugene and Leah Falkovitz. 2004. "The *Vibrio shiloi/Oculina patagonia* Model System of Coral Bleaching." *Annual Review of Microbiology,* no. 58: 143–59.

Ruccio, David F. 2011. "Anthropocene—or How the World Was Remade by Capitalism," (March 4), https://anticap.wordpress.com/2011/03/04/anthropocene%E2%80%94or-how-the-world-was-remade-by-capitalism/.

Ruddiman, William F. 2005. *Plows, Plagues, Petroleum*. Princeton: Princeton Univ. Press.

———. 2013. "The Anthropocene." *Annual Reviews in Earth and Planetary Science*, no. 41: 45–68.

Rudwick, Martin J.S. 2005. *Bursting the Limits of Time*. Chicago: Univ. of Chicago Press.

Russ, Joanna. 1975. *The Female Man*. New York: Bantam Books.

Russell, Ed. 2001. *War and Nature*. Cambridge; New York: Cambridge Univ. Press.

Sanderson, Eric, Malanding Jaiteh, Marc A. Levy, Kent H. Redford, Antoinette V. Wannebo, and Gillian Woolmer. 2000. "The Human Footprint and the Last of the Wild." *BioScience* 52 (10): 891–904.

Sartre, Jean-Paul. 1964. *Les Mots*. Paris: Gallimard.

Sayer, Derek. 1987. *The Violence of Abstraction*. Oxford: Blackwell.

Sayre, Nathan F. 2012. "The Politics of the Anthropogenic." *Annual Review of Anthropology*, no. 41: 57–70.

Schluchter, Wolfgang. 1980. *Rationalismus und Weltbeherrschung*. Frankfurt: Suhrkamp Verlag.

Schmitt, Carl. 2003. *The Nomos of the Earth in the International Law of the Jus Publicum Europaeum*. Translated by G.L. Ulmen. Candor, NY: Telos Press.

Schumpeter, Joseph A. 1950. *Capitalism, Socialism and Democracy*. New York: Harper & Row.

Schwägerl, Christian. 2010. *Menschenzeit. Zerstörten oder gestalten? Wie wir heute die Welt von morgen erschaffen*. München: Goldmann.

Schwartz, Stuart B. 1970. "The Macambo: Slave Resistance in Colonial Bahia." *Journal of Social History* 3 (4): 313–33

———. 1985. *Sugar Plantations in the Formation of Brazilian Society*. Cambridge: Cambridge Univ. Press.

Seccombe, Wally. 1992. *A Millennium of Family Change: Feudalism to Capitalism in Western Europe*. London: Verso.

———. 1995. *Weathering the Storm*. London: Verso.

Sella, Domenico. 1974. "European Industries 1500–1700." In *The Fontana Economic History of Europe II*, edited by Carlo M. Cipolla, 354–426. New York: Fontana Books.

Sevilla-Buitrago, Alvaro. 2015. "Capitalist Formations of Enclosure." *Antipode* 47 (4): 999–1020.

Shapiro, Stephen. 2013. "The World-System of Capital's Manifolds: Transformation Rips and the Cultural Fix." Unpublished paper. Department of English and Comparative Literary Studies, Univ. of Warwick.

———. 2014. "From Capitalist to Communist Abstraction: *The Pale King*'s Cultural Fix" *Textual Practice* 28 (7): 1249–71.

Shellenberger, Michael, and Ted Nordhaus, eds. 2011. *Love Your Monsters: Postenvironmentalism and the Anthropocene*. San Francisco: The Breakthrough Institute.

Shepard, Paul. 2002. *Man in the Landscape*. Athens: Univ. of Georgia Press.

Simmons, A.J. 2001. "On the Territorial Rights of States." *Philosophical Issues*, no. 11: 300–326.

Slicher van Bath, B.H. 1963. *The Agrarian History of Western Europe, 500–1850 A.D.* Translated by Olive Ordish. New York: St. Martin's Press.

———. 1977. "Agriculture in the Vital Revolution." In *The Cambridge Economic History of Europe*, vol. 5, edited by E.E. Rich and C.H. Wilson, 42–132. Cambridge: Cambridge Univ. Press.

Smith, Adam. [1776] 1937. *An Inquiry into the Nature and Causes of the Wealth of Nations.* New York: Modern Library.

Smith, Felisa A., Scott M. Elliott, and S. Kathleen Lyons. 2010. "Methane Emissions from Extinct Megafauna." *Nature Geoscience* 3 (6): 374–75.

Smith, Neil. 1984. *Uneven Development.* Oxford: Basil Blackwell.

———. 1987. "Rehabilitating a Renegade? The Geography and Politics of Karl August Wittfogel." *Dialectical Anthropology* 12 (1): 127–36.

———. 2006. "Nature as an Accumulation Strategy." In *Socialist Register 2007: Coming to Terms with Nature*, edited by Leo Panitch and Colin Leys, 16–36. London: Merlin Press.

Snow, C.P. 1964. *The Two Cultures: And a Second Look.* Cambridge: Cambridge Univ. Press.

Snyder, Gary. 1974. *Turtle Island.* New York: New Directions.

Soufan Group, The. 2014. "Geostrategic Competition in the Arctic: Routes and Resources." http://soufangroup.com/tsg-intelbrief-geostrategic-competition-in-the-arctic-routes-and-resources/.

Special Commission on Weather Modification. 1965. *Weather and Climate Modification.* Washington, DC: National Science Foundation.

St. Louis Post-Dispatch. 2013. "Decades Later, Baby Tooth Survey Lives On." *St. Louis Post-Dispatch* (August 1).

Steffen, Will. 2010. "The Anthropocene." Lecture, TEDx Canberra (November 14). https://www.youtube.com/watch?v=ABZjlfhNoEQ.

Steffen, Will, Paul J. Crutzen, and John R. McNeill. 2007. "The Anthropocene: Are Humans Now Overwhelming the Great Forces of Nature?" *Ambio* 36 (8): 614–21.

Steffen, Will, Jacques Grinevald, Paul Crutzen, and John McNeill. 2011a. "The Anthropocene: Conceptual and Historical Perspectives." *Philosophical Transactions of the Royal Society A* 369 (1938): 842–67.

Steffen, Will, Åsa Persson, Lisa Deutsch, Jan Zalasiewicz, Mark Williams, Katherine Richardson, Carole Crumley, et al. 2011b. "The Anthropocene: From Global Change to Planetary Stewardship." *Ambio* 40 (7): 739–61.

Steffen, Will, Wendy Broadgate, Lisa Deutsch, Owen Gaffney, and Cornelia Ludwig. 2015. "The Trajectory of the Anthropocene." *Anthropocene Review* 2 (1): 81–98.

Steinberg, Theodore L. 1986. "An Ecological Perspective on the Origins of Industrialization." *Environmental Review: ER* 10 (4): 261–76.

Steiner, Gary. 2005. *Anthropocentrism and its Discontents.* Pittsburgh: Univ. of Pittsburgh Press.

Stengers, Isabelle. 2009. *Au temps des catastrophes.* Paris: La Découverte.

———. 2011. "Relaying a War Machine?" In *The Guattari Effect*, edited by Eric Alliez and Andrew Goffey, 134–55. London: Continuum.

Stengers, Isabelle, and Vinciane Despret. 2014. *Women Who Make a Fuss.* Translated by April Knutson. Minneapolis: Univocal Publishing.

Stephens, Beth. *Goodbye to Gauley Mountain: An Ecosexual Love Story.* http://goodbyegauleymountain.org/.

Strathern, Marilyn. 1990. *The Gender of the Gift.* Berkeley: Univ. of California Press.

———. 1991. *Partial Connections.* Lanham, MD: Rowman and Littlefield.

———. 1992. *Reproducing the Future.* Manchester: Manchester Univ. Press.

———. 1995. *The Relation: Issues in Complexity and Scale.* Cambridge: Prickly Pear Press.

———. 2005. *Kinship, Law and the Unexpected.* Cambridge: Cambridge Univ. Press.

Studnicki-Gizbert, Daviken, and David Schecter. 2010. "The Environmental Dynamics of a Colonial Fuel-Rush," *Environmental History* 15 (1), 94–119.

Sundberg, Ulf. 1991. "An Energy Analysis of the Production at the Great Copper Mountain of Falun During the Mid-seventeenth Century." *International Journal of Forest Engineering* 1 (3): 4–16.

Swyngedouw, Erik. 1992. "Territorial Organization and the Space/Technology Nexus." *Transactions of the Institute of British Geographers* 17 (4): 417–33.

———. 1996. "The City as a Hybrid." *Capitalism Nature Socialism* 7 (2): 65–80.

———. 2013. "Apocalypse Now! Fear and Doomsday Pleasures." *Capitalism Nature Socialism* 24 (1): 9–18.

Szcygielski, W. 1967. 'Die Okonomische Aktivitat des Polnischen Adels im 16–18. Jahrhundert." *Studia Historiae Oeconomicae*, no. 2: 83–101.

Tainter, Joseph A. 1988. *The Collapse of Complex Societies.* Cambridge: Cambridge Univ. Press.

Taylor, Marcus. 2015. *The Political Ecology of Climate Change Adaptation.* New York: Routledge.

TeBrake, William H. 2002. "Taming the Waterwolf: Hydraulic Engineering and Water Management in the Netherlands During the Middle Ages." *Technology & Culture*, no. 43: 475–99.

Teschke, Benno. 2006. "The Metamorphoses of European Territoriality." In *State, Territoriality and European Integration*, edited by Michael Burgess and Hans Vollaard, 37–67 London: Routledge.

Thomas, Brinley. 1985. "Escaping from Constraints: The Industrial Revolution in a Malthusian Context." *Journal of Interdisciplinary History* 15 (4): 729–53.

Thomas, Peter D. 2009. "Gramsci and the Political." *Radical Philosophy*, no. 153: 27–36.

Thompson, Edward P. 1971. "The Moral Economy of the English Crowd in the Eighteenth Century." *Past & Present* 50 (1): 76–136

Thoreau, Henry David. 1991. *Walden; or, Life in the Woods.* New York: First Vintage Books.

Topolski, Jerzy. 1962. "La Regression Economique en Pologne du XVIe au XVIIIe Siecle." *Acta Polonaie Historica*, no. 7: 28–49.

Topolski, J., and A. Wyczanski. 1982. "Les fluctuations de la production agricole en Pologne XVIe–XVIIIe siècles." In *Prestations paysannes, dîmes, rente foncière et mouvement de la production agricole à l'époque préindustrielle*, vol. 1., edited by J. Goy and E. Le Roy Ladurie. Paris: Editions de l'EHESS.

Toynbee, Arnold. 1894. *Lectures on the Industrial Revolution of the Eighteenth Century in England.* London: Longmans, Green, and Co.

Tsing, Anna. 2005. *Friction: An Ethnography of Global Connection*. Princeton: Princeton Univ. Press.

———. 2015. *The Mushroom at the End of the World: On the Possibility of Life in Capitalist Ruins*. Princeton, NJ: Princeton University Press.

Tsing, Anna, et al. 2014. "Anthropocene: Arts of Living on a Damaged Planet." Conference, Institute for Humanities Research, Univ. of California, Santa Cruz, May 8–10. http://ihr.ucsc.edu/portfolio/anthropocene-arts-of-living-on-a-damaged-planet/.

Tuathail, G.Ó. 1997. "At the End of Geopolitics?" *Alternatives* 22 (1): 35–55.

Turner, Frederick Jackson. 1961. "The Significance of the Frontier in American History" In *Frontier and Section: Selected Essays of Frederick Jackson Turner*, edited by Ray Allen Billingon, 37–62. Englewood Cliffs, NJ: Prentice-Hall.

Unger, Richard W. 1975. "Technology and Industrial Organization: Dutch Shipbuilding to 1800." *Business History* 17 (1): 56–72.

———. 2011. "Dutch Nautical Sciences in the Golden Age: The Portuguese Influence." *E-Journal of Portuguese History* 9 (2): 68–83.

U.S. Department of the Interior. 1879. "Organic Act of the U.S. Geological Survey." *U.S. Statutes at Large* 20, Stat. 394. Washington, DC: U.S. Government Printing Office.

van Dooren, Thom. 2013. "Keeping Faith with Death: Mourning and De-extinction." Accessed May 12, 2015. http://extinctionstudies.org/2013/11/10/keeping-faith-with-death-mourning-and-de-extinction/.

———. 2014. *Flight Ways: Life and Loss at the Edge of Extinction*. New York: Columbia Univ. Press.

van Dooren, Thom, and Deborah Rose. 2012. "Storied-Places in a Multispecies City." *Humanimalia* 3 (2): 1–27

Vansina, Jan. 1996. "Quilombos on São Tomé, or in Search of Original Sources." *History in Africa* 23: 453–59.

Varchmin, Jochim, and Joachim Radkau. 1981. *Kraft, Energie und Arbeit: Energie und Gesellschaft*. Hamburg: Deutsches Museum.

Vaughn, Megan. 1991. *Curing Their Ills*. Palo Alto: Stanford Univ. Press.

Vaver, David, ed. 2006. *Intellectual Property Rights: Critical Concepts in Law*, vol. 4. New York: Taylor & Francis.

Vince, Gaia. 2011. "An Epoch Debate." *Science* 334 (7): 32–37.

Virilio, Paul. 2007. *The Original Accident*. Cambridge: Polity.

Voosen, Paul. 2012. "Geologists Drive Golden Spike toward Anthropocene's Base." *Greenwire*, Sept. 17. Accessed May 5, 2013. http://eenews.net/public/Greenwire/2012/09/17/1?page_type=print.

Wackernagel, Mathis, Larry Onisto, Patricia Bello, Alejandro Callejas Linares, Ina Susana, López Falfán, Jesus Méndez García, Ana Isabel Suárez Guerrero, and Ma. Guadalupe Suárez Guerrero. 1999. "National Natural Capital Accounting with the Ecological Footprint Concept." *Ecological Economics* 29 (3): 375–90.

Wackernagel, Mathis, and William E. Rees. 1996. *Our Ecological Footprint*. Gabriola Island, BC: New Society Publishers.

Wallerstein, Immanuel. 1974. *The Modern World-System I*. New York: Academic Press.

———. 1980. *The Modern World-System II*. New York: Academic Press.

Ward, Peter Douglas. 2009. *The Medea Hypothesis*. Princeton: Princeton Univ. Press.

Warde, Paul. 2006a. *Ecology, Economy and State Formation in Early Modern Germany*. Cambridge: Cambridge Univ. Press.

———. 2006b. "Fear of Wood Shortage and the Reality of the Woodland in Europe, c. 1450–1850." *History Workshop Journal* 62 (1): 28–57.

———. 2009. "Energy and Natural Resource Dependency in Europe, 1600–1900." BWPI Working Paper 77, Univ. of Manchester.

Warde, Paul, and Antonio Marra. 2007. *Energy Consumption in England and Wales, 1560–2000*. Naples: Consiglio nazionale delle ricerche, Istituto di studi sulle società del Mediterraneo.

Wark, McKenzie. 2015. *Molecular Red: Theory for the Anthropocene*. London: Verso.

Watts, David. 1987. *The West Indies*. Cambridge: Cambridge Univ. Press.

Watts, Michael J. 2005. "Nature:Culture." In *Spaces of Geographical Thought*, edited by P. Cloke and R. Johnston, 142–74. London, Sage.

Weart, Spencer. 2008. *The Discovery of Global Warming*. Cambridge, MA: Harvard Univ. Press.

Weber, Max. 1947. *The Theory of Social and Economic Organization*. New York: Free Press.

———. 1964. *The Religion of China*. New York: Free Press.

———. 1978. *Economy and Society*. Berkeley: Univ. of California Press.

———. 1992. *The Protestant Ethic and the Spirit of Capitalism*. New York: Routledge.

Webb, James. 2009. *Humanity's Burden*. Cambridge: Cambridge Univ. Press.

Webb, Walter Prescott. 1964. *The Great Frontier*. Austin: Univ. of Texas Press.

Weis, Tony. 2013. *The Ecological Hoofprint*. London: Zed.

Wente, Margaret. 2013. "Can Enviro-optimists Save the Movement from Itself?" *Globe and Mail* (April 20).

Wermuth, T.S. 1998. "New York Farmers and the Market Revolution." *Journal of Social History* 32 (1): 179–96.

Wexler, Harry. 1958. "Modifying Weather on a Large Scale." *Science*, no. 128: 1059–63.

White, Richard. 1995. *The Organic Machine*. New York: Hill & Wang.

———. 2010. "Containing Communism by Impounding Rivers." In *Environmental Histories of the Cold War*, edited by J.R. McNeill and Corinna R. Younger, 139–66. Cambridge: Cambridge Univ. Press.

Williams, Michael. 2003. *Deforesting the Earth*. Chicago: Univ. of Chicago Press.

Williams, Raymond. 1963. *Culture and Society: 1780–1950*. Harmondsworth: Penguin.

———. 1972. "Ideas of Nature." In *Ecology: The Shaping Enquiry*, edited by Jonathan Benthall, 146–64. London: Longman.

———. 1983. *Keywords*. London: Fontana Press.

———. 2005. *Culture and Materialism*. London: Verso.

Wilson, Charles H. 1968. *The Dutch Republic and the Civilisation of the Seventeenth Century*. New York: McGraw Hill.

Wing, John T. 2012. "Keeping Spain Afloat: State Forestry and Imperial Defense in the Sixteenth Century." *Environmental History*, no. 17: 116–45.

Wittfogel, Karl. 1957. *Oriental Despotism*. New Haven: Yale Univ. Press.

Wittman, Hannah, Annette Aurélie Desmarais, and Nettie Wiebe, eds. 2011. *Food Sovereignty in Canada*. Halifax, NS: Fernwood.

Wolf, Eric R. 1982. *Europe and the People without History*. Berkeley: Univ. of California Press.

Worster, Donald. 1985. *Rivers of Empire*. New York: Pantheon.

———. 1990. "Transformations of the Earth" *Journal of American History* 76 (4): 1087–1106.

———. 1993. *The Wealth of Nature*. New York: Oxford Univ. Press.

———. 1994. *Nature's Economy*. Cambridge: Cambridge Univ. Press.

van der Woude, Ad. 2003. "Sources of Energy in the Dutch Golden Age." *NEHA-Jaarboek voor economische, bedrijfs, en techniekgeschiedenis*, no. 66: 64–84.

Zalasiewicz, Jan, Mark Williams, Alan Smith, Tiffany L. Barry, Angela L. Coe, Paul R. Bown, Patrick Brenchley, et al. 2008. "Are We Now Living in the Anthropocene?" *GSA Today* 18 (2): 4–8.

Zalasiewicz, Jan, Mark Williams, Will Steffen, and Paul Crutzen. 2010. "The New World of the Anthropocene." *Environmental Science & Technology* 44 (7): 2228–31.

Zalasiewicz, Jan, Mark Williams, Richard Fortey, Alan Smith, Tiffany L. Barry, Angela L. Coe, Paul R. Bown, et al. 2011a. "Stratigraphy of the Anthropocene." *Philosophical Transactions of the Royal Society A* 369 (1938): 1036–55.

Zalasiewicz, Jan, Mark Williams, Alan Haywood, Michael Ellis. 2011b. "The Anthropocene: A New Epoch of Geological Time?" *Philosophical Transactions of the Royal Society A* 369 (1938): 835–41.

Zanden, Jan Luiten van. 1993. *The Rise and Decline of Holland's Economy*. Manchester: Manchester Univ. Press.

———. 2002. "The 'Revolt of the Early Modernists' and the 'First Modern Economy.'" *Economic History Review*, 55 (4): 619–41.

———. 2009. *The Long Road to the Industrial Revolution*. Leiden: Brill.

Zeeuw, J.W. de. 1978. "Peat and the Dutch Golden Age." *A.A.G. Bijdragen*, no. 21: 3–31.

Zins, Henryk. 1972. *England and the Baltic in the Elizabethan Era*. Manchester: Manchester Univ. Press.

Contributors

Elmar Altvater is professor emeritus of political science, Free University of Berlin. Areas of research and teaching: international political economy, Marxist theory, development theory with particular emphasis on the Amazon, international environmental policy, and social movements. He is the author of *The Future of the Market* (Verso, 1993) and the author and editor of numerous books and articles in German. Altvater was a member of a study commission of the German Parliament on the globalization of the world economy. His most recent publications are on the limits of globalization, the informalization of labor, and money and politics on a global scale. He is a member of several scientific societies and of the scientific council of ATTAC-Germany.

Eileen Crist received her BA from Haverford College (sociology, 1982) and her PhD from Boston University (sociology, 1994). She has been teaching at Virginia Tech in the Department of Science and Technology in Society since 1997. She is author of *Images of Animals: Anthropomorphism and Animal Mind*. She is also coeditor of a number of books, including *Gaia in Turmoil: Climate Change, Biodepletion, and Earth Ethics in an Age of Crisis; Life on the Brink: Environmentalists Confront Overpopulation*; and *Keeping the Wild: Against the Domestication of Earth*. She is the author of numerous academic and popular papers and a contributor to the late journal *Wild Earth*. Her work focuses on biodiversity loss and destruction of wild places and pathways to halt these trends. More information and publications can be found on her website: www.eileencrist.com.

Donna Haraway is distinguished professor emerita in the History of Consciousness Department at the University of California, Santa Cruz. She earned her PhD in biology at Yale in 1972 and has taught the history of science, science and technology studies, feminist theory, and multispecies studies at the University of Hawaii, the Johns Hopkins University, and the University of California, Santa Cruz. In 2000, she was awarded the JD Bernal Prize from the Society for Social Studies of Science for distinguished lifetime contributions to the field. Attending to the webs of biological sciences, cultures, and politics, Haraway explores string figures composed by science fact, science fiction, speculative feminism, speculative fabulation, science and technology studies, and multispecies worlding. Her books include *Crystals, Fabrics, and Fields* (1976, 2004); *Primate Visions* (1989); *Simians, Cyborgs, and Women* (1991); *Modest_Witness@ Second_Millennium* (1997); *The Companion Species Manifesto* (2003); *The Haraway Reader* (2004); *When Species Meet* (2008); and *Manifestly Haraway*, reprinting the Cyborg Manifesto and Companion Species Manifesto with an extended conversation with Cary Wolfe (2016). Her new book on response-ability in times of great ecosocial urgency is *Staying with the Trouble: Making Kin in the Chthulucene*.

Daniel Hartley is lecturer in English and American literature and culture at the University of Giessen (Germany). He is the author of *The Politics of Style: Marxist Poetics in and beyond Raymond Williams, Terry Eagleton and Fredric Jameson* (Brill, 2016). He is now working on a book focusing on depersonalization and temporality in contemporary literature.

Justin McBrien is PhD candidate in environmental history at the University of Virginia. His work examines the historical relationship between the military-industrial complex, climate science, environmentalism, and theories of planetary catastrophe. He is currently completing his dissertation, "Making the World Safe for Disaster: The Rise of the Biosecurity State and the Globalization of Catastrophe in Cold War America."

Jason W. Moore is a historical geographer and world historian at Binghamton University, where he is associate professor of sociology and Research Fellow at the Fernand Braudel Center. He is author of *Capitalism in the Web of Life* (Verso, 2015), *Transformations of the Earth: Nature in* *the Making and Unmaking of the Modern World* (in Chinese, Commercial, 2015); and *Ecologia-mondo e crisi del capitalismo: La fine della natura a buon mercato* (Ombre Corte, 2015). He writes frequently on the history of capitalism, environmental history, and social theory. Moore is currently completing *Ecology and the Rise of Capitalism*, an environmental history of the rise of capitalism, and with Raj Patel, *Seven Cheap Things: A World-Ecological Manifesto*—both with the University of California Press. He is coordinator of the World-Ecology Network. Many of his essays can be found on his website: www.jasonwmoore.com.

Christian Parenti teaches in New York University's Global Liberal Studies program. He has published four books, most recently, *Tropic of Chaos: Climate Change and the New Geography of Violence* (Nation Books, 2011). As a journalist he has reported extensively from Afghanistan, Iraq, and various parts of Africa, Asia, and Latin America. His work has appeared in the *Nation*, *Fortune*, the *London Review of Books*, the *New York Times*, and many other publications. He has a PhD in sociology and geography from the London School of Economics.

Index

Page numbers in *italic* refer to illustrations. "Passim" (literally "scattered") indicates intermittent discussion of a topic over a cluster of pages.

Suess, Hans, 130
sugar industry, 85, 92, 96–100 passim, 105, 109, 110, 120
surplus value, 92, 118, 143, 145, 168
surveillance, 112, 125, 139, 141, 162
surveying, 183n4
Sweden, 107
sympoiesis, 10, 36–37, 40, 52, 59, 65n16

tariffs, 176
tar sand oil extraction, 71–72n41
technology, 15, 25, 109–12 passim, 125, 134–35, 140–44 passim, 157; determinism, 156; in early capitalism, 100, 101; Hamilton view, 176; Haraway views, 50; Kurzweil view, 138; Moore views, 82–83, 92, 98; time-marking, 87. *See also* steam power
tentacles, 35, 36, 37, 56, 58, 63n8
theft of data. *See* data theft
Theogony (Hesiod), 57, 69n32, 74n52
Thomas, Peter D., 163
Thoreau, Henry David, 26
thoughtlessness, 39–40
"tipping points," 149–50
toxicity, 118
trade, international. *See* international trade
transportation, 176–81 passim
Trotsky, Leon, 173
Tsing, Anna, 40, 69–70n37
Turtle Island (Snyder), 26

UNESCO, 132
uniformitarianism, 122
unpaid work, 79, 85, 89–93 passim, 110–12 passim, 158–59, 162
urbanization, 99, 102
use values, 139, 148, 167–77 passim
U.S. Export-Import Bank. *See* Export-Import Bank of the United States
U.S. federal lands. *See* federal lands: U.S.
U.S. Geological Survey, 171

value, 93, 98; Marxist theory, 158. *See also* surplus value; use values
van der Donck, Adriaen. *See* Donck, Adriaen van der
van der Woude, Ad, 103
van Dooren, Thom: *Flight Ways*, 41, 61n5
Varley, John: Gaea trilogy, 64n14
"Venus Effect," 133
Vernant, Jean-Pierre, 76n63
Vibrio (bacteria), 76n65
Virgin Mary, 74n56
Von Neumann, John, 125, 136n7

wage labor and wages, 99–100, 102, 113
war, 46–47, 124; robotic, 139
Ward, Peter Douglas, 134, 135
Wark, McKenzie, 111
Washington, George, 183n4
Washington University: Baby Tooth Survey, 127
waste, 19, 147, 148, 149, 151. *See also* nuclear waste
water supply, California, 123
weather, extreme, 128–29
weather control, 125, 126
Weber, Max, 173
Weis, Tony: *The Ecological Hoofprint*, 5
Wermuth, T.S., 181
Werner, Brad, 50–51
whaling, 108–9
wheat, 99, 102, 181
White, Richard, 90
Wiener, Norbert, 125–26, 136n7
wilderness, 15, 30n2, 30n4, 30–31n10, 53
Williams, Raymond, 107, 154, 163, 164, 165
witch-hunts, 161–62
women, violence against, 161–62
women's work, 99, 100, 101, 162
wooly mammoth, 121
Word for World Is Forest, The (Le Guin), 44
work. *See* labor

ABOUT PM PRESS

PM Press was founded at the end of 2007 by a small collection of folks with decades of publishing, media, and organizing experience. PM Press co-conspirators have published and distributed hundreds of books, pamphlets, CDs, and DVDs. Members of PM have founded enduring book fairs, spearheaded victorious tenant organizing campaigns, and worked closely with bookstores, academic conferences, and even rock bands to deliver political and challenging ideas to all walks of life. We're old enough to know what we're doing and young enough to know what's at stake.

We seek to create radical and stimulating fiction and non-fiction books, pamphlets, T-shirts, visual and audio materials to entertain, educate, and inspire you. We aim to distribute these through every available channel with every available technology—whether that means you are seeing anarchist classics at our bookfair stalls, reading our latest vegan cookbook at the café, downloading geeky fiction e-books, or digging new music and timely videos from our website.

PM Press is always on the lookout for talented and skilled volunteers, artists, activists, and writers to work with. If you have a great idea for a project or can contribute in some way, please get in touch.

PM Press
PO Box 23912
Oakland, CA 94623
www.pmpress.org

FRIENDS OF PM PRESS

These are indisputably momentous times—the financial system is melting down globally and the Empire is stumbling. Now more than ever there is a vital need for radical ideas.

In the years since its founding—and on a mere shoestring—PM Press has risen to the formidable challenge of publishing and distributing knowledge and entertainment for the struggles ahead. With over 300 releases to date, we have published an impressive and stimulating array of literature, art, music, politics, and culture. Using every available medium, we've succeeded in connecting those hungry for ideas and information to those putting them into practice.

Friends of PM allows you to directly help impact, amplify, and revitalize the discourse and actions of radical writers, filmmakers, and artists. It provides us with a stable foundation from which we can build upon our early successes and provides a much-needed subsidy for the materials that can't necessarily pay their own way. You can help make that happen—and receive every new title automatically delivered to your door once a month—by joining as a Friend of PM Press. And, we'll throw in a free T-shirt when you sign up.

Here are your options:

- **$30 a month** Get all books and pamphlets plus 50% discount on all webstore purchases

- **$40 a month** Get all PM Press releases (including CDs and DVDs) plus 50% discount on all webstore purchases

- **$100 a month** Superstar—Everything plus PM merchandise, free downloads, and 50% discount on all webstore purchases

For those who can't afford $30 or more a month, we're introducing **Sustainer Rates** at $15, $10 and $5. Sustainers get a free PM Press T-shirt and a 50% discount on all purchases from our website.

Your Visa or Mastercard will be billed once a month, until you tell us to stop. Or until our efforts succeed in bringing the revolution around. Or the financial meltdown of Capital makes plastic redundant. Whichever comes first.

In, Against, and Beyond Capitalism: The San Francisco Lectures

John Holloway
with a Preface by Andrej Grubačić

ISBN: 978-1-62963-109-7
$14.95   112 pages

In, Against, and Beyond Capitalism is based on three recent lectures delivered by John Holloway at the California Institute of Integral Studies in San Francisco. The lectures focus on what anticapitalist revolution can mean today—after the historic failure of the idea that the conquest of state power was the key to radical change—and offer a brilliant and engaging introduction to the central themes of Holloway's work.

The lectures take as their central challenge the idea that "We Are the Crisis of Capital and Proud of It." This runs counter to many leftist assumptions that the capitalists are to blame for the crisis, or that crisis is simply the expression of the bankruptcy of the system. The only way to see crisis as the possible threshold to a better world is to understand the failure of capitalism as the face of the push of our creative force. This poses a theoretical challenge. The first lecture focuses on the meaning of "We," the second on the understanding of capital as a system of social cohesion that systematically frustrates our creative force, and the third on the proposal that we are the crisis of this system of cohesion.

"His Marxism is premised on another form of logic, one that affirms movement, instability, and struggle. This is a movement of thought that affirms the richness of life, particularity (non-identity) and 'walking in the opposite direction'; walking, that is, away from exploitation, domination, and classification. Without contradictory thinking in, against, and beyond the capitalist society, capital once again becomes a reified object, a thing, and not a social relation that signifies transformation of a useful and creative activity (doing) into (abstract) labor. Only open dialectics, a right kind of thinking for the wrong kind of world, non-unitary thinking without guarantees, is able to assist us in our contradictory struggle for a world free of contradiction." —Andrej Grubačić, from his Preface

"Holloway's work is infectiously optimistic."
—Steven Poole, the *Guardian* (UK)

"Holloway's thesis is indeed important and worthy of notice"
—Richard J.F. Day, *Canadian Journal of Cultural Studies*

Birth Work as Care Work: Stories from Activist Birth Communities

Alana Apfel, with a foreword by Loretta J. Ross, preface by Victoria Law, and introduction by Silvia Federici

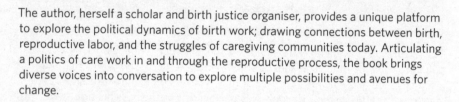

ISBN: 978-1-62963-151-6
$14.95   128 pages

Birth Work as Care Work presents a vibrant collection of stories and insights from the front lines of birth activist communities. The personal has once more become political, and birth workers, supporters, and doulas now find themselves at the fore of collective struggles for freedom and dignity.

The author, herself a scholar and birth justice organiser, provides a unique platform to explore the political dynamics of birth work; drawing connections between birth, reproductive labor, and the struggles of caregiving communities today. Articulating a politics of care work in and through the reproductive process, the book brings diverse voices into conversation to explore multiple possibilities and avenues for change.

At a moment when agency over our childbirth experiences is increasingly centralized in the hands of professional elites, *Birth Work as Care Work* presents creative new ways to reimagine the trajectory of our reproductive processes. Most importantly, the contributors present new ways of thinking about the entire life cycle, providing a unique and creative entry point into the essence of all human struggle—the struggle over the reproduction of life itself.

"I love this book, all of it. The polished essays and the interviews with birth workers dare to take on the deepest questions of human existence."
—Carol Downer, cofounder of the Feminist Women's Heath Centers of California and author of *A Woman's Book of Choices*

"This volume provides theoretically rich, practical tools for birth and other care workers to collectively and effectively fight capitalism and the many intersecting processes of oppression that accompany it. Birth Work as Care Work *forcefully and joyfully reminds us that the personal is political, a lesson we need now more than ever."*
—Adrienne Pine, author of *Working Hard, Drinking Hard: On Violence and Survival in Honduras*

Capital and Its Discontents: Conversations with Radical Thinkers in a Time of Tumult

Sasha Lilley

ISBN: 978-1-60486-334-5
$20.00   320 pages

Capitalism is stumbling, empire is faltering, and the planet is thawing. Yet many people are still grasping to understand these multiple crises and to find a way forward to a just future. Into the breach come the essential insights of *Capital and Its Discontents*, which cut through the gristle to get to the heart of the matter about the nature of capitalism and imperialism, capitalism's vulnerabilities at this conjuncture—and what can we do to hasten its demise. Through a series of incisive conversations with some of the most eminent thinkers and political economists on the Left—including David Harvey, Ellen Meiksins Wood, Mike Davis, Leo Panitch, Tariq Ali, and Noam Chomsky—*Capital and Its Discontents* illuminates the dynamic contradictions undergirding capitalism and the potential for its dethroning. At a moment when capitalism as a system is more reviled than ever, here is an indispensable toolbox of ideas for action by some of the most brilliant thinkers of our times.

"*These conversations illuminate the current world situation in ways that are very useful for those hoping to orient themselves and find a way forward to effective individual and collective action. Highly recommended.*"
—Kim Stanley Robinson, *New York Times* bestselling author of the *Mars Trilogy* and *The Years of Rice and Salt*

"*In this fine set of interviews, an A-list of radical political economists demonstrate why their skills are indispensable to understanding today's multiple economic and ecological crises.*"
—Raj Patel, author of *Stuffed and Starved* and *The Value of Nothing*

"*This is an extremely important book. It is the most detailed, comprehensive, and best study yet published on the most recent capitalist crisis and its discontents. Sasha Lilley sets each interview in its context, writing with style, scholarship, and wit about ideas and philosophies.*"
—Andrej Grubačić, radical sociologist and social critic, co-author of *Wobblies and Zapatistas*

From ■SPECTRE▶ from PM Press

Catastrophism: The Apocalyptic Politics of Collapse and Rebirth

Sasha Lilley, David McNally, Eddie Yuen, and James Davis with a foreword by Doug Henwood

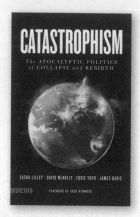

ISBN: 978-1-60486-589-9
$16.00   192 pages

We live in catastrophic times. The world is reeling from the deepest economic crisis since the Great Depression, with the threat of further meltdowns ever-looming. Global warming and myriad dire ecological disasters worsen—with little if any action to halt them—their effects rippling across the planet in the shape of almost biblical floods, fires, droughts, and hurricanes. Governments warn that no alternative exists than to take the bitter medicine they prescribe—or risk devastating financial or social collapse. The right, whether religious or secular, views the present as catastrophic and wants to turn the clock back. The left fears for the worst, but hopes some good will emerge from the rubble. Visions of the apocalypse and predictions of impending doom abound. Across the political spectrum, a culture of fear reigns.

Catastrophism explores the politics of apocalypse—on the left and right, in the environmental movement, and from capital and the state—and examines why the lens of catastrophe can distort our understanding of the dynamics at the heart of these numerous disasters—and fatally impede our ability to transform the world. Lilley, McNally, Yuen, and Davis probe the reasons why catastrophic thinking is so prevalent, and challenge the belief that it is only out of the ashes that a better society may be born. The authors argue that those who care about social justice and the environment should eschew the Pandora's box of fear—even as it relates to indisputably apocalyptic climate change. Far from calling people to arms, they suggest, catastrophic fear often results in passivity and paralysis—and, at worst, reactionary politics.

"This groundbreaking book examines a deep current—on both the left and right—of apocalyptical thought and action. The authors explore the origins, uses, and consequences of the idea that collapse might usher in a better world. Catastrophism *is a crucial guide to understanding our tumultuous times, while steering us away from the pitfalls of the past."*
—Barbara Epstein, author of *Political Protest and Cultural Revolution: Nonviolent Direct Action in the 1970s and 1980s*